THE REPORTER AS ARTIST:

A Look at the New Journalism Controversy

THE REPORTER

AS ARTIST: A Look at The New Journalism Controversy

Edited by Ronald Weber

COMMUNICATION ARTS BOOKS

Hastings House, Publishers   NEW YORK

Copyright © 1974 by Ronald Weber

Library of Congress Cataloging in Publication Data

Weber, Ronald, comp.   The reporter as artist.

CONTENTS: Weber, R. Some sort of artistic excitement.–Wolfe, T. Introduction to the kandy-kolored tangerine-flake streamline baby.–Talese, G. Author's note to fame and obscurity. [etc.]

1. Journalism—United States. 2. American prose literature—20th century—Addresses, essays, lectures. I. Title.

PN4867.W4   818'.08   73-19896
ISBN 0-8038-6330-6
ISBN 0-8038-6333-0 (pbk.)

Published simultaneously in Canada by Saunders of Toronto, Ltd., Don Mills, Ontario

Designed by Al Lichtenberg
Printed in the United States of America

"We want to pursue reporting as an art form. I think that is wonderful: the reporter as the artist. Wonderful."

—Gay Talese in an interview
with John Brady

Contents

Preface

This book reprints a number of documents—articles, reviews, chapters of books, interviews—dealing in one way or another with the New Journalism. The documents weren't selected or arranged to suggest a particular attitude toward the New Journalism but rather to stimulate and enlighten debate on the subject. Readers are invited to use the documents as they will to come to their own conclusions.

To provide a rough clarity the material is divided into four sections. Part One, Personal Journalism, contains pieces that offer background on the development of the New Journalism and discuss its characteristic attitudes and methods. Most of the writers who appear in this section are themselves New Journalists and, predictably, take an affirmative stand on the subject. Part Two, The Article as Art, offers works that argue for the magazine article or the literary essay as an art form uniquely suited to the time. Not surprisingly, most of the writers in this section are or were magazine editors.

Part Three, Fact in the Fiction Void, continues the thrust of Part Two with emphasis on the artistic potential of journalistic writing. Part Four, Dissent and Qualification, contains pieces that take a stand against the New Journalism or offer significant reservations. Inevitably, there's some overlapping here; some writers appearing elsewhere in the book reappear in this section to voice complaints. Following Part Four are some suggestions for further readings that treat the New Journalism.

Finally, a reminder that the term "New Journalism" is anything but a precise one. When it's used in the documents here it doesn't always refer to the same thing; and in some documents it isn't used at all, or used with the capital letters, and what writers have in mind is simply a new awareness of the literary and journalistic potential of nonfiction writing. But however vague and slippery a term, the New Journalism has become the convenient label for recent developments in nonfiction writing and for the sharp critical controversy this writing has stirred up—and it's in such an admittedly loose sense that it's used to draw together the materials in this book.

R. W.

Acknowledgments

Michael J. Arlen, "Notes on the New Journalism." Copyright © 1972, by The Atlantic Monthly Company, Boston, Mass. Reprinted with permission.

Daniel J. Balz, "Bad Writing and New Journalism." Reprinted with permission from the *Columbia Journalism Review*, September/October, 1971. ©.

John Brady, "Gay Talese: An Interview." Copyright © 1973 by *Writer's Digest*. Reprinted with permission.

Brock Brower, "The Article." From the book *On Creative Writing*. Edited by Paul Engle. Copyright © 1963, 1964 by Paul Engle. Published by E. P. Dutton & Co., Inc., and used with their permission.

Benjamin DeMott, "In and Out of Universal City." From the book *Supergrow: Essays and Reports on Imagination in America* by Benjamin DeMott. Copyright © 1969, 1968, 1967, 1966 by Benjamin DeMott. Published by E. P. Dutton & Co., Inc., and used with their permission. The article originally appeared in a somewhat different form in *The Antioch Review*.

Herbert Gold, "On Epidemic First Personism." Reprinted by permission of the author and his agents, James Brown Associates, Inc. Copyright © 1971 by Herbert Gold. The article originally appeared in *The Atlantic Monthly*.

Herbert Gold, "How Else Can a Novelist Say It?" From *First Person Singular*, edited by Herbert Gold. Copyright © 1963. Reprinted by permission of the publisher, The Dial Press.

Gerald Grant, "The 'New Journalism' We Need." Reprinted with permission from the *Columbia Journalism Review*, Summer, 1970. ©.

Harold Hayes, "Editor's Notes on the New Journalism." Reprinted by permission of *Esquire Magazine*. Copyright © 1971 by Esquire, Inc.

Harold Hayes, "Introduction to *Smiling Through the Apocalypse: Esquire's History of the Sixties*." Reprinted from *Smiling Through the Apocalypse*, edited by Harold Hayes, by permission of Saturday Review Press. Copyright © 1960, 1961, 1962, 1963, 1964, 1965, 1966, 1967, 1968, 1969 by Esquire, Inc.

Nat Hentoff, "Behold the New Journalism—It's Coming After You!" Reprinted with permission from *Evergreen Review*, July, 1968.

Seymour Krim, "The Newspaper as Literature/Literature as Leadership." From the book *Shake It For The World, Smartass* by Seymour Krim. Copyright © 1970 by Seymour Krim. Reprinted by permission of the publisher, The Dial Press.

Dwight Macdonald, "Parajournalism, Or Tom Wolfe and His Magic Writing Machine." Reprinted with permission from *The New York Review of Books*. Copyright © 1965 by the New York Review, Inc.

Lester Markel, "So What's New?" Reprinted with permission from *The Bulletin* of the American Society of Newspaper Editors, January, 1972.

David McHam, "The Authentic New Journalists." Reprinted with permission from the September, 1971, issue of *The Quill*, published by Sigma Delta Chi, professional journalistic society.

Jack Newfield, "Journalism: Old, New and Corporate." From the book *The Dutton Review*. Edited by Susan Stern *et ors*. Copyright © 1970 by *The Dutton Review*. Published in a paperback edition by E. P. Dutton & Co., Inc., and used with their permission.

Jack Newfield, "Is There a 'New Journalism'?" Reprinted by permission of *The Village Voice*. Copyright © 1972 by The Village Voice, Inc.

George Plimpton, "Truman Capote: An Interview." Copyright © 1966 by The New York Times Company. Reprinted by permission.

Donald Pizer, "Documentary Narrative as Art: William Manchester and Truman Capote." Reprinted with permission from the *Journal of Modern Literature*, September, 1971.

Norman Podhoretz, "The Article as Art." Reprinted with permission of Farrar, Straus & Giroux, Inc., from *Doings and Undoings* by Norman Podhoretz. Copyright © 1958, 1964 by Norman Podhoretz.

William L. Rivers, "The New Confusion." Reprinted with permission from *The Progressive*, December, 1971.

Some Sort of Artistic Excitement

RONALD WEBER

Tom Wolfe says he doesn't know who coined the term or when it was coined—and if he doesn't know probably no one does. For one decent working definition of the New Journalism is that it's what Tom Wolfe writes. If not exactly the founder of the movement (or whatever you prefer to call it: phenomenon, breakthrough, *menace*) Wolfe has for some years now been its major theorist and of course among its most visible practitioners. Though there were strong rumblings before, it was with the publication of his *Kandy-Kolored Tangerine-Flake Streamline Baby* in 1965 that the subject burst with full Day-Glo coloring on the literary-journalistic scene—and with the book's strong sales (note Dwight Macdonald's review) came the first winds of acclaim and denial, soon rising to a broadly joined and often noisy critical controversy (though one that involved, oddly, little real debate). Then in the summer of 1973 Wolfe gave the affair a new turn, and fresh fuel, by providing his subject with a capsule history plus an aesthetic and elevating it to the status of a genre in a rambling essay * and an anthology of New Journalism examples published with the blandly unWolfian title *The New Journalism.*

At this late date about the only thing beyond dispute is that the New Journalism is badly named. Even Wolfe doesn't much like the term on grounds that the the "New" is just begging for trouble by

---

* The essay is drawn from material that appeared earlier in *New York* and *Esquire* magazines.

13

evoking memories of other revolutionary developments—the New Criticism, the New Poetry, the New Frontier—that now ride the "garbage barge of history." Others have taken heavier bead on the term by arguing that the New Journalism is neither all that new nor, at least in common understanding, strictly journalism. They point out that writers like James Agee, Lillian Ross, and John Hersey functioned as New Journalists long before the term was invented—as did an earlier breed of newspapermen like Jimmy Cannon, Paul Gallico, and Jim Bishop. And they note that the New Journalism has largely found its way into print between the covers of magazines and books rather than in newspapers (with the exception of Sunday supplements, and notably that of Wolfe's beloved *New York Herald Tribune*) and so, to prevent confusion with the still unreconstructed world of daily journalism, might better be called the New Nonfiction. Finally, there's the radical common-sense position that the New Journalism is a poor term because it proposes categories in an activity, writing, in which the only meaningful distinction is between good and bad. In this view (Jack Newfield's) all the New Journalism amounts to is good writers being turned loose by wise editors on real subjects—and that's no reason to coin a presumptuous term.

Yet when all this and more is admitted it remains that the New Journalism is the term that caught on in the 1960s and 70s to describe what Wolfe calls "some sort of artistic excitement in journalism." It became the catchall term to classify the nonfiction work of writers as diverse as Wolfe, Gay Talese, Norman Mailer, Terry Southern, and Truman Capote as well as that of Seymour Krim, Joan Didion, Pete Hamill, Garry Wills, Jimmy Breslin, George Plimpton, Joe McGinniss, Gloria Steinem, and Hunter Thompson. It became the overarching term for such subtypes as saturation reporting, advocacy journalism, participatory journalism, underground journalism, journalit, and the nonfiction novel. It became, in short, *the* term, and whatever difficulties it offered in precise definition it referred clearly enough to a significant stir in American writing—to its advocates, a stir that amounted to a fundamental shift in our understanding of what constitutes serious writing. The real problem posed by the New Journalism wasn't so much one of definition as evaluation of that claim.

Any try at evaluation requires noticing first of all (rather obviously, perhaps, but a necessary point of departure if the slippery beast is to be tamed at all) that there are two basic strains at work in the New Journalism—and second that the strains are opposed, even contradictory. When Wolfe talks about finding "artistic" excitement in journalism he has in mind one such strain—the effort to draw literary effect from nonfiction materials, to render literature from reporting, art from fact. In this sense the New Journalism is fundamentally a literary rather than journalistic development in that while dealing with factual rather than invented materials and using traditional (though often intensified) methods of reporting it draws its most characteristic techniques from the legacy of realistic fiction.

In fact it tends to think of itself (if the thinker is Tom Wolfe) as the sole surviving heir of the literary tradition of realism at a time when the serious novel, abandoning the events and figures of the world around us, has sailed off on thin seas of romance and fable and into the introspection and parody of various forms of metafiction. In other words, as the novel has become increasingly nonrealistic journalism has stepped into the abandoned territory of manners and morals to create a new literary realism, or a New Journalism, that differs from the work of Trollope and Balzac, John Steinbeck and Sinclair Lewis, only in that it's free of the old-fashioned need to invent stories.

The case of course is wildly overstated, if only in the assumption that serious novelists have totally given up on the realities of the day. Good novelists—Bellow and Updike, to name two—continue to treat ordinary life and times; nothing so far has come out of the new realism of the New Journalism to rival a *Mr. Sammler's Planet,* or maybe even a *Rabbit Redux* (though *The Electric Kool-Aid Acid Test, The Armies of the Night,* and *In Cold Blood* are clearly works of real importance). But whatever the exaggerations involved in thinking of the New Journalism rising like the phoenix from the ashes of an abandoned literary realism, the point is that the New Journalism is on one side a distinctly literary development. It's intention is fundamentally literary, as is its hoped for effect.

That effect—what Hemingway, distinguishing literature from journalism, called "magnification"—is gained by using familiar literary devices on factual material. According to Wolfe the devices are essentially four in number: the telling of a story through scenic construction, extensive use of dialogue, a third-person point of view that allows the writer to reveal what goes on inside the mind as well as exterior detail, and the recording of the concrete particulars of manners, customs, and events. Wolfe thinks the last trick has stirred up the most controversy—perhaps because he's often charged with being interested only in the flow of fashion—but it's the revelation of interior states that probably has been the most debated of the New Journalism's literary methods.

Reporters who take us inside the heads of people they write about, the argument goes, have stepped over the line into *creative* writing, thus forfeiting any claim to journalism. Not so, the New Journalists maintain. The portrayal of interior states is admittedly a novelistic device but it can be harmonized with the factual basis of journalism since the material is derived from reporting. The writer simply interviews the subject about his thoughts and emotions as well as everything else, then renders the response in dramatic form. Such intimate, inside-the-skin reporting obviously requires the full cooperation of the subject and makes hard demands on the time and sensitivity of the reporter. But New Journalists like Gay Talese remain convinced that it's possible, "by asking the right question at the right time, to learn and to report what goes on within other people's minds."

So the New Journalism must in part be approached as a literary development. It has claimed public attention in a period of declining interest in realistic fiction or the fiction of illusion—of declining interest in fiction generally. It has reared its well-publicized head (a matter to turn to later) at a time when it's commonplace to remark that if the novel isn't dead the age of the novel surely is, or that the center of American writing has shifted from fiction to the magazine article or the occasional journalistic piece. The New Journalism has revived literary techniques that appear exhausted or outmoded to novelists and storywriters (some of them) and returned them to serious service. It has taken as its particular terrain the world of manners and morals, public events and social existence, that has been abandoned (though not completely) as burnt-over territory by imaginative writers. There is a sense then in which the New Journalism offers itself as a new fiction—a fiction for an age suspicious or weary of fiction or not up to its tough intellectual and spiritual demands—with of course the qualification that it's based on verifiable fact. It's a new factual fiction in that, following Wolfe's line of thought, it maintains the old realistic impulse of fiction,* as well as its spellbinding attraction, while traditional fiction writers (those still writing fictional fiction) have misadventured into an esoteric fabulism. The new factual fiction returns to the novel's fascination with the detailed depiction of social reality and its concern to interest the reader while offering the added attraction, dear to the American heart, of being *true*. As such, its advocates say, it has taken over as the hottest game in town—what Seymour Krim calls "the *de facto* literature of our time."

There's another reason for emphasizing the literary side of the New Journalism to the extent of labeling it a new fiction, one not often mentioned but of basic importance. Serious literature, realistic as well as fabulistic, never holds up an entirely authentic mirror to nature. That's the aim of journalism. Literature as opposed to journalism is always a refracting rather than reflecting mechanism; it always to some degree distorts (or, as Hemingway said, magnifies) life, if only

---

* For Wolfe realism isn't just one of the available fictional devices but *the* device, the one that raised the art to its highest point with the work of Dickens and Balzac. He likens the introduction of realism into fiction to the introduction of electricity into machine technology; it was, in other words, the real juice.

to give it a shape or clarity that can't otherwise be detected. And the roots of literary distortion are always located in the person of the writer himself, in the individual stamp he puts on his work. It's the deflection and refraction of the material in the filter of the self that gives a piece of writing its special edge, that perhaps lifts it to levels of art. In literature it's really distortion we prize—the distortion of the uniquely individual.

Wolfe's work is a perfect case in point. His brand of nonfiction functions every bit as much as a distorting mechanism as does good fiction—and for the same reason: it bears his individual, idiosyncratic mark in its every aspect. Which isn't to imply that the facts are faked or that the reporting is less arduous or complete than Wolfe contends. The New Journalists insist that every fact they offer, as well as every thought or emotion attributed to a character, is verifiable—and nothing has come to light (excepting maybe the attacks on Wolfe's *New Yorker* piece or the Redpants affair involving Gail Sheehy) to discredit the claim. But in Wolfe's case it's not really the facts, interior or exterior, that we read for but the fun-house mirror (in Wilfrid Sheed's phrase) he holds up to them. It's the Wolfian imagination brought to bear on the materials, rather than the Bernsteins or the Pranksters or the car people themselves, that finally holds our interest—or fails to. As Sheed shrewdly observes, Wolfe imposes upon the truths of reporting and research "his own consciousness, his own selection and rhetoric, and they become Wolfe-truths, and he is halfway over the border into the hated Novel." Only halfway, it's true—held back, limited, by the constraints of fact; the imagination can range only so far before it's hauled back by the nonfiction need to stick to what can be verified. But up to this point—and in Wolfe's case it's a *far* point—it's the distorting magic of the artist that gives the New Journalism its deepest literary quality.

The other basic strain at work in the New Journalism is more strictly journalistic.* It's rooted not so much in the effort to turn reporting into art as to bend the stultifying conventions of traditional journalistic practice and to extend the range and power of nonfiction writing. Partly this involves a freedom of style and construction that permits the writer to abandon the tonal simplicities and ready-made structures of newspaper and magazine writing—a freedom to experiment with language and to align manner and form with material. But the central journalistic convention against which the New Journalism

---

* This side to the New Journalism, keeping thoughts about art and rivalry with fiction in the background and concentrating more on loosening up rigid journalistic attitudes and practices, has lacked a spokesman of Wolfe's zeal and stature and consequently tends to seem of less importance. But this could be deceptive. It could be that in the long run, the literary New Journalists having switched (or switched back) to writing old novels, the less publicized changes at work in newspaper and magazine journalism will have the more lasting effect.

has tilted is that of the proper attitude or point of view for the journalist. Traditionally—though going back only so far as the beginnings of the mass-circulation press—the newsman is supposed to take a detached attitude toward his material, dispassionate while reporting and objective while writing. His function is largely that of conduit between event and reader, and he performs the function well when he keeps the line open and flowing, unclogged by emotional or intellectual intrusions on his part.

Over the past decade professional newsmen have felt increasingly restive with such a bland, impersonal conception of their role. They have argued that the journalist can never in reality be a totally neutral figure, wholly detached and wholly objective, and that furthermore such an ideal may hinder rather than serve his primary function: the pursuit of topical truth. The journalist is always present at events as a person, a more or less active consciousness situated between those events and the reader, and everything he writes is to some extent shaped by this fact. To deny the shaping presence of the reporter because of the theoretical demands of detachment and objectivity is to be fundamentally dishonest with the reader as well as oneself. It's also to erroneously imply that detachment is accuracy, that what is seemingly stripped of personal opinion and individual feeling is therefore to be trusted and relied upon. At its worst the detached stance can lead not only to being less than candid with the reader but to positively misinforming him; it can allow the reporter to print what he believes to be false merely because someone in authority said it, without indicating personal dissent or without soliciting balancing views from other news sources. In such case it's the conventions of journalism that are served, not the reporter's commitment to truth.

The journalist and novelist Dan Wakefield neatly catches the professional reporter's unease with the tradition of impersonal journalism in his book *Between the Lines: A Reporter's Personal Journey Through Public Events,* published the year after Wolfe's *Kandy-Kolored.* In an opening section called "The Shadow Unmasked"—meaning the reporter revealed—Wakefield explains that the book is for readers "who have grown increasingly mistrustful of and bored with anonymous reports about the world, whether signed or unsigned, for those who have begun to suspect what we reporters of current events and problems so often try to conceal: that we are really individuals after all, not all-knowing, all-seeing Eyes but separate, complex, limited, particular 'I's'." To demonstrate the point he reprints a number of past magazine pieces done in an impersonal manner but adds to them personal information about what was happening to him at the time of the writing, how what he gathered and wrote was affected by people and circumstance. The idea is to reveal what was hidden in the reports all along, between the lines—the presence of the writer himself and the pressure of his consciousness on what was finally written.

Impersonal, objective reporting, Wakefield argues, is really a kind of special code that can deceive the reader who isn't fully aware of the limitations of the convention. His book, on the other hand, is an attempt to "hold those official coded reports [the previously printed pieces] over a flame and allow the warmth to bring out the other, more interesting words that were there in the white space, written in the invisible ink of personal experience." Only in this way, with the reporter fully revealed as a functioning presence, can the reader be certain of his ground and begin the groping movement toward the truth of events.

Other journalists, professionals and part timers, have offered similar arguments against impersonal journalism. Seymour Krim echoes Wakefield when he insists that the reporter must "declare his credentials [to the reader] by revealing the concrete details and particular sweat of his own inner life; otherwise he (or she) will not have earned the right to speak openly about everything or be trusted." Norman Mailer takes a similar stand in *The Armies of the Night* when he contends that the long, personal, novelistic first part of the book is a necessary prelude to the brief, impersonal (more or less), historical second part. Because of the intimate confessions of the first part the reader is in a better position to measure the reportage of the second. The first part informs the reader that the reporter-novelist-historian Mailer is "crooked," his telescopes "warped," but this is all to be expected since "the instruments of all sciences—history so much as physics—are always constructed in small or large error." What redeems their use by Mailer "is that our intimacy with the master builder of the tower [Mailer himself], and the lens grinder of the telescopes [Mailer again] . . . has given some advantage for correcting the error of the instruments and the imbalance of his tower." In other words, because Mailer has revealed himself to us in personal detail we can place more trust in his reporting on the Pentagon march (more than in *Time's* or *Newsweek's*) because it allows for the adjustment and correction demanded by the use of any human instrument. All of which of course is to take the same position that James Agee adopted to his material in *Let Us Now Praise Famous Men*—a work that offers classic inspiration (or, depending on your view, classic warning) for all recent efforts at personal journalism. Wakefield fittingly takes a famous passage of that book as one of the epigraphs for *Between the Lines:*

> George Gudger is a man, et cetera. But obviously, in the effort to tell of him (by example) as truthfully as I can, I am limited. I know him only so far as I know him, and only in those terms in which I know him; and all of that depends as fully on who I am as on who he is.

To writers of deep social concern—Agee being one—impersonal journalism is not only a technical issue but a moral one. Jack Newfield insists that certain facts about our society that have recently drawn the attention of journalists—racism, prison conditions, the Vietnam war— are not morally neutral and consequently can't be written about in neutral fashion. As an advocate of truth the journalist has no choice in these areas but to follow the course of advocacy journalism. He can't hide behind the impersonal conventions of his medium when they prevent him from speaking out for what he believes to be true. "Objectivity," Newfield says with an irony aimed at traditional journalistic practice, "is not shouting 'liar' in a crowded country." To shout, let alone shout liar, is inappropriate given the familiar notions of responsible journalism—but it might well be appropriate given equally familiar and more important notions of responsible morality.

The two basic strains in the New Journalism—the one to lift reporting to art, the other to personalize it and thus strengthen its credibility—come together (uneasily, as I'll try to indicate) in an emphasis on the writer himself, on his individual imprint on the material of fact. This is evident enough in the razzle-dazzle stylistics of Tom Wolfe, the center-stage participatory manner of Norman Mailer and Hunter Thompson, the committed moralism of Jack Newfield and Nat Hentoff —and it's also true, though in less apparent ways, in the more traditional journalistic work of Truman Capote and Gay Talese. In books like *In Cold Blood, The Kingdom and the Power,* and *Honor Thy Father* the writer remains an "eye," an omniscient shadow slipping unannounced from scene to scene, character to character, yet in the obvious meticulousness of the reporting and the novelistic artistry of scene and characterization the writer makes his presence and his shaping consciousness known.

The "I" is absent from such books, their authors tell us, not because of disagreement with the arguments for personal journalism but on technical grounds that once you start using the "I" you have to keep using it throughout the work and it gets in the way. It directs attention away from character and situation and inhibits easy shifts from scene to scene. But the absence of the "I" remains to some extent a matter of appearance for the presence of the writer is strongly felt in the shaping and dramatizing of his material and in managing its implications. In such work the writer is never as directly or powerfully present nor the journalism so personal as in the reporting of Agee or Mailer or the revised articles of Wakefield, but the work is still given the mark of a distinctive consciousness, a signature that is uniquely if not assertively its own.

So the New Journalism, on both its literary and journalistic sides, comes down to personal writing, with wide variations in how personal the writer chooses to get and how deeply an artistically distorting mechanism his individual consciousness becomes. And therein, in its essential "I" quality, is a good part of the explanation for the attention that has greeted the New Journalism—as well as for much of the criticism it has drawn.

One way of thinking about the popularity of the New Journalism is to say that it's "I" writing for an "I" time, personal writing for an age of personalism.* All about us ego seems loosed into the cultural air as never before. Notions of detachment, objectivity, and neutrality conflict in every sphere with a passion for uninhibited individual expression. Both ones first and last duty now belong to oneself. Wolfe's work has effectively portrayed this pervasive concentration on the self, on the discovery of *me*—my life, my needs, my uniqueness. "Fifteen years ago," Wolfe intones, "it was popular among historians to say that the great 19th-century wave of individualism was over and that America was now in the era of the 'mass man.' Thirty years from now historians will record the widespread discovery of the Self in the 1960s and 1970s as one of the most extraordinary developments in American history. . . ." The New Journalism, one might suggest, Wolfe's and everyone else's, is merely a sympton of the times—the journalist unmasking his shadow and often unburdening his soul in a period when everyone else is doing the same. If everyone nowadays is saying (as Wolfe says they are), "Look at *me* . . . I'm unique . . . I'm *me*," then the New Journalism, in varying degrees, is merely following suit.

Marshall McLuhan notes that an unstated corollary to the admonition to "do your own thing" is that others will watch. And that's another aspect of the New Journalism's popularity: it's very watchable. Richard Poirier tells us in a recent book called *The Performing Self* that what most matters about contemporary literature and the modern arts in general is not so much performance itself (the finished book, the completed article) as the feats of performance that go into the making, the "pacing, economies, juxtapositions, aggregations of tone, the whole conduct of the shaping presence." Poirier argues that it's here the reader should seek his pleasures in modern writing, in the "thousands of tiny movements" of the performing self, the writer at his work, rather than in old-hat ideas about character and story, meaning and significance. Mailer of course becomes Poirier's chief object of atten-

---

* Another way is to offer the point, with Theodore Solotaroff and Herbert Gold, that personal journalism always flourishes in times of change and tumult when literary men feel compelled to speak directly to events and issues. In an essay called "Autobiography and America" (*Virginia Quarterly Review*, Spring, 1971) James M. Cox puts it this way: "For when politics and history become dominant realities for the imagination, then the traditional prose forms of the essay and the autobiography both gain and attract power and the more overtly 'literary' forms of prose fiction—the novel and the short story—are likely to be threatened and impoverished."

tion since he's a literary performer without peer. Though Bellow and others may write better books in some cosmic objective sence, they are no match for Mailer as a dazzling performer, a writer who uses his work as stage or scene for the dramatization of the self.

Poirier could have drawn on the New Journalism as conducted by Mailer and others to illustrate his point. It has been talked about by writers and commentators, analyzed, dissected, pronounced dead or alive, largely in terms of the details and technicalities of performance rather than in light of the thing performed, the finished product. It has been celebrated, and celebrated itself, by drawing attention to how the work is done (by saturation reporting, by asking questions about thoughts and feelings, by free-form writing, by training the memory to avoid note taking, by revealing the presence of the writer, etc.) or in light of its implications for literary-journalistic history (a revival of the realistic tradition, a breakthrough to a new form called the nonfiction novel, a return to the personal essay, etc.). Fittingly enough for a self-conscious development in a self-conscious age, far more printed space and far more talk time in interviews and panel discussions have been given to the technical ins and outs of the New Journalism, to its inventive feats of reporting and writing—in other words, to the performing self, the journalist at his work—than to careful considerations of the work by and of itself.

Yet it's exactly here that the most troublesome critical difficulty with the New Journalism seems to lie. Michael J. Arlen holds that much of the New Journalism fails because of "the New Journalist's determination and insistence that we shall see life largely on *his* terms." He's willing to allow most of the objections to rigid journalistic objectivity but still finds something "troubling and askew in the arrogance—and perhaps especially in the personal unease—that so often seems to compel the New Journalist to present us our reality embedded in his own ego." Arlen's complaint rests primarily on established journalistic notions of detachment (though he's as quick as any New Journalist to disassociate himself from the on-the-one-hand . . . on-the-other-hand style of reporting). The journalist should subordinate himself to his material and render it in *its* term, not his own. An account of reality itself, not the journalist's private version of it, is what's required.

But if that's the way of journalism it's not the way of literature. In good literature the whole point is to get the reader to see life on the writer's terms. Serious literature is always in a sense escape literature in that it removes us from ourselves and to some degree locks us within another's vision of things—with of course the paradoxical hope that, through sharpened perception or broadened awareness, we will plunge back into our own reality to a greater depth than was possible before. Modern experimental literature, it's true, disdains the mesmerizing effect of traditional literature and tends (for various theoretical reasons) to keep the reader at arm's distance, interested in a narrative but not absorbed in it, within his own realm of reality. Yet the essential (if greatly oversimplified) aim of good writing, experimental or traditional, is to draw the reader into what Poirier has called a "world elsewhere," a world of the writer's own imaginative making, and however much that world at times resembles our own it's the writer's capacity to persuade us into *his* vision that we most deeply respond to. No one, as the critic Philip Young points out, "really wants to read about life precisely and exactly as he knows it"—which helps explain why we celebrate tragedy in our books though not in our lives, why we find happy endings suspect in literature but totally desirable in reality.

Journalism is wholly another story. If art is not life journalism is supposed to be. If we don't want to read about life in serious literature exactly as we know it that's precisely what we want to do in journalism. Journalism brings us the news not of worlds elsewhere but of this world, with all its familiar foolishness and comedy, pain and tragedy. The New Journalism, however, tries to draw together, or draw closer, the conflicting worlds of journalism and literature. It carries over into traditional journalism a variety of literary techniques and attitudes—the most important of which being the artist's need (as Sheed puts it) to drag everything back to *his* cave, to stamp everything, character, events, language, with the imprint of his person.

Obviously the New Journalists attempt such blending in varying degrees. Most locate themselves on one side or the other—as journalists trying to extend journalism's reach or as literary types using fact for artistic purpose. But however the New Journalists view themselves, what they are up to is neither exactly literature nor exactly journalism but a rough mixture of the two—and that's the heart of the critical problem. The New Journalism is vulnerable on both sides. It can be argued that it misses literary quality because it remains bound to fact, hence inhibiting the full play of artistry which the imaginative writer can bring to bear. Thus a book as artfully shaped as *In Cold Blood* is classified only as a superior piece of journalism (or what Donald Pizer calls a "documentary narrative"), an engrossing account of crime and punishment—and not another *Crime and Punishment*. But it likewise can be argued that the New Journalism lacks real journalistic quality because in the very imaginative artistry it *does* employ it leaves itself suspect as solid reporting.

To the degree that journalism pushes toward literature it opens itself to attack both as second-rate literature and second-rate journalism. It comes to resemble what Dwight Macdonald calls parajournalism, "a bastard form, having it both ways, exploiting the factual authority of journalism and the atmospheric license of fiction." Parajournalism appears in the guise of journalism and touts itself as journalism but in fact isn't journalism since its aim isn't to convey information (even though the information may be totally accurate) but create entertainment. Its tendency to personalize issues and events and, depending on how much literary apparatus is warmed up, to dramatize situations through novelistic scene setting and character building makes for interesting reading but dubious history. The result, despite repeated claims to accuracy, is widespread disregard of the New Journalism as serious journalism, let alone serious literature, and the inclination to view it as yet another branch of the entertainment industry. Or to suggest with Sheed that it's only to be trusted with small units of material and not with deep issues or significant events—in other words, not with real history.

Is there any way out of such a critical crunch? Probably not. So long as the New Journalism continues to claim positions within the territory of traditional journalism and serious literature it's open to attack from both sides—in Wolfe's polar terms, from the clerks of fact and the men of letters. As personal writing the New Journalism will most likely continue to draw journalistic fire for too much intrusion by the writer, literary fire for too little. But one thing that might help— to offer, at this late stage, a light suggestion—would be to shift the level of the controversy, hence changing the angle of criticism. It might be put forward, for example, that what the rise of the New Journalism mostly signifies is the emergence of a new kind of popular literature, and that it's on this level, the level of new trends in popular culture, that acclaim and denial might best be offered.

As popular literature the New Journalism whips together a mixture of feature-story journalism, true confessions, mass-magazine fiction, the middlebrow novel, and narrative history—though in extent of reporting and quality of writing it usually ranks a far cut above all its ingredients. The mass audience it seeks is not the old middlebrow audience but the large and growing liberally-educated population that has been through the required surveys of literature yet holds fast to the national fascination with fact. It's an audience that wants to know what's going on, that feels compelled to Keep Up, but prefers its information—if it has to read to get it—dispatched entertainingly and with familiar literary trimmings.* Information plus art . . . an up-to-date factual fiction that leaps over the dreariness of day-to-day journalism yet doesn't fly off in the strange ways of Barth and Borges and Barthelme . . . rather like Herman Wouk's *The Winds of War* (currently atop the best-seller lists), in other words, except that it's *true*, every last detail of it: the rough formula for a new style of popular literature.

---

* Dwight Macdonald suggests that Wolfe's *Kandy-Kolored* is addressed not so much to the young, as it might at first appear, as to "a large and growing public that feels it really should Take An Interest and is looking for guidance as to what is, currently, The Real Thing."

From this angle Tom Wolfe may well have something in linking the New Journalism to the origins of the realistic novel. The New Journalism may be beginning to function in something of the same way for an educated middle class as the early novel did for an emerging economic middle class—it's bringing the news in engaging fashion (about such matters as the Mafia and the Detroit Lions and moon shoots and politicians and Hell's Angels and the Bernsteins—and soon, from Gay Talese, about new sexual manners). It's offering itself, in Seymour Krim's words, as a "literature for the majority." That's worth the doing of course and it can be done with high degrees of skill and genuine artistry, as many New Journalists have demonstrated. But it's clearly not the only thing worth doing nor necessarily the best. There's still the serious novel—and still serious journalism and serious history. Of course some New Journalists might interpose at this point (well, Tom Wolfe might interpose) that for that super-inflated highbrow word "serious" one really ought to read "dull"—an understated, "pale beige" kind of writing that bores readers to tears because it lacks all the New Journalism's "personality, energy, drive, bravura . . . style, in a word." That, alas, may now and then be the case—and for the good enough reason that not every subject yields easily to kandy-kolored treatment, not every subject can—or should—end up as an entertainment, even in an amusement society such as our own. The point is simply that there are some hard historical, journalistic, and literary tasks around that require hard, demanding, dispassionate treatment— minority tasks, admittedly, appealing to small and necessarily elite audiences but searching beyond information and technique and entertainment to the deepest truth. This kind of writing has been around for a long time and will doubtless continue; the New Journalism is neither threatening nor replacing it—nor is it seriously confusing distinctions. The New Journalism simply operates on different levels and must be understood by different standards.

Just how different those standards ought to be can perhaps be gauged by quoting from a house ad carried in *Harper's* a short time ago in which the magazine tried to describe with a geographic metaphor its brand of New Journalism:

> Somewhere west of journalism and this side of history . . . there is a place where reporting becomes literature. There are those— namely one million readers—who think Harper's Magazine is the place.

> For Harper's Magazine is dedicated to the idea that fine writing need not buckle under the pressure of a deadline, nor should literature be solely confined to the dim distant past or the recent inventions of a novelist's mind. It can deal with *now*—with the angers of our time, the beautiful beginnings of a changed society and the sad vestiges of a violent past. . . .

Even with normal allowances for the heady inflations of advertising, the gripping rhetoric of the ad ("the angers . . . the beautiful beginnings . . . the sad vestiges. . . .") might appear to give the game away. Somewhere west of journalism and this side of history there's a place where reporting becomes . . . *popular* literature. Call it the New Journalism.

But really now, isn't that just the old hidebound man-of-letters view, the typical put-down via pigeonholing of the likes of Wolfe's Literary Gentleman In The Grandstand? So the New Journalism is maybe better understood as a new development directed to a new and educated mass audience within the familiar genre of popular literature; so you drop it down a notch or two in some vague literary-journalistic pecking order; so what? So it might help to tone down the controversy a little, put it in a slightly more sensible perspective if not the absolutely correct pigeonhole—a perspective from which it might be suggested that the New Journalism has resulted in some good, fresh writing but not the discovery of a new art form (or the rediscovery, in journalistic dress, of an old one) that's wiping out the serious novel or even coming close. A perspective from which it might be suggested that what the New Journalism involves is not a Great Take Over of journalism or literature but the application of intensified journalistic practices, literary techniques, and artistic intentions on nonfiction materials mostly on levels (so far) of mass consumption and mass (though college trained) taste. All of which isn't to say very much of course—but maybe it's all that *can* be said, with a passably straight face.

As even Tom Wolfe seems to know. Near the end of his *New Journalism* treatise he offers a suddenly narrowed summary:

> The status of the New Journalism is not secured by any means. In some quarters the contempt for it is boundless . . . even breathtaking. . . . With any luck at all the new genre will never be sanctified, never be exalted, never given a theology. I probably shouldn't even go around talking it up the way I have in this piece. All I meant to say when I started out was that the New Journalism can no longer be ignored in an artistic sense. The rest I take back.

Fair enough. But if the New Journalism shouldn't be ignored in an artistic sense neither should it be puffed entirely out of its league, characterized as the great word wave of the future, the last best hope of writing man, sweeping all distinctions before it. It's simply what Wolfe, in another of his clear-eyed moments, says it is: some sort of artistic excitement in journalism. That's exciting enough.

Part One

PERSONAL JOURNALISM

Introduction to
THE KANDY-KOLORED TANGERINE-FLAKE STREAMLINE BABY

TOM WOLFE

I don't mean for this to sound like "I had a vision" or anything, but there was a specific starting point for practically all of these stories. I wrote them in a fifteen-month period, and the whole thing started with the afternoon I went to a Hot Rod & Custom Car show at the Coliseum in New York. Strange afternoon! I was sent up there to cover the Hot Rod & Custom Car show by the New York *Herald Tribune*, and I brought back exactly the kind of story any of the somnambulistic totem newspapers in America would have come up with. A totem newspaper is the kind people don't really buy to read but just to *have*, physically, because they know it supports their own outlook on life. They're just like the buffalo tongues the Omaha Indians used to carry around or the dog ears the Mahili clan carried around in Bengal. There are two kinds of totem newspapers in the country. One is the symbol of the frightened

Tom Wolfe acknowledges that the first time he realized there was something new going on in journalism was in 1962 when he read an *Esquire* article by Gay Talese on Joe Louis. But the New Journalism became a subject, with appropriate capital letters, in 1965 with the publication of Wolfe's first collection of articles and the introduction in which he explained his now-celebrated breakthrough to a new style and new material. The later Wolfe exercises in the New Journalism are *The Pump House Gang, The Electric Kool-Aid Acid Test,* and *Radical Chic & Mau-Mauing the Flak Catchers.*

chair-arm-doilie Vicks Vapo-Rub *Weltanschauung* that lies there in the solar plexus of all good gray burghers. All those nice stories on the first page of the second section about eighty-seven-year-old ladies on Gramercy Park who have one-hundred-and-two-year-old turtles or about the colorful street vendors of Havana. Mommy! This fellow Castro is in there, and revolutions may come and go, but the picturesque poor will endure, padding around in the streets selling their chestnuts and salt pretzels the world over, even in Havana, Cuba, assuring a paradise, after all, full of respect and obeisance, for all us Vicks Vapo-Rub chair-arm-doilie burghers. After all. Or another totem group buys the kind of paper they can put under their arms and have the totem for the tough-but-wholesome outlook, the Mom's Pie view of life. Everybody can go off to the bar and drink a few "brews" and retail some cynical remarks about Zora Folley and how the fight game is these days and round it off, though, with how George Chuvalo has "a lot of heart," which he got, one understands, by eating mom's pie. Anyway, I went to the Hot Rod & Custom Car show and wrote a story that would have suited any of the totem newspapers. All the totem newspapers would regard one of these shows as a sideshow, a panopticon, for creeps and kooks; not even wealthy, eccentric creeps and kooks, which would be all right, but lower class creeps and nutballs with dermatitic skin and ratty hair. The totem story usually makes what is known as "gentle fun" of this, which is a way of saying, don't worry, these people are nothing.

So I wrote a story about a kid who had built a golden motorcycle, which he called "The Golden Alligator." The seat was made of some kind of gold-painted leather that kept going back, on and on, as long as an alligator's tail, and had scales embossed on it, like an alligator's. The kid had made a whole golden suit for himself, like a space suit, that also looked as if it were covered with scales and he would lie down on his stomach on this long seat, stretched out full length, so that he appeared to be made into the motorcycle or something, and roar around Greenwich Village on Saturday nights, down Macdougal Street, down there in Nut Heaven, looking like a golden alligator on wheels. Nutty! He seemed like a Gentle Nut when I got through. It was a shame I wrote that sort of story, the usual totem story, because I was working for the *Herald Tribune*, and the *Herald Tribune* was the only experimental paper in town, breaking out of the totem formula. The thing was, I knew I had another story all the time, a bona fide story, the real story of the Hot Rod & Custom Car show, but I didn't know what to do with it. It was outside the system of ideas I was used to working with, even though I had been through the whole Ph.D. route at Yale, in American Studies and everything.

Here were all these . . . *weird* . . . nutty-looking, crazy baroque custom cars, sitting in little nests of pink angora angel's hair for the purpose of "glamorous" display—but then I got to talking to one of the men who make them, a fellow named Dale Alexander. He was a very serious and soft-spoken man, about thirty, completely serious about the whole thing, in fact, and pretty soon it became clear, as I talked to this man for a while, that he had been living like the *complete artist* for years. He had starved, suffered—the whole thing—so he could sit inside a garage and create these cars which more than 99 per cent of the American people would consider ridiculous, vulgar and lower-class-awful beyond comment almost. He had started off with a garage that fixed banged-up cars and everything, to pay the rent, but gradually he couldn't stand it anymore. Creativity—his own custom car art—became an obsession with him. So he became the complete custom car artist. And he said he wasn't the only one. All the great custom car designers had gone through it. It was the *only way. Holy beasts!* Starving artists! Inspiration! Only instead of garrets, they had these garages.

So I went over to *Esquire* magazine after a while and talked to them about this phenomenon, and they sent me out to California to take a look at the custom car world. Dale Alexander was from Detroit or some place, but the real center of the thing was in California, around Los Angeles. I started talking to a lot of these people, like George Barris and Ed Roth, and seeing what they were doing, and—well, eventually it became the story from which the title of this book was taken, "The Kandy-Kolored Tangerine-Flake Streamline Baby." But at first I couldn't even write the story. I came back to New York and just sat around worrying over the thing. I had a lot of trouble analyzing exactly what I had on my hands. By this time *Esquire* practically had a gun at my head because they had a two-page-wide color picture for the story locked into the printing presses and no story. Finally, I told Byron Dobell, the managing editor at *Esquire*, that I couldn't pull the thing together. O.K., he tells me, just type out my notes and send them over and he will get somebody else to write it. So about 8 o'clock that night I started typing the notes out in the form of a memorandum that began, "Dear Byron." I started typing away, starting right with the first time I saw any custom cars in California. I just started recording it all, and inside of a couple of hours, typing along like a madman, I could tell that something was beginning to happen. By midnight this memorandum to Byron was twenty pages long and I was still typing like a maniac. About 2 A.M. or something like that I turned on WABC, a radio station that plays rock and roll music all night long, and got a little more manic. I wrapped up the memorandum about 6:15 A.M., and by this time it was 49 pages long. I took it over to *Esquire* as soon as they opened up, about 9:30 A.M. About 4 P.M. I got a call from Byron Dobell. He told me they were striking out the "Dear Byron" at the top of the memorandum and running the rest of it in the magazine. That was the story, "The Kandy-Kolored Tangerine-Flake Streamline Baby."

What had happened was that I started writing down everything I had seen the first place I went in California, this incredible event, a "Teen Fair." The details themselves, when I wrote them down, suddenly made me see what was happening. Here was this incredible combination of form plus money in a place nobody ever thought about finding it, namely, among teen-agers. Practically every style recorded in art history is the result of the same thing—a lot of attention to form, plus the money to make monuments to it. The "classic" English style of Inigo Jones, for example, places like the Covent Garden and the royal banquet hall at Whitehall, were the result of a worship of Italian Palladian grandeur . . . form . . . plus the money that began pouring in under James I and Charles I from colonial possessions. These were the kind of forms, styles, symbols . . . Palladian classicism . . . that influence a whole society. But throughout history, everywhere this kind of thing took place, China, Egypt, France under the Bourbons, every place, it has been something the aristocracy has been responsible for. What has happened in the United States since World War II, however, has broken that pattern. The war created money. It made massive infusions of money into every level of society. Suddenly classes of people whose styles of life had been practically invisible had the money to build monuments to their own styles. Among teen-agers, this took the form of custom cars, the twist, the jerk, the monkey, the shake, rock music generally, stretch pants, decal eyes—and all these things, these teen-age styles of life, like Inigo Jones' classicism, have started having an influence on the life of the whole country. It is not merely teen-agers. In the South, for example, all the proles, peasants, and petty burghers suddenly got enough money to start up their incredible car world. In fifteen years stock car racing has replaced baseball as the number one sport in the South. It doesn't make much difference what happens to baseball or stock car racing, actually, but this shift, from a fixed land sport, modeled on cricket, to this wild car sport, with standard, or standard-looking, cars that go 180 miles an hour or so—this symbolizes a radical change in the people as a whole. Practically nobody has bothered to see what these changes are all about. People have been looking at the new money since the war in economic terms only. Nobody will even take a look at our incredible new national pastimes, things like stock car racing, drag racing, demolition derbies, sports that attract five to ten million more spectators than football, baseball and basketball each year. Part of it is a built-in class bias. The educated classes in this country, as in every country, the people who grow up to control visual and printed communication media, are all plugged into what is, when one gets down to it, an ancient, aristocratic aesthetic. Stock car racing, custom cars—and, for that matter, the jerk, the monkey, rock music—still seem beneath serious consideration, still the preserve of ratty people with ratty hair and dermatitis and corroded thoracic boxes and so forth. Yet all these rancid people are creating new styles all the time and changing the life of the whole country in ways that nobody even seems to bother to record, much less analyze.

A curious example of what is happening in Society, in the sense of High Society, in New York City today. Only it isn't called High Society or even Café Society anymore. Nobody seems to know quite what to call it, but the term that is catching on is Pop Society. This is because socialites in New York today seem to have no natural, aristocratic styles of their own—they are taking all their styles from "pop" groups, which stands for popular, or "vulgar" or "bohemian" groups. They dance the jerk, the monkey, the shake, they listen to rock music, the women wear teen-age and even "sub-teen" styles, such as stretch pants and decal eyes, they draw their taste in art, such as "underground" movies and "pop" painting, from various bohos and camp culturati, mainly. New York's "Girl of the Year"—Baby Jane Holzer—is the most incredible socialite in history. Here in this one girl is a living embodiment of almost pure "pop" sensation, a kind of corn-haired essence of the new styles of life. I never had written a story that seemed to touch so many nerves in so many people. Television and the movies all of a sudden went crazy over her, but that was just one side of it. A lot of readers were enraged. They wrote letters to the publisher of the *Herald Tribune*, to the *Herald Tribune* magazine, *New York*, where it appeared, they made phone calls, they would confront me with it in restaurants, all sorts of things—and in all of it I kept noticing the same thing. Nobody ever seemed to be able to put his finger on what he was enraged about. Most of them took the line that the *Herald Tribune* had no business paying that much attention to such a person and such a life as she was leading. Refreshing! Moral Outrage! But it was all based on the idea that Jane Holzer was some kind of freak they didn't like. Jane Holzer—and the Baby Jane syndrome—there's nothing freakish about it. Baby Jane is the hyper-version of a whole new style of life in America. I think she is a very profound symbol. But she is not the super-hyper-version. The super-hyper-version is Las Vegas. I call Las Vegas the Versailles of America, and for specific reasons. Las Vegas happened to be created after the war, with war money, by gangsters. Gangsters happened to be the first uneducated . . . but more to the point, un-aristocratic, *outside* of the aristocratic tradition . . . the first unedu-cated, prole-petty-burgher Americans to have enough money to build a monument to their style of life. They built it in an isolated spot, Las Vegas, out in the desert, just like Louis XIV, the Sun King, who pur-posely went outside of Paris, into the countryside, to create a fantastic baroque environment to celebrate his rule. It is no accident that Las Vegas and Versailles are the only two architecturally uniform cities in Western history. The important thing about the building of Las Vegas is not that the builders were gangsters but that they were proles. They celebrated, very early, the new style of life of America—using the money pumped in by the war to show a prole vision . . . *Glamor!* . . . of style. The usual thing has happened, of course. Because it is prole, it gets ignored, except on the most sensational level. Yet long after Las Vegas' influence as a gambling heaven has gone, Las Vegas' forms and symbols will be influencing American life. That fantastic skyline! Las Vegas' neon sculpture, its fantastic fifteen-story-high display signs, parabolas, boomerangs, rhomboids, trapezoids and all the rest of it, are already the staple design of the American landscape outside of the oldest parts of the oldest cities. They are all over every suburb, every subdivision, every highway . . . every *hamlet*, as it were, the new crossroads, spiraling Servicenter signs. They are the new landmarks of America, the new guideposts, the new way Americans get their bearings. And yet what do we know about these signs, these incredible pieces of neon sculpture, and what kind of impact they have on people? Nobody seems to know the first thing about it, not even the men who design them. I hunted out some of the great sign makers of Las Vegas, men who design for the Young Electric Sign Co., and the Federal Sign and Signal Corporation—and marvelous!—they come from completely outside the art history tradition of the design schools of the Eastern universities. I remember talking with this one designer, Ted Blaney, from Federal, their chief designer, in the cocktail lounge of the Dunes Hotel on "The Strip." I showed him a shape, a boomerang shape, that one sees all over Las Vegas, in small signs, huge signs, huge things like the archway entrance to the Desert Inn—it is not an arch, really, but this huge boomerang shape—and I asked him what they, the men who design these things, call it.

Ted was a stocky little guy, very sunburnt, with a pencil mustache and a Texas string tie, the kind that has strings sticking through some kind of silver dollar or something situated at the throat. He talked slowly and he had a way of furling his eyebrows around his nose when he did mental calculations such as figuring out this boomerang shape.

He stared at the shape, which he and his brothers in the art have created over and over and over, over, over and over and over in Las Vegas, and finally he said,

"Well, that's what we call—what we sort of call—'free form.'"

Free form! Marvelous! No hung-up old art history words for these guys. America's first unconscious avant-garde! The hell with Mondrian, whoever the hell he is. The hell with Moholy-Nagy, if anybody ever heard of him. Artists for the new age, sculptors for the new style and new money of the . . . Yah! lower orders. The new sensibility—*Baby baby baby where did our love go?*—the new world, submerged so long, invisible, and now arising, slippy, shiny, electric—Super Scuba-man!—out of the vinyl deeps.

Author's Note to
FAME AND OBSCURITY

GAY TALESE

My thanks to my editor, Robert A. Gutwillig, for assembling this collection. Most of the selections are representative of a form of reporting being referred to these days as the "new journalism," the "new nonfiction," or "parajournalism," the latter a derogatory description coined by the critic Dwight Macdonald, who is somewhat suspicious of the form, feeling, as a few other critics do, that its practitioners compromise the facts in the interest of more dramatic reporting.* I do not agree.

The new journalism, though often reading like fiction, is not fiction. It is, or should be, as reliable as the most reliable reportage although it seeks a larger truth than is possible through the mere compilation of verifiable facts, the use of direct quotations, and adherence to the rigid organizational style of the older form. The new journalism allows, demands in fact, a more imaginative approach to reporting, and it permits the writer to inject himself into the narrative if he wishes, as many writers do, or to assume the role of a detached observer, as other writers do, including myself.

Gay Talese's collection of magazine articles was published under the title *Fame and Obscurity* in 1970. His most recent work is *Honor Thy Father*.

---

* [Editor's note: See Dwight Macdonald, "Parajournalism, or Tom Wolfe and His Magic Writing Machine," page 223.]

I try to follow my subjects unobtrusively while observing them in revealing situations, noting their reactions and the reactions of others to them. I attempt to absorb the whole scene, the dialogue and mood, the tension, drama, conflict, and then I try to write it all from the point of view of the persons I am writing about, even revealing whenever possible what these individuals are *thinking* during those moments that I am describing. This latter insight is not obtainable, of course, without the full cooperation of the subject, but if the writer enjoys the confidence and trust of his subjects it is possible, through interviews, by asking the right question at the right time, to learn and to report what goes on within other people's minds.

I did this extensively in my book of last year, *The Kingdom and the Power*, and I hope to experiment still further with it in a book that I am involved with now, a study of tradition and change within three successive generations of an Italo-American family between 1900 and 1970. However, in this collection, *Fame and Obscurity*, I do not achieve all of what I suggest is possible in nonfiction because most of the selections included here were written originally as magazine articles, each having been produced within a period of between four and eight weeks. One exception is the DiMaggio profile, which took about ten weeks; another is the Sinatra profile, which took closer to three months (neither man was very cooperative, although I believe that this was ultimately more a help than a hindrance); and a third exception is the portrait of the bridge-builders, which was originally published as a short book entitled *The Bridge* and was researched, sporadically, over a period of several months—less research time than I think I would settle for today, particularly since one of my ambitions is to remain with my subjects long enough to see their lives change in some way. By way of comparison, I spent three years researching and writing *The Kingdom and the Power*, a human history of *The New York Times*, where I had once worked; and I have been researching the book about the Italian-American family, on and off, for about six years to date.

Still, *Fame and Obscurity* does include some of the best reporting and writing that I have done during the nineteen-sixties, representing a shift from the "old" journalism that I had practiced at *The Times* to the freer, more challenging approach that *Esquire* magazine permitted and encouraged under the editorship of Harold Hayes. My first contribution to *Esquire*, in 1960, was an essay on obscurity in New York City, a series of vignettes on the unnoticed people, the odd facts and bizarre events that had caught my fancy during my travels around town as a newspaperman. This was a beginning of what later became a book that Harper & Row published in 1961 entitled, *New York—A Serendipiter's Journey*. Rereading that book now, in the closing section of *Fame and Obscurity*, I recognize it as a young man's view of New York, envisioned with a mixture of wonderment and awe, and yet with a realization, too, of how destructive the city is, how it promises so much more than it fulfills, and how right E. B. White was when he wrote many years ago: "No one should come to New York to live unless he is willing to be lucky." There is also in *Serendipiter's Journey* some early signs of my interest in using the techniques of fiction, an aspiration on my part to somehow bring to reportage the tone that Irwin Shaw and John O'Hara had brought to the short story. But I did not get very far with this in *Serendipiter's Journey*, finally relying more on the selection of my material than on style to reflect the glamour and gloom that I have always felt so strongly in New York.

After this tentative beginning, my first attempt at what would be called the "new journalism" began with some of the profiles on famous people that I did for *Esquire*. In the Joe Louis piece, for example, the article opens with Louis, fatigued after three frolicsome days and nights in New York City, arriving at the Los Angeles airport and being met by his wife, the lawyer—a scene that could have led into a short story situation; later in the article, the writing style falls back on straighter reportage, indicating my own uncertainty with the form at that point, but still later the approach is again scene-setting and dialogue and away from rigid reporting.

A more successful attempt at using fictional techniques for factual situations is in the profile of Joshua Logan, the theatrical director. I happened to be in the theater one afternoon watching Logan rehearse his play when, suddenly, he and his star, Claudia McNeil, got into an argument that not only was more dramatic than the play itself, but revealed something of the character of Logan and Miss McNeil in ways that I could never have done had I approached the subject from the more conventional form of reporting.

While researching the Frank Sinatra piece I also happened to be at the right place at the right time: on the night that Sinatra objected to the attire of the young man playing pool in the game room of the Daisy Discotheque, in Beverly Hills, I had been standing near the bar in the other room. While I missed the opening exchange between Sinatra and the young man, I did arrive in time to hear most of what transpired; later, with the cooperation of witnesses who had heard it all, I was able to reconstruct the scene.

As I noted earlier, Sinatra was not very cooperative during my stay in Beverly Hills. I had arrived at a bad time for him, he being upset by a head cold among other irritants, and I was unable to get the interview that I had expected. Nevertheless I did observe him periodically during the six weeks that I spent on research, watching him at recording sessions, on a movie set, at the gambling tables in Las Vegas, and I was able to perceive his changing moods, his irritation and suspicion when he thought that I was getting too close, his pleasure and courtesy and charm when he was able to relax among those whom he trusted. I gained more by watching him, overhearing him, and watching the reaction of those around him than if I had actually been able to sit down and talk to him.

Joe DiMaggio was an even more reluctant subject when I began the research on him in San Francisco. I had met DiMaggio six months before in New York, at which time he indicated that he would cooperate on the article; but his attitude was radically different after I had appeared outside his restaurant on Fisherman's Wharf. And yet the tense and chilly reception that I received, initially, provided me with an interesting opening scene in which I was not only a witness but a participant being ejected from the premises by DiMaggio himself. The fact that I was able to become reacquainted with DiMaggio a few days later was the result of a request that I had made through one of DiMaggio's friends and golfing partners that I be allowed to follow their foursome through one eighteen-hole round. During the golfing session, DiMaggio, who hates to lose golf balls, lost three of them. I found them. After that, DiMaggio's attitude toward me improved noticeably; I was invited to other golf matches and to join him in the evening with his other friends at Reno's bar, where much of my work was done.

Except for some minor word changes, such as restoring the colorful profanity of Peter O'Toole that *Esquire's* editors had toned down, I have not updated any of these profiles in *Fame and Obscurity*. They appear in this volume as I wrote them years ago, and they stand simply as a collection of my earlier work. It is always gratifying to an author to have his work remain in print; and for his suggestion to do so, and for his arrangement of the pieces, I am again grateful to Mr. Gutwillig as well as to *Esquire's* editor, Harold Hayes, who published most of them originally, and to the editors of Harper & Row, who permitted the reprinting of *New York—A Serendipiter's Journey, The Bridge,* and some of the profiles that had been included in an obscure earlier collection of mine entitled *The Overreachers.*

The Personal Voice
and the
Impersonal Eye

DAN WAKEFIELD

The negative sound of the term "nonfiction" always seemed to me sadly reflective of the common cultural attitude toward that vast and various field of writing. The term itself indicates that "fiction" is the standard, central sort of serious writing, and anything else is basically defined by being "not" of that genre. (I have sometimes thought that writers of this "non" category ought to strike back by calling novels and stories "nonreality.") Among the subheads beneath the general nonfiction category, such fields as biography and history stand up as respectable, if somewhat plodding, cousins to the major literary practice of fiction. There is also an important and large but even less culturally stylish vein of the nonfiction field that, whether it is referred to as journalism, reporting, or, the fancier term, reportage, is usually preceded by the adjective "mere" in discussions of serious literature. And yet, in the past year nonfiction works by Tom Wolfe and Truman Capote have catapulted the reportorial kind of writing to a level of social interest suitable for cocktail party conversation and little-review comment. As Wolfe might put it, nonfiction has suddenly become . . . *fashionable*.

Dan Wakefield's article in the *Atlantic,* June, 1966, was one of the earliest commentaries on new developments in nonfiction writing. His nonfiction books include *Island in the City* and *Supernation at Peace and War.* He has written two novels, *Going All the Way* and *Starting Over.*

But long before it was announced that Mr. Capote intended to raise reporting to an "art"—somewhat like a benevolent industrialist disclosing his plans for helping out an underdeveloped country—there was, and has continued to be, a growing amount of imaginative and artfully rendered writing in the field. Since the 1950s, Murray Kempton in his newspaper columns and James Baldwin in his personal essays (most notably in *Notes of a Native Son*) have demonstrated that journalism can be practiced at the level of art. Increasing numbers of novelists—among them Harvey Swados, Gore Vidal, George P. Elliott, and Norman Mailer—have tried their hand at journalism and often turned out work of unquestionable literary as well as informational merit. The critic Norman Podhoretz has even suggested that some of Mailer's journalism has been more interesting and important than his fiction.

Whatever the validity or necessity of such comparison, there is no doubt that Mailer's journalistic pieces, especially the long takeouts in *Esquire*, are charged with energy of art. Whether or not his piece in that magazine on the 1960 Democratic convention—"Superman Comes to the Supermarket"—did, as Mailer himself believes, tip the scales of that whole election to John Kennedy in some mysterious, mystical, psycho-hipsterical manner, it certainly proved that a good, factual, and keenly observed account of a political convention doesn't have to be dull. To cite only one section of one enormous, snakelike, shimmering sentence from that report, Mailer described how

> . . . it was in the Gallery of the Biltmore where one first felt the mood which pervaded all proceedings until the convention was almost over, that heavy, thick, witless depression which was to dominate every move as the delegates wandered and gawked and paraded and set for a spell, there in the Gallery of the Biltmore, that huge depressing alley with its inimitable hotel color, that faded depth of chiaroscuro which unhappily has no depth, that brown which is not a brown, that grey which has no pearl in it, that color which can be described only as hotel-color because the beiges, the tans, the walnuts, the mahoganies, the dull blood rugs, the moaning yellows, the sick greens, the greys and all those dumb browns merge into that lack of color which is an over-large hotel at convention time, with all the small-towners wearing their set, starched faces, that look they get at carnival, all fever and suspicion, and proud to be there, eddying slowly back and forth in that high block-long tunnel of a room with its arched ceiling and square recesses filling every rib of the arch with art work, escutcheons and blazons and other art, pictures I think, I cannot even remember, there was such a hill of cigar smoke the eye had to travel on its way to the ceiling, and at one end there was galvanized pipe scaffolding and workmen repairing some part of the ceiling, one of

them touching up one of the endless squares of painted plaster in the arch, and another worker, passing by, yelled up to the one who was working on the ceiling: "Hey, Michelangelo!"

That is of course not the style of cold, clipped, just-the-facts-please daily newspaper journalism, and in an effort to categorize it, some observers have referred to that kind of approach as "fictional." This confuses the issue, and I think it is partly a result of the old prejudice that any "good writing" must by definition be "fictional" writing. Yet the label suggests that the reporting done in such a style is not factual, but rather something the reporter made up. This is not the case. Such reporting is "imaginative" not because the author has distorted the facts, but because he has presented them in a full instead of a naked manner, brought out the sights, sounds, and feel surrounding those facts, and connected them by comparison with other facts of history, society, and literature in an artistic manner that does not diminish but gives greater depth and dimension to the facts.

Mailer is not the first or the last writer to approach an event, person, or subject in this manner, nor is the imaginative method limited to use by novelists. Brock Brower has written persuasively of what he calls the Art of the Fact,* and he has effectively practiced that art, along with Gay Talese, Thomas B. Morgan, and later, Tom Wolfe, most often in the pages of *Esquire*. The graceful, witty, and precise reporting of Meg Greenfield on subjects ranging from The Prose of Richard Nixon to A Tenth Class Reunion at Smith College has brightened and distinguished the pages of *The Reporter;* and Willie Morris, up from the *Texas Observer,* has also demonstrated in personal journalistic accounts like his piece on Texas rightwingers in *Commentary* that reporting has been practiced as an art in our own times.

American magazines have opened up a great deal from the standard cut-and-dried formula-article approach that was generally the rule in the post-war era and into the early fifties, yet I think special credit must be given to *Esquire* for leading the way to many of the newer, freer, more imaginative forms of nonfiction. If their own willingness to experiment has sometimes resulted in an uneven product, in stylistic failures as well as successes, I think on the whole it has had a happy effect on the magazine, the writer, and journalism in general. *Esquire's* editorial attitude seems to be anything goes as long as it is interesting and true. The magazine has a research department, and every fact in every nonfiction piece is checked and verified. The license they offer writers is not for distortion of facts but experimentation in style.

---

* [Editor's note: See Brock Brower, "The Article," page 137.]

The most recent and controversial result of that policy has been the emergence of Tom Wolfe, whose best-selling collection of articles, published last year, was named after one of his *Esquire* pieces, "The Kandy-Kolored Tangerine-Flake Streamline Baby." Wolfe had been assigned to cover a custom car show in California, and when he returned, he found he could not put his notes together into any customary magazine-article form.* *Esquire* needed the copy right away, and asked Wolfe to type up his notes so someone else might try to write the piece. Wolfe did just that, addressing his report to the managing editor and writing up his impressions as he might in a personal letter, beginning "Dear Byron." When the editors read the result they simply struck off the salutation and ran the report as it was. The beginning (it is not a standard "lead") is the key to what Wolfe was going to do and how:

> The first good look I had at customized cars was at an event called a "Teen Fair," held in Burbank, a suburb of Los Angeles beyond Hollywood. This was a wild place to be taking a look at art objects—eventually, I should say, you have to reach the conclusion that these customized cars *are* art objects, at least if you use the standards applied in a civilized society. But I will get to that in a moment. Anyway, about noon you drive up to a place that looks like an outdoor amusement park, and there are three serious-looking kids, like the cafeteria committee in high school, taking tickets, but inside the scene is quite mad.

Such a beginning indeed has the quality and tone of a personal letter from someone who respects my intelligence as a reader, who assumes I can get the message without having it watered down into banal language or dressed up with throat-grabbing urgency. There is a sense that the writer is going to tell the story in his own way and at his own pace ("I will get to that in a moment"), that he is going to describe as well as he can the thing he has witnessed, and explain what he thinks its interest and importance are. There is no pretense of omniscience, self-importance, or the sort of pseudo-gravity that passes for "seriousness." It promises a civilized, casual, and colorful account of a phenomenon unfamiliar to many of us but important to our time; and it delivers.

I think these qualities and characteristics of Wolfe's style are more important than his notorious and easily parodied use of abundant dots and exclamation marks and italics. Yes, there are times when his leads do *not* have a "letterlike" tone, but perhaps come pounding out in something like his start to a piece on Baby Jane Holzer:

---

* [Editor's note: See Tom Wolfe, "Introduction to *The Kandy-Kolored Tangerine-Flake Streamline Baby*," page 29.]

Bangs manes bouffants beehives Beatle caps butter faces brush-on eyelashes decal eyes puffy sweaters French thrust bras flailing. . . .

This descriptive assault turns out to be entirely appropriate to the opening scene of jet-setters attending a concert of the Rolling Stones; and appropriate to the subject of the piece, who moves in such a milieu. The critic should remember that Wolfe's sometimes "mad" style is after all fitted to the madness of what he is writing about, for his social reporting often comes, as he put it himself, "out of the vinyl deep."

Wolfe's critics have accused him of championing the "youth cult" as it is expressed in such phenomena as stock cars, frugging, tight pants, and Beatle caps. This accusation seems to me to miss the whole point of Wolfe's work. As a reader it is clear to me that Wolfe is describing rather than defending the "vinyl" world he is writing about. Dwight Macdonald, the dean of Wolfe's critics, surely misinterprets when he cites as an example of Wolfe's pro-youth and anti-middle-age outlook the end of a piece on stock-car racer Junior Johnson, "The Last American Hero":

. . . up with the automobile into their America, and the hell with arteriosclerotic old boys trying to hold onto the whole pot with arms of cotton seersucker. Junior!

It is "their" America Wolfe is talking about, not his; and it is clear from reading the piece that the ending is an evocation of the feelings of the people he has been describing rather than his own. He has described them and their world—a world that is encroaching on us everywhere in this country—with an artistry that conveys not the attractiveness of it but the hollowness; it is not an alluring but a frightening view of what seems to be building into the main wave of the future in America. Tom Wolfe is the first and so far the best reporter who has told us about it.

When Wolfe's collection of pieces first appeared as the *KKTFSB*, the book was generally received with great praises, including a *Time* magazine judgment that it "might well be required reading in courses like American studies," and a verdict that the author was a "genius" in the *Sunday Times Book Review*. Wolfe was *in*, until he made the mistake of trying to poke some unsupported gibes at the *New Yorker* and its editor in two articles for the *Herald Tribune* Sunday magazine. The furor over that exercise has been comparable in literary circles with the tizzy caused in the sports world by Cassius Clay's declaration that he had "nothing against them Viet Congs." Wolfe's disrespect for the *New Yorker*, like Clay's for his country's foreign policy, resulted in his becoming a cultural *persona non grata*. Everyone from

Murray Kempton to Muriel Spark jumped to attack him, with such usually disparate spirits as Nat Hentoff and Joseph Alsop joining in the bombardment. Not only had Wolfe written two disrespectful pieces with factual errors, but the criticism included charges that his methods smacked of Communism, and yes, McCarthyism. Attention has been lavished on the two offending pieces as if they were the Dead Sea Scrolls, culminating (at least at the time of this writing) in a heavily documented refutation in the *Columbia Journalism Review* by two young *New Yorker* staff members, plus a comment on their own comment on Wolfe's comments by free-lancer Leonard Lewin, which, like a journalistic Supreme Court judgment on the case, ruled that

> Although their indictment is diluted by overzealous refutation of trivial errors (who played the trumpet? what was hung on the walls of Thurber's old office?) they nevertheless make a convincing case, if their allegations are correct, that Wolfe's articles were informed by a remarkable unconcern over the factual basis of his more serious charges, as well as of his atmospheric touches and of his "documented" literary judgments.

Until the inevitable Ph.D. theses come along on the case, I can only judge by evidence extant that Wolfe botched the job, which is all the more regrettable since the nature and intensity of the furor over it indicate that this particular job, as the New York *Post* might put it, "cries out to be done." I am not for condoning Wolfe's factual errors in these pieces, but neither am I for condemning his entire work, style, *persona*, and the magazines he has written articles for because on this occasion he muffed one.

That sort of blanket condemnation, however, has been made at exhaustive length in two articles on Wolfe in the *New York Review of Books* by Dwight Macdonald.* Mr. Macdonald seems to have appointed himself to play the Inspector to Wolfe's Jean Valjean in an endless Tale of Two Articles. Macdonald has also set himself up as a combination detective, prosecutor, and judge over modern journalism, a province one senses that Macdonald feels is his own exclusive turf ("others have discovered our teenage culture, including myself, seven years ago, in a New Yorker series. . . . Mr. Kluger asked me to review it [a Mailer novel reviewed by Wolfe] and I declined for lack of time").

Macdonald attempts to eradicate Wolfe, the *Herald Tribune*, *Esquire*, and some other rival journalists by the invention of the term "parajournalism," which of course is bad journalism, or not the kind, one assumes, Macdonald writes. He defines this evil method as "a

---

* [Editor's note: See Dwight Macdonald, "Parajournalism, or Tom Wolfe and His Magic Writing Machine," page 223.]

bastard form, having it both ways, exploiting the factual authority of journalism and the atmospheric license of fiction." He identifies the *Herald Tribune* as the citadel of this heresy, though he points the finger of accusation at *Esquire* as the place where "the genre originated" and where it has also flourished. He does not mention the fact that he has written for *Esquire* himself for more than five years, or that he is a regular movie critic for that magazine. Whether his own contributions in that magazine are to be considered "parajournalism," or perhaps in the case of his movie criticism, "parareviewing," he does not say. Nor does he explain what he means by the "atmospheric license of fiction," though it sounds like a license to make things up, a charge which his own experience in being queried by the *Esquire* research department must surely have illustrated as untrue in the case of that magazine.

It is difficult to pinpoint exact and usable definitions of this para-journalism. But let us try, following Macdonald as he castigates a Wolfe review of Mailer's latest novel and berates the reviewer as again playing parajournalist because his technique was "to jeer at the author's private life and personality—or rather his *persona*. . . ."

Surely then, the following passages, taken from a piece written shortly after the death of Ernest Hemingway, could rank as para-journalism:

> He was a big man and he was famous and he drank a great deal now and wrote very little. . . .
>
> The position is outflanked the lion can't be stopped the sword won't go into the bull's neck the great fish is breaking the line and it is the fifteenth round and the champion looks bad. . . .
>
> Now it is that morning in the house in Ketchum, Idaho. He takes his favorite gun down from the rack. . . . He puts the end of the gun barrel into his mouth and he pulls both triggers.

It is hard to match that for bad taste, and for jeering at the *persona* rather than criticizing the work of an author. Surely then it ranks as "parajournalism." And yet it was written by Dwight Macdonald. You see, this becomes very confusing. After all Macdonald's complaints about errors, it is surprising to find that in an addendum to the Hemingway piece, in which he included a letter from George Plimpton that refuted much of what Macdonald said, Macdonald admitted on at least the significant point of Hemingway's turning to drinking instead of writing that "I was wrong factually. . . ." Mr. Macdonald was also wrong factually in a nasty piece he wrote about William F. Buckley, Jr., in which Macdonald refers to Buckley's mother's "private chapel," which Buckley claims was actually a steeple on their horse barn; his mother has no private chapel. Mr. Buckley wrote Macdonald a letter about this and other errors, but Macdonald evidently didn't think it a serious enough matter to correct them when he reprinted the essay in book form. Nor did he, of course, alter his attack on Mr. Buckley's *persona,* including the judgment that Buckley is "an indecorous young man." I don't think any of this disqualifies Mr. Macdonald as a serious journalist, but perhaps it disqualifies him as a watchdog over the sins of his colleagues.

Bad taste and errors of fact can crop up in any kind of journalism, as indeed in any kind of writing, and I don't think recent journalism with its freer style is any more guilty of distortion than the older, more traditional forms. The important and interesting and hopeful trend to me in the new journalism is its personal nature—not in the sense of personal attacks, but in the presence of the reporter himself and the significance of his own involvement. This is sometimes felt to be egotistical, and the frank identification of the author, especially as the "I" instead of merely the impersonal "eye," is often frowned upon and taken as proof of "subjectivity," which is the opposite of the usual journalistic pretense. And yet, as Thoreau pointed out in *Walden,* "It is, after all, always the first person that is speaking."

Since I feel that this admission and use of the first singular is the most exciting, challenging, and potentially fruitful course for modern journalism, I naturally was not inclined to find favor with Truman Capote's third-person omniscient, "novelistic" account of a murder case, *In Cold Blood.* By the pretense or device of keeping himself, as the reporter, out of the book altogether, and reconstructing the chain of events leading up to and following the murder in a straight flow of descriptive narrative and dialogue, Capote has produced what he calls a "nonfiction novel." That may sound like a contradiction in terms, and I think it is.

I don't think Capote was the Columbus of the "nonfiction novel" because no one had thought of it before, but rather because it had been rejected as a journalistic, if not an artistic, possibility. As a matter of fact, the closest thing to it I know of was not done in serious journalism at all, but in those magazines for men with titles like *Male He-Man* and *Brawny Adventure.* A free-lance writer friend of mine in New York used to write sometimes for such publications when he was broke, and he explained to me that the sort of "article" he did for them was called by the editors "fact-fiction." The method was to take a somewhat innocuous news account of a murder or accident or other potentially dramatic event and then build it up into a story with invented dialogue and "fictional development" of the characters involved. The technique of invented dialogue is also sometimes used in stories in confessional and "fan" magazines, which, again, are not regarded as organs of serious or responsible journalism.

Now this was, of course, not Capote's method. He spent countless hours over a period of years examining facts, interviewing, and re-searching his story. He has said that he is blessed with a memory that can retain the details of two- and three-hour conversations, without transcribing them on the spot by notes or tape recorder, and I have no reason to doubt this gift. Nor do I question the repeated assertion in the book that one of the murderers (most fortunately for Capote) was blessed with a "brilliant memory." But I cannot believe that everyone in the town of Holcomb, Kansas, the scene of the crime, possessed the faculty of total recall; yet that would have to be the case for Capote's book to be a true, journalistically accurate rendering of dialogue as well as scene and event. Try to remember conversations you had a few weeks ago or even days ago; you can recall the content, but rarely can you remember the verbatim exchange or set it down in the form of a transcript. I am convinced that Capote did as honest and skillful a job as possible in his re-creation; I simply am skeptical of the journal-istic validity of any such re-creation—and I wince at the thought of the inevitable legions of less skillful and less scrupulous imitators of Capote's "new form." They will soon be upon us, wave on wave.

From the artistic as well as the journalistic viewpoint, I am dis-appointed that Capote chose to go off in the opposite direction from the personal "I" approach in his effort to revitalize modern journalism. If reporting is, as Capote says, "the great unexplored art form of the future," I think it will develop along the direction taken by a writer who, ironically, is, or at least was once, greatly admired by Capote. In an interview with Capote in the *Paris Review* published in 1958, he named among those writers who had most influenced him "James Agee, a writer whose death over two years ago was a real loss." And yet it was Agee, in his great *sui generis* book on the tenant farmers in Ala-bama, *Let Us Now Praise Famous Men*, who recognized and made art and illumination of the presence and personality of the reporter as he entered and inevitably affected the scene and events he was watching, or as Agee put it, "spying" upon. For Agee this was not a matter of egotism or of art, but a practical matter of honesty and communication. As he explained, referring to one of the tenant farmers he was writing about:

> George Gudger is a man, et cetera. But obviously, in the effort
> to tell of him (by example) as truthfully as I can, I am limited.
> I know him only so far as I know him, and only in those terms in
> which I know him; and all of that depends as fully on who I am
> as on who he is.

Capote, trained in the *New Yorker*-LillianRoss school of dead-pan journalism, which he first practiced in book-length form in his series on the trip of the *Porgy and Bess* troupe to Russia (*The Muses Are Heard*), betrayed or revealed his own view of the nature of reporting in that same *Paris Review* interview. The interviewer noted Capote's unusual "detachment" in writing *The Muses*, and in discussing that and other issues of journalistic style, Capote remarked of the *Porgy and Bess* pieces: "That was reporting, and 'emotions' were not much involved—at least not the difficult and personal territories of feeling that I mean."

This sort of "detachment" seems to me particularly—and even understandably—sacred in America, where advanced degrees are offered in journalism, and in general the trend is to justify and elevate all endeavors by making them more "scientific"—that is, less personal. But I think it is precisely in those "difficult and personal territories of feeling" Capote rejects that the future of reporting, as an art, will most likely be found.

Behold the New Journalism— It's Coming After You!

NAT HENTOFF

I saw it begin to happen in my own work several years ago. I was no longer the "visitor" to whom the person I was writing about spoke. (You know the old style: "I'm going to kill myself," Roberta Himmelfarb said to a visitor as she jumped out the window.) During my early years as a journalist, I wrote many long pieces without a single "I" in them. In traditional journalism, it was bad form to put yourself in. You might be accused of lack of "objectivity," and stripped, like Dreyfus, of press cards, copy paper, and big, soft black pencils while your former colleagues jeered, "He thought he was more important than the story!"

Sure, there were a few "personal journalists" in the 1950's. I don't mean political analysts, but rather working reporters who not only got the story but told you how they felt as they were getting it, what was still missing, and how the story affected *them*. They, however, were considered special cases. They were a bonus in the paper, but for the real, hard news, you had to read the *Times*.

Well, the times, they have changed—though not the paper of that name nearly enough. Aside from the continuing collected works of Murray Kempton, the best single model of the rapidly increasing new

Nat Hentoff is a novelist, columnist, jazz critic, and author of such nonfiction books as *A Doctor Among the Addicts, Our Children Are Dying,* and *The New Equality.* His article appeared in the *Evergreen Review,* July, 1968.

personal journalism is Norman Mailer's *The Armies of the Night*—first published in *Harper's* and *Commentary*, and now a New American Library book. An account of Mailer's participation in the October, 1967 peace demonstrations in Washington, the work could hardly be more personal and yet it simultaneously digs more deeply into the essences—and some of the putrescences—of the way we live now than the total wordage moved by AP and UPI during the past year.

Two examples. First, Mailer describing the club-swinging Marshals: ". . . the hollows in their faces spoke of men who were rabid and toothless, the tenderness had turned corrosive, the abnegation had been replaced by hate, dull hate, cloud banks of hate, the hatred of failures who had not lost their greed. Se he [Mailer] was reminded of a probability he had encountered before: that, nuclear bombs all at hand, the true war party of America was in all the small towns, even as the peace parties had to collect in the cities and the suburbs. Nuclear warfare was dividing the nation. The day of power for the small-town was approaching—who else would be left when atomic war was done would reason the small-town mind, and in measure to the depth of their personal failure, would love Vietnam, for Vietnam was the secret hope of a bigger war, and that bigger war might yet clear the air of races, faces, in fact—technologies—all that alienation they could not try to comprehend."

Secondly, there is Mailer, in jail, wanting OUT, and seeing Tuli Kupferberg refuse to agree to stay away from the Pentagon for six months and thereby condemned to serve his five days: "Kupferberg was not particularly happy; with his beard and long hair, he did not think it was going to be altogether routine when the majority of the Pentagon protesters were gone, and he was then dropped in with the regular prison population. But he did not see any way out of it. To agree not to return to the Pentagon for six months was to collaborate with the government—what then had they been protesting?"

Herewith the new journalism: "Seen from one moral position . . . prison could be nothing but an endless ladder of moral challenges. Each time you climbed a step, as Kupferberg just had, another higher, more disadvantageous step would present itself. Sooner or latter, you would have to descend. It did not matter how high you had climbed. The first step down in a failure of nerve always presented the same kind of moral nausea. Probably, he [Mailer] was feeling now like people who had gone to the Pentagon, but had chosen not to get arrested, just as such people, at their moment of decision, must have felt as sickened as all people who should have marched from Lincoln Memorial to the Pentagon, but didn't. The same set of emotions could be anticipated for all people who had been afraid to leave New York. One ejected oneself from guilt by climbing the ladder—the first step back, no matter where, offered nothing but immersion into nausea. No wonder people hated to disturb their balance of guilt. To become less guilty, then weaken long enough to return to guilt was worse than to remain cemented in your guilt."

Now, there, right there, is what the new journalism is all about. It is not only that Mailer is so personally, so vulnerably involved in the events he is reporting, but also *his* involvement draws *you* in as no traditional news account possibly could. If you're not entirely anesthetized, reading that passage is bound to have an unlocking effect on you, quite beyond those particular events at the Pentagon. That passage brings you the news about the rest of your life.

Obviously this kind of journalism is by no means pervasive as yet. Clifton Daniel, managing editor of the *New York Times,* still says— and God save the mark, still believes!—that "newspapers—this one included—hold up a mirror to the world." The reporter must not get "involved."

And this past March, Dr. Lincoln Gordon, President of Johns Hopkins University, told 5,000 student journalists meeting in New York that it is a "bizarre notion" and a "disastrous myth to assume that objectivity is impossible and therefore, . . . not worth striving for. Write the news not how it feels, but how it is happening."

What is bizarre is Dr. Gordon's omission of the fact that a reporter does feel. What is he to do with that feeling? Bill Moyers, of all people, has quite different advice for journalists. When Moyers was at the White House, manipulating the news, he once told a free-lance writer, "That must be great—to be your own man." Now that Moyers is publisher of *Newsday,* he apparently feels better, and is certainly thinking more clearly.

During an interview on a Public Broadcasting Laboratory (PBL) television show on the press, Moyers spoke for the new journalism: "For a long time, there's been a myth about journalism, a myth shared by people who read us and view us, and a myth shared by those of us who are in the profession. That myth has been that newspapers are . . . simply mirrors of the world . . . that we simply reflect what is happening in the world." In the process of discarding that myth, Moyers went on to say that we're on the edge of "a major development in the history of journalism in this country because there really is no such thing, in journalism, as an innocent bystander. If a man is a bystander, he isn't innocent, and to really understand what's going on so that he can make sense to the reader, he has to be part of it and see it as a participant, and record what he feels."

"You do not have to accept it," Moyers concluded, "if you're the reader. You do not have to subscribe to it, but you do have to get a feeling that here's a man trying to do his best to tell you, another man, what he has seen and felt about something that has happened, and this will open the creative processes of journalism in a way that writing the five W's of the old traditional newslead will never do."

For this to happen to any significant extent in the dailies there'll have to be a new generation of editors, successors to the Clifton Daniels. But it is already happening in the underground press, in magazines such as this one, in Mailer's body of journalistic work (look back on some of the reporting in *Cannibals and Christians*). And the result is that a new generation of young readers is being brought into the news in ways that make more and more of them realize that they need not remain only voyeurs of living history. The new journalism, because it is powered by feeling as well as intellect, can help break the glass between the reader and the world he lives in. A citizen has to be more than informed; he has to act if he is to have some say about what happens to him; and the new journalism can stimulate active involvement.

It can, that is, if it continues to grow and if it extends much more deeply than it has so far to television and to films. The fundamental affliction of this society—what William Sloan Coffin defines as "original sin"—is that we do not feel. On a very basic, pragmatic level, if not enough of the citizenry, for example, feel urgently about the waste of black people, their elected representatives engage in the ritual dance of rhetoric but do not reallocate resources and redistribute power. Martin Luther King, Jr. is mourned pietistically by public officials but the dull beat of white auto-anesthesia goes on.

I have often wondered how the *Times* would look on any given day if it were edited and written by people from Bedford-Stuyvesant. Norman Mailer, in *The Armies of the Night,* tells of a similar fantasy: "He would buy a television station, and a commentator would read the news each day, and a chorus of street kids would give comments."

Neither of these fantasies is about to become real. But for the best of the younger journalists, the old ways are dead. And if institutions like the *Times* do not open themselves to the new journalism— a start has been made in the *Times* with Tom Wicker's column—they will no longer attract the best of the younger journalists. And this new generation of readers will increasingly turn to other sources of real news.

When Adlai Stevenson was ending his life telling lies for his country at the United Nations, nearly all the reportage on his disintegration missed the marrow of the story because the journalists then did not allow their own feelings to become part of what they were writing. They knew he was telling lies, but they hardly ever said so, and never directly. And so most of the citizenry *didn't* know he was telling lies. The reporters, many of them, felt the pathos of this man deadening himself to the last of the life within him, but they didn't write about it. And so most of the citizenry was unaware of a proto-typical tragedy of this time. It would not happen that way now across the journalistic board. The wire services and many of the dailies would still be "objective," but a sizable number of papers and report-ers—among them Tom Wicker—could no longer pretend to be innocent bystanders.

Admittedly, the new journalism has a long way to go, but as a sometime journalist, I'm convinced there has not for decades been a better time than now to practice the profession. The subtitle of *The Armies of the Night* is: *History as a Novel/The Novel as History*. The novel, Mailer says, "is, when it is good, the personification of a vision which will enable one to comprehend other visions better; a microscope if one is exploring the pond; a telescope upon a tower if you are scrutinizing the forest."

And so is history, when it is good—Gibbon, for instance. Jour-nalism, too, because it is living history. Of course, as a journalist, you still get all the facts you can. But then you tell what the facts mean to you, how you react to them. And in that way you can bring the reader into living history. The new journalist, then, will have to have something of the novelist's eye and ear, the novelist's ability to project himself into the head and viscera of others, the novelist's cauterizing skill at self-exploration. This does not mean he has to be able to write novels. Mailer is unusual, to say the least. A clearer paradigm is Murray Kempton. He is entirely a journalist, but with a novelist's creative vision.

To be personal—and how could I not be in *this* piece?—I'll keep on writing novels because I enjoy the total unpredictability of that act. But increasingly I find that much of the freedom of feeling I have in fiction can also be part of journalism, and so I intend to continue being a journalist too. However, that "visitor," that faceless, note-taking onlooker has gone for good from my nonfiction articles. It's I who am there; it's I telling you where I've been, what I've seen, how I felt about it, what changes it made and did not make in me. As Bill Moyers says, "You don't have to subscribe to it; you don't have to accept it." The way journalism is going is the way it has to go, and if I'm any good at all, you're going to react to what I write with your feelings.

Like the Beatles say, "I read the news today oh boy." And as they say it, they feel, you feel, "God, it is, it could be, about me."

Journalism: Old, New and Corporate

JACK NEWFIELD

To give the news impartially, without fear or favor, regardless of any party, sect, or interest involved.

> first published on August 19, 1896
> —Credo of *The New York Times*

You walk into the room with your pencil in your hand,
You see somebody naked and you say, who is that man?
You try so hard, but you don't understand what you
          say when you get home
Because something is happening here, but you don't
          know what it is, do you, Mister Jones?
> —Bob Dylan, Ballad of a Thin Man

    When I am asked what is my gripe against the respectable gray pillars of American journalism, I explain it isn't, at bottom, any of the polite criticisms. It's not just that the journalism schools have become impersonal factories that mass produce what Pete Hamill of the *New York Post* calls "clerks of fact." It isn't just that there is

Jack Newfield is an editor of the *Village Voice*. His books include *A Prophetic Minority*, *Robert Kennedy: A Memoir*, and *Bread and Roses Too: Reporting About America*, in which "Journalism: Old, New and Corporate" is reprinted. The article originally appeared in *The Dutton Review*, No. 1.

monopoly ownership in too many cities by publishers who care little about professionalism, and everything about profits. It isn't just that the newspaper unions have become conservative, dominated by non-writing commercial employees, and perpetuate a seniority system that protects the lazy and punishes the imaginative. It isn't just that advertisers have a suble say about what goes into a newspaper.

My root criticism of the old journalism is simply that it is blind to an important part of reality, that it just doesn't print all of the truth. It has a built-in value system that influences every editorial, every decision on hiring, what syndicated columnist to buy, what stories to cover, what copy to spike, what reporter to promote.

Spiro Agnew was right, although for the wrong reasons. A few individuals *do* control the mass media in America. Only most of them are Republicans and Conservatives.

For example, in 1968, sixty percent of the nation's daily papers editorially endorsed Richard Nixon, and only fifteen percent endorsed Hubert Humphrey. According to a survey compiled by the perceptive press gadfly Ben Bagdikian, eighty-five percent of the syndicated columns published across the country can be generally classified as conservative.

The Vice President, in his famous Des Moines and Montgomery speeches, did not choose to mention the power of conservative media complexes like the *Chicago Tribune,* which owns two Chicago papers, a Chicago FM radio station, a Chicago VHF franchise, WPIX in New York, and *The New York Daily News.* He did not mention the giant publishing empires of Hearst and Annenberg (Triangle Publications, Inc.) or that Mr. Annenberg had recently been appointed by the President to be Ambassador to England. He also did not mention that Nixon had recently appointed Robert Wells to the FCC, and that Mr. Wells owns seven newspapers and four television stations in the Midwest. (One of Wells' first decisions as an FCC member, according to the *Wall Street Journal,* was a vote against "even holding a hearing on the TV license renewal of a Cheyenne, Wyo. broadcaster who owns that city's only TV station, only full-time AM radio station, only community antenna TV franchise, one of two FM stations, and whose associates control Cheyenne's only newspapers.")

The knee-jerk liberals and the panicked network moguls responded to Agnew's jeremiad against the media by screaming "government censorship."

But the disturbing reality is that the press censors itself, through superficiality, through bias, through incompetence, and through a desire to be the "responsible" fourth branch of government.

A few examples of this self censorship. Geoff Cowan and Judith Colburn exposed Operation Phoenix in *The Village Voice* in November of 1969. Operation Phoenix is a top-secret CIA and Army intelligence program to train counter-insurgency teams to torture and assassinate the NLF's civilian cadre. George Wilson, the *Washington Post's* Pentagon reporter, was on to the story, and wanted to pick it up. But at a special meeting of the *Post's* senior editors it was decided not to publish the damaging story.

The story of the My Lai massacre was first uncovered by Seymour Hersh and his tiny Dispatch News Service. Yet, when he offered the story initially to both *Life* and *Look*, it was rejected. And it was only after the respected dailies in Europe began to front page the story, that the television networks finally picked up on it.

And then there is the story Gay Talese shares with us in his book, *The Kingdom and the Power*, of how the *Times* editors invited former CIA director John McCone to visit the *Times* building in 1966 to read a series of articles on the Agency before it was published. According to Talese, McCone suggested some changes "where the facts might imperil national security." Can anyone imagine the *Times* inviting Tom Hayden up for a look at a series on SDS before it was printed?

So the men and women who control the technological giants of the mass media are not neutral, unbiased computers. They have a mind-set. They have definite life styles and political values, which are concealed under a rhetoric of objectivity. But those values are organically institutionalized by the *Times*, by AP, by CBS (remember the Smothers Brothers?), into their corporate bureaucracies. Among these unspoken, but organic, values are belief in welfare capitalism, God, the West, Puritanism, the Law, the family, property, the two-party system, and perhaps most crucially, in the notion that violence is only defensible when employed by the State. I can't think of any White House correspondent, or network television analyst, who doesn't share these values. And at the same time, who doesn't insist he is totally objective.

And it is these assumptions—or prejudices—that prevent publishers and editors from understanding, or even being open to, any new reality that might be an alternative to those assumptions. Potential alternatives are buried deep inside the black liberation movement, the white new left, the counter-culture of rock music, long hair, underground newspapers and drugs, as well as in the nonwhite revolutionary movements of the third world. And it is these threatening and unfamiliar social movements that the mass media most systematically misrepresent. And it is their sympathizers who are excluded from positions of real power within the media hierarchies.

Why is it that of the dozens of nationally syndicated daily columnists, with the possible exception of Tom Wicker, not one represents a radical point of view? Why is it that Jimmy Breslin, when his column was offered for syndication, was bought by only five daily papers in the whole country? And Murray Kempton by just one? While the dull, predictable muzak-prose of Max Lerner and Marquis Childs is printed in more than one hundred papers. Why is it that Andrew Kopkind or I.F. Stone or Seymour Hersh are never invited to join the panel on "Meet the Press"?

Insurgent movements are also distorted because they tend to get covered only in terms of immediate confrontations and personalities, rather than in the context of issues, ideas or historical backgrounds. How many of the news stories written during the 1968 Democratic Convention, for example, took the trouble to mention that the street demonstrators had applied for legal permits to march and assemble in a peaceful rally, and had been denied these elemental rights by the Chicago court system? How many wire service dispatches on the rebellion at Columbia University in April 1968 spread the myth on a conspiracy hatched months before by SDS cadres? Many more, I think, than bothered to report the lengthy history on the Columbia campus of student agitation, through legitimate channels, against the University's real estate expansionism, and its relationship with the military-industrial-security complex.

A textbook case of the differences between the old journalism and the new, might be found in rereading the back issues of *The New York Times* and the underground and campus press during the student movement at Columbia in April and May of 1968. The *Times*, prizing objectivity, underplayed the police violence, misstated facts, ignored the substantive issues in dispute, slanted news stories in favor of the Administration, and editorialized emotionally against the students.

Some examples. The *Times* editorial in its April 29 issue said: "The faculty, trustees and administration of Columbia have closed ranks against capitulation to the rule-or-ruin tactics of a reckless minority of students. . . . It was apparent from the start that the youthful junta which has substituted dictatorship by temper tantrum for undergraduate democracy neither cared about, nor received, the support from the majority of students."

But the fact-finding Cox Commission Report, released six months later, and based on 1,790 pages of testimony, concluded that: "By its final days, the revolt enjoyed both wide and deep support among the students and junior faculty. . . . The grievances of the rebels were felt equally by a still larger number, probably a *majority* of the students." (Italics added)

On April 26 the *Times* chose to describe the Institute for Defense Analysis, which was central to the whole controversy, in this benign fashion: "The institute specializes in finding the answers to many of mankind's most pressing problems."

The Cox Report, which was drafted by a commission headed by the former U.S. Assistant Solicitor General, described the IDA as being "established by the Department of Defense and the Joint Chiefs of Staff in 1955 in order to obtain organized university research and counsel upon such matters as weapons systems and the conditions of warfare."

The police bust took place at Columbia at 2:30 a.m. on the night of April 29th. More than one hundred forty students were injured and ninety-two hospitalized as a result of the police violence. The Cox Report would later judge that "the police engaged in acts of individual and group brutality for which a layman can see no justification."

The next morning the *Times* reported only "several scuffles," in its news lead on the raid that resulted in six hundred twenty-eight arrests. The following day, after twenty-four hours to reflect, interview victims, and look at the extensive newsreel footage of the wild, stick-swinging bust, the *Times* managed to write an entire editorial without once mentioning the extraordinary police violence. And in the lead news story by Sylvan Fox, "charges" of police brutality were not even mentioned until the twenty-third paragraph. The *Times* story did not mention at all the obvious fact that the police violence had united the students and faculty against the Trustees, as it had done on many other campuses.

One of those hospitalized by the police was *Times* reporter Robert Thomas, who required twelve stitches in his scalp. But the *Times'* editors didn't think of him when they needed a sidebar story on police brutality. Instead they asked Martin Arnold, who wrote: "To an experienced antiwar or civil rights demonstrator, yesterday morning's police action on the Columbia campus, was, for the most part, relatively gentle."

The next day the following sign was tacked to the door of the office of the Columbia student paper:

"The Columbia Daily Spectator hereby announces open hostility toward the cretins who form the bulk of the working national press. Your insensitive misrepresentations will receive no aid from this office."

In contrast, *Rat* and *Ramparts* published the documents the students "liberated" from Grayson Kirk's office, including an exchange of letters that indicated that *Times* editor A. M. Rosenthal was once used by Columbia University to plant a favorable story in the *Times*. The *Voice* printed stories by Richard Goldstein and myself based on conversations with the students inside the five liberated buildings. The *Times* did have one reporter (John Kifner) inside the Math building at the moment of the police raid, but wouldn't let him write a description of that event. Kifner was told instead to write a follow-up on "student vandalism inside the liberated buildings." And when the troubles were all over, the student *Spectator* published a content analysis by sophomore Michael Stern, carefully documenting the "continual and flagrant disregard for both professional ethics and the facts," by the *Times, Post* and *News.*

Two final points on the *Times'* coverage of Columbia. The one *Times* reporter whose sympathies were with the students, Steven Roberts, ended up publishing his views not in the *Times* but in *The Village Voice* ("The University that Refused to Learn," *Voice,* May 9th). And the *Columbia Journalism Review,* in its summer 1968 issue editorialized that the *Times,* in its news columns, "appeared not only to be trying to tell people what they ought to know about Columbia, but what they ought to think."

The corollary to the mass media's presumption against insurgency, is its bias in the direction of authority. This is not an imperialist conspiracy, as the more paranoid factions of SDS believe. It is just that the editors of *Time,* Eric Sevareid, Walter Cronkite, and James Reston all happen to share many values, friends, fears, and class interests with Richard Nixon's WASP cabinet. So in the *Times,* Tom Hayden generally alleges something, but John Mitchell always announces something. The organs of the old journalism automatically print the press releases and White Papers of the government without any note of scepticism. The presumption of truth is always with the President, or the University dean, or the local police chief. The burden of proof is always put on the inarticulate poor, who can never afford, like GM or S. I. Hayakawa, to hire a press agent.

But the recent historical evidence suggests that the government—any government—lies as a matter of casual policy. President Eisenhower lied about Gary Power's U-2 flight over the Soviet Union. John Kennedy lied about America's role in the Bay of Pigs landing. Lyndon Johnson lied to the country at each new step of the Vietnam escalation. And Richard Nixon lied to us last November 3, during his nationally televised address to the nation, when while giving wholly distorted history of the Vietnam War, he tried to deny that it was originally a civil war in the south. He also lied to us when he first denied that the CIA was involved in Laos.

The truth, and even the hard news, usually rests beneath the public surface of any event or social conflict. Yet, reporters rarely question what they are told by any politician with a title. But no traditional publication has on its staff a muckraker of the distinction of I. F. Stone, or Sy Hersh or James Ridgeway. Ralph Nader, the consumer's tribune, has shown us just how many scandals and skeletons are waiting to be exposed inside the coils of the federal bureaucracy. But no national columnist, or network reporter, is doing that necessary work.

In the last few years a new kind of journalism has grown up in the space abdicated by the old, just as a new radicalism, and a new cinema, and a new music has grown up beyond the frozen frontiers of the older forms. This new journalism exists, and is flourishing, because it meets real needs. Fashion followers, undercover narcs, and sexual deviates cannot constitute all of *The Village Voice's* 160,000 readers, or *Rolling Stone's* 200,000 or *New York's* 250,000.

Daily newspapers cannot possibly compete with the immediacy and authenticity of color television news. The only way print can compete is to provide something television can't. And that is advocacy, complex detail, personal feeling. Linear weeklies that have been generally closed to the new journalists, like *The New Yorker* and *The New Leader,* have failed to gain in readership during a period when *The Village Voice, Rolling Stone* and *New York Magazine* have grown enormously. And the mortality rate among daily newspapers during the 1960's probably had as much to do with their inability to adjust to television, as with the selfishness on the craft unions.

Before I attempt any definition of this new journalism, let me make four qualifying points to prevent any possible misunderstanding. I am not suggesting here that the new journalism is a substitute or replacement for the more orthodox variety. Although I am an advocate of the newer writers and publications, I understand that they cannot realistically become anything more than a corrective, or example, or gadfly to media corporations as powerful as *Time, Life,* or the *Newsweek-Washington Post* Corporation. Second, the new journalism is still in its infancy, and it remains quite a mixed bag. Some of it is brilliant and important, but some of it is also indulgent, repetitive and paranoid. For example, I would probably rather read the Oakland telephone book than the *East Village Other.* And obviously, some of the underground press is indifferent to good writing and guilty of mindless propaganda.

Third, I am not here making the argument that Norman Podhoretz and Seymour Krim have made elsewhere that articles and journalism have become a new, superior literature replacing the novel.* Jimmy Breslin and Pete Hamill are journalists, not city room Balzacs. Their special gift is to write quickly and perceptively about real people and real experiences. As long as Roth, Pynchon and Heller are writing novels, that form does not need any obituary writers.

And last, just as there are some very bad new journalists, there are some excellent traditional daily reporters whose work I continually admire and respect. Among them are Anthony Lukas of the *Times,* Joseph Lelyveld of the *Times,* Richard Harwood of the *Washington*

---

* [Editor's note: See Norman Podhoretz, "The Article as Art," page 125 and Seymour Krim, "The Newspaper as Literature/Literature as Leadership," page 169.]

Post, Nick Kotz of the *Des Moines Register and Tribune,* John Kifner of the *Times,* and Robert Maynard of the *Washington Post.*

One dimension of the new journalism are those individual writers, some of whom publish in quite conventional publications, like *Esquire* and *Life,* whose choice of language, structure and subject break new ground. They have successfully appropriated the forms and techniques of the short story to enrich and expand the more immediate genre of journalism. They have exploded the old, impersonal, objective journalism school formulas, to get closer to the human core of reality, to tell more of how it really is after the press agents and ghost-writers go home, to be more than "clerks of fact."

They use symbols, imagery, and imaginative language and structure. They set a mood, and experiment with character development, and try wild stabs of intuitive insight. They have a point of view and they are personally involved in whatever they are writing about.

And most distinctively, the new journalism challenges the central myth of objectivity. The new journalist does not call the anonymous source or the official expert for a quote. He does not try to speak for an institution, only for his own conscience. He does not take into account "the national interest," but only what he sees and thinks. As Andrew Kopkind put it in his *New York Review of Books* essay on James Reston, "Objectivity is the rationalization for moral disengagement, the classic cop-out from choice-making."

The participatory journalist does for his profession exactly what new, activist historians like Howard Zinn and Staughton Lynd do for theirs.

What is also distinctive about the new journalists is that they are working reporters. They go out, and see, and react to real, living events and people. And they examine these spontaneous reactions honestly in print. The very best ones—Breslin, Hamill, Wolfe, Mailer— keep getting better because they keep getting stretched by their own confrontations with raw experience.

The point to keep in mind about Breslin is how his own explosion of talent has kept forcing him to expand his journalistic form. He started off writing 900-word sports columns for the old *Journal American,* and later Runyonesque copy for the *Herald Tribune.* Then he began to write politically unorthodox 2,000- and 3,000-word pieces for *New York Magazine.* After a while, he found even that space inhibiting his imagination, so he wrote his comic, episodic, short novel on the Mafia, *The Gang that Couldn't Shoot Straight.* And now Breslin is trying to write a long, serious novel.

But while Breslin was exploding his form and exposing himself to new, raw experiences—Vietnam, Watts, Selma, Oceanhill-Brownsville, the Chicago convention violence—most old journalists remained trapped inside a system that insulated them from consciousness-changing situations. *Newsweek* editors wrote about distant events they never smelled and touched by reading impersonal files and clippings. And then published their authoritative, "objective" stories with no names attached, stories written to fit a pre-existing formula. The editors of the *New York Times* wrote sober editorials expressing an "institutional point of view," about events they never witnessed, from the Chicago conspiracy trial, to the Black Panther fund raising party given by Mrs. Leonard Bernstein, and without ever consulting the *Times* reporters who did cover them in person.

At a shop like *Newsweek*, which is probably the most permissive and politically liberal incarnation of Luce-style group journalism, senior editors still have the power to arbitrarily change or invert the point of view expressed by the reporter who actually covered the event. In the June 1970 issue of *Scanlan's* magazine, for example, Kate Coleman, an ex *Newsweek* researcher, described how her copy on the 1968 Columbia University uprising was mutilated beyond recognition:

> During the Columbia strike, I was on campus every day and almost every night. The only building that was taken that I did not get into was the hall occupied by the black students. No reporters from the overground press were being admitted into the student-occupied offices of President Kirk in Lowe Library. I managed to gain entry to the office by slipping past police onto the second story ledge on the opposite side from Kirk's offices and then inching my way along the ledge to circumnavigate all of Lowe Library, until I gained entry through the window of the offices. . . .
>
> I duly wrote up my lengthy reports at the end of the week and gave them to the education editor, Peter Janssen, who had also spent a lot of time up on the scene. He had also witnessed the late-night arrests and clubbings of the students. He wrote a cover story that was accurate as well as sympathetic, based on my files, his own reporting, and that of another reporter. Originally, the story had three paragraphs devoted to the beatings of the demonstrators and their injuries. I left early Friday night, exhausted from the whole effort. But the story had not yet been edited, and my leaving was a sorry mistake. On Monday I read a cover story that was filled with vicious inaccuracies, many of them facts taken from my own files but twisted past recognition.
>
> In the past, *Newsweek* education stories on demonstrations had not been unsympathetic: both Janssen and former education writer Joe Russin were understanding of student attempts to reshape the university system. Both writers were radicalized by the job that put them in frequent contact with student activists and their thinking. Why then was the Columbia cover story as rabid as

the New York *Daily News?* The likely answer lies in the fact that Ed Diamond was on vacation. And whatever infighting he may have been into, as an editor he was infinitely preferable to his substitute, Dwight Martin, who still told stale racist jokes and seemed never to have left the era of World War II. He edited Peter's manuscript with a rightist meat cleaver, while downstairs, Kermit Lansner was busy on the phone talking to an old crony who fed him lies about students pissing all over Kirk's office. Taking his friend's word for gospel, he dutifully inserted the tasty tidbit into the story.

When I confronted Elliott with the charge that the magazine had simply lied, he listened carefully as I enunciated each point in the story that was false, and then urged me to put it into a memo. And that was it.

Among the catholic group of writers I would place under the new journalism umbrella are: Tom Wolfe (who has no politics), Jimmy Breslin, Jeremy Larner, Gay Talese, Richard Goldstein, Pete Hamill, Gloria Steinem, Larry Merchant, Sally Kempton, Ron Rosenbaum, Griel Marcus, Gail Sheehy, Michael Lydon, Mike Royko, Norman Mailer, Marshall Frady, Paul Cowan, David Halberstam, Nicholas Von Hoffman, Joe McGinniss and Pete Axthelm. And those over-40 pioneers, Al Aronowitz, Murray Kempton, Jimmy Cannon and W. C. Heinz. (Look up Heinz' piece on Rocky Graziano in *Sport Magazine* in 1947.)

Whether it is Breslin writing about the white working class of horse players, cops, priests, and bartenders, or Michael Lydon writing about the music, groupies, and life style of The Grateful Dead, or Jeremy Larner writing about Eugene McCarthy's campaign from the point of view of his speechwriter, it is reportage about experiences that are an integrated part of the writer's biography. This is the exact opposite of the anonymous group journalism of the news magazines. It is journalism so personal that it becomes almost memoir; writing that is too immediate to be called literature; reportage that is too honest to be called propaganda.

The second dimension of the new journalism—and much more ambiguous—are those publications that are actually new and original. These seem to be divided into three generations. The older, and now established ones whose roots go back into the wasteland of the 1950's: *I. F. Stone's Weekly, The Texas Observer,* and *The Village Voice.* The second generation emerged out of the flowering of the drug subculture in the mid-1960's, like *EVO,* the *Oracle, Inner Space* and *Grass Roots.* And third, the current generation of underground and antiestablishment papers like *Rat, Old Mole, Rolling Stone, Hard Times,* the *Ann Arbor Argus,* Atlanta's *Great Speckled Bird,* and *The Chicago Journalism Review.*

Although reflections of their region and staffs, these current publications share a few distinctive characteristics. One is that they are dominated by the sensibilities of their young writers, rather than by the decisions of desk-bound committees of editors. Second, they benefit from liberated language, and experimental layout, and quick publication and impact. Third, they view themselves more as communities based on energy than as institutions dependent on profits. And last, they are all committed to some variety of social change.

Also, these underground papers keep springing up and flourishing despite severe police and right-wing harassment in the more uptight sections of the country.

There were four examples of this just during the first two weeks of August 1969. In New Orleans, police busted the *Nola Express* three times in one week, for pornography, corrupting minors and peddling merchandise on the streets without a permit. The paper had to put up $2,500 in bail.

In Houston, vigilantes hurled a bomb into the offices of the *Space City News*, causing minor damage.

In Ann Arbor, John Sinclair, one of the founders of the *Argus* (and the White Panthers, and the former manager of the MC5 band) was sentenced to ten years in prison for possession of two joints of marijuana.

And in Atlanta, street vendors of the *Great Speckled Bird* were picked up and harassed by police.

In the last month I have read through the back issues of about thirty-five underground papers (there are over one hundred fifty) and have been astonished to notice that in the six or seven that are really first rate, there are frequently stories and subjects ignored by the old journalism, and fresh angles on other stories that have received saturation coverage in the mass media. Women's lib and ecology, for example, received sensitive coverage in the underground press before they became media fads, and continue to do so now.

Rat, for example, printed excerpts from the film script of "Che" before it was released, and incorporated them into a tough-minded analysis of Hollywood commercialization and exploitation of the "youth market." *Hard Times* has consistently printed the most original material on the G. I. Organizing movement and on conditions in military stockades. *El Gritto del Norte* publishes the most extensive and reliable coverage of the growing militancy of the Chicano movement in the Southwest. *Old Mole* was the first paper in the country to print the documents "liberated" from Administration files at Harvard, documents that revealed how a university Dean had tried to circumvent the vote of the faculty against ROTC on campus. *Ramparts* broke the scandal of the CIA-NSA covert relationship.

Reading these underground papers is like visiting another country, which remains invisible to the well-paid, middle-aged white, male editors of the *Times*.

Participation and advocacy remain the touchstones of the new insurgent journalism. The evidence now seems overwhelming that the closer a serious writer gets to his material, the more understanding he gets, the more he is there to record those decisive moments of spontaneity and authenticity. He gets inside the context and sees scenes and details that distance and neutrality deny to the more conventional reporters. He does not have to write about impersonal public rituals like ghost-written speeches, well-rehearsed concerts, and staged and managed press conferences. He is there to see and react to the human reflexes exposed late at night that illuminate a man's character.

The advocacy journalist breaks down the artificial barrier between work and leisure; between private and public knowledge. He can do this because he is writing, by choice, about subjects that excite his imagination, rather than fulfilling an assignment made by the city desk, and that needs to be approved and edited by the copy desk. He is a free man, relying on his instincts, intelligence, and discipline, liberated from all the middlemen who try to mediate between the writer and reality.

There is now a considerable body of literature based on direct personal involvement. Norman Mailer's seminal *Armies of the Night* is just the most praised example. There is also Sally Belfrage's book *Freedom Summer*, based on her experiences as a civil rights worker in Mississippi during the watershed summer of 1964, a volume that contains truthful (but not neutral) reportage from inside the heart of the movement. There is Tom Wolfe's *Electric Kool-Aid Acid Test*, written with intelligence from inside the drug subculture of Ken Kesey and the Merry Pranksters. And there is Hunter Thompson's powerful book on the Hell's Angels, also written out of the emotions of personal encounter.

Participation and advocacy, yoked to integrity, were also the literary and personal values that inspired James Agee as he worked on *Let Us Now Praise Famous Men*, Orwell as he fought and wrote from the trenches of the Spanish Civil War, and Albert Camus as he wrote for *Combat* as a member of the French Resistance.

American is now in great danger from a new, white collar McCarthyism centered in the Justice Department. Historic constitutional guarantees are now menaced by conspiracy indictments, subpoenas, wire taps, preventive detention, mail checks, repressive no-knock legislation, and pre-dawn police raids.

And so we are in special need of writers, who like Agee, Orwell and Camus, are committed in their bones, to not just describing the world, but changing it for the better.

The New Journalism:
A Panel Discussion
with Harold Hayes,
Gay Talese, Tom Wolfe and
Professor L. W. Robinson

LEONARD WALLACE ROBINSON

Last year Professor Lawrence Pinkham here at the Columbia Graduate School of Journalism created a course called Subjective Realism for the winter and spring term. During the course of those sessions, the following remarks got made: "The so-called Outside Reality you are generally asked to accept as true is under suspicion today. There is a general conviction we are being lied to, by politicians, by TV, by advertising, by magazines, by mothers and fathers, and by professors. All external reality as it's being presented in the multimedia of today seems less and less like reality as we individuals experience it. Now, what does one do when he finds out the world does not correspond to the world as described by authority? He is forced back on his own subjective reactions, for one thing, or he's apt to be. He may do any number of things, he may just explode, or he may go mad. But as a writer he's forced inward, to some extent."

Here's something else that was said by the *New American Review* last year, and it seems to me very pertinent: "The role of many American writers today is that of a witness. This does not necessarily mean that they provide a first-hand account of the political and cultural warfare of today, though many more write about events and demonstra-

The panel discussion on the New Journalism was printed in *Writer's Digest,* January, 1970. It was conducted by Leonard Wallace Robinson, then a member of the faculty of the Columbia Graduate School of Journalism.

tions and trials than was formerly the case; it *does* mean that they provide a firsthand account of their involvement in what has been happening in and to America. This is true of fiction, poetry and drama, as well as of the essay; in all of them one senses a movement toward 'bloody crossroads,' as Lionel Trilling puts it, 'where art and politics meet.' Similarly, the contemporary essay tends toward reportage, or interior journalism, which at its best places the writer's own values on the line and turns the merely topical piece into a form of testimony."

I think these words describe better than I could, the New Journalism. It represents man in a deep quandry, man trying to define himself in the world about him. Now would you, Mr. Wolfe, tell how you would describe the New Journalism—because I suppose we'll have many different ways of expressing the matter.

Tom Wolfe: I think the New Journalism is the use by people writing nonfiction of techniques which heretofore had been thought of as confined to the novel or to the short story, to create in one form both the kind of objective reality of journalism and the subjective reality that people have always gone to the novel for.

Professor Robinson: Mr. Hayes, what do you, as an editor, think?

Harold Hayes: What interests me is the promise that the very best literary form offers for reportage. And it seems to me what has been going on in the last ten years has been a greater tendency on the part of magazines and book publishers to encourage nonfiction writers, particularly to extend themselves into forms which were not previously seen as nonfiction. Len Robinson, a managing editor of *Esquire* back at the time when this whole movement was just beginning, knows from his own past experience that the magazine article was a form very largely taken for granted among editors and writers. They knew precisely what we required of the writer on any given assignment. The magazine article was a convention of writing, and those who were successful at it were those who understood the convention in the same way that a reporter understands the demands of a news story. There was an anecdotal lead opening into the general theme of the piece; then some explanation, followed by anecdotes or examples. If a single individual was important to the story, some biographical material was included. Then there would be a further rendering of the subject, and the article would close with an anecdote. Now that's a crude expression of the form, but it was a form up until that time; it was a form that was commercially successful in almost all the consumer magazines with the exception of the *New Yorker*, with *Esquire* to some extent, the *Atlantic* and *Harper's*. With these magazines, there was some feeling that the possibilities of nonfiction were greater. This conventional form could be seen regularly in *Collier's, Saturday Evening Post, Redbook, The American*, the works, right across the board. And writers were interchangeable for those magazines; it *was* a time when there was a profession of freelance writers, because they all thought alike and the magazines ordered the same kind of work from them, and the magazines thrived on it. At the other magazines I mentioned, there was a greater willingness to experiment. It's really fascinating to go back and look up, I think, some of the things that appeared in the *New Yorker* in the Forties in this area, and perhaps back even into the Thirties. In *Esquire*, F. Scott Fitzgerald was writing through a form that was hard to categorize—it was nonfiction, it was revelatory, it dealt with his emotional experiences, it wasn't reporting exactly. Hemingway was writing his letters at the time; discursive letters, which kept him in the center of events and he described the events that he saw, and he did it on a very high level of literary writing. So again I think that the distinction I would raise is that if there's been any great change to accelerate the possibility of writers dealing more flexibly with the language and with form, it's not because of the birth of a new journalistic form, but because there is a commercial disposition among magazines to see the imaginative writing now is more appealing to their readers.

Their magazines express themselves better because the writers are expressing themselves better. Now I don't think a writer can sit down and say, I'm going to be a New Journalist. Many of them are trying to do that today, and I think that it's one of the by-products, and a bad one, of this tendency of ours to find a label for everything that comes along. I don't think Tom Wolfe started as a New Journalist; I don't think Gay Talese started as a New Journalist. I think they started as marvelously original writers. There was an opportunity for them to express this unique way they had towards their materials, and they took it. The great premium is not upon the existence of a form, but on originality. And a writer's own personal sense of deciding precisely what he should respond to, and how he will go about it.

Professor Robinson: Mr. Talese, would you describe your entry into New Journalism?

Gay Talese: Well, I started as a newspaperman, as Tom did. And what got me into this so-called New Journalism was a realization on my part that I couldn't tell through the old journalism the whole story. Or maybe it wasn't so old. I'm from the *New York Times* school, the fundamental old school of journalism, that's the citadel of old-fashioned reporting. Granted this was daily reporting but I found I was leaving the assignment each day, unable with the techniques available to me or permissible to the *New York Times*, to really tell, to report, all that I saw; to communicate through the techniques that were permitted by the archaic copy desk. So I don't know at what point I got into another form of journalism, more ambitious, more suspect. The heroes that I had certainly were not journalists. They were two fiction writers, short story writers, John O'Hara and Irwin Shaw. Right out of the Forties and Fifties. Irwin Shaw was my favorite writer of the short story because of his style, mood, and economy of words. Both of these writers, I so much admire because of their ability to convey so much, with so few words, and with an almost artless style. I started with trying to use the techniques of the short story writer. In some of the *Esquire* pieces I did in the early Sixties. I remember one particularly on the director Joshua Logan. Underlying all of what I did then and do now and will do in the future is one fundamental thing, and that is care in reporting. It may read like fiction, it may give some critics the impression that it was made up, faking quotes or faking scenes, or over-dramatizing incidents for the effect those incidents may cause in the writing, but without question in my own case and I'm sure this is true of Tom and other people we admire, there is reporting. There is reporting that fortifies the whole structure. Fact reporting, leg work. In the Joshua Logan incident, I was just trying to write a piece for Harold about this once famous and now somewhat obscure theatrical director who was trying to make a new success of an old play on Broadway, and his failure to do so. I was writing really about failure. It is a subject that intrigues me much more than success. Here you have in Tom and myself two people about the same age, who in reporting have gone off in quite different directions, although admiring many of the same things, including my admiration for him. But Tom is interested in the new, the latest, the most current; Tom is way ahead in knowing these things, and relays them to those who read him, including myself. What is so contemporary, or what will be. I'm more interested in what has held up for a long time and how it has done; I'm more interested in old things, the Joshua Logan trying to make a comeback, the Joe DiMaggio become an old hero, how his life is, a Frank Sinatra, who seems to symbolize, at least to me, fame and how a man lives with it. I keep getting off the point. The point was to try to say something about how I got into New Journalism. Or old journalism. Parajournalism is Dwight Macdonald's description of it.

Professor Robinson: Parajournalism?

Gay Talese: Parajournalism. He is one of the critics who believes that we are fake artists.* There was a scene during a rehearsal of his play Logan was directing in which he and the star, an actress named Claudia McNeil, got into a great argument. This was an afternoon rehearsal and I was one of the three people in the theatre watching these two people battle one another on the stage, she calling him various

---

* [Editor's note: See Dwight Macdonald, "Parajournalism, or Tom Wolfe and His Magic Writing Machine," page 223.]

names, he calling her names, threatening to walk off, close the production. I just got my pencil and with some of the light that was left (it was a seat on the aisle), started writing down the dialogue; remembering what I couldn't write. I don't use a tape recorder, never will. And I thought, this is a marvelous scene, it revealed so much more of those characters, Logan and his actress, than I could have done by reporting it with the techniques of journalism as taught me in the journalism department. The scene as it read in that magazine article reads just like fiction. And yet every fact is verifiable. And that's been true, I think, of everything that I've written since then. And in the *New York Times* book, it's New Journalism on the old journalism. If I may take the liberty again of considering this new. There is not one fact in that book that I think is not verifiable. And yet verifiable facts aren't enough for me. I'm sure they're not enough for Tom. Not enough to get a fraction of the truth. Or not even that we are getting at the whole truth, but we are closer to the telling on a much broader scale, with the techniques of fiction: the dialogue, the scenes, than we could do with the more restricted form allowed us by the traditional journalism as expressed in some of the old magazines. And the last point, what I'm doing now is to try to carry this New Journalism further, I'm trying to use interior monologue in reporting. Things that I've gotten away from are direct quotations. I rarely if ever will use a direct quotation any more. I'll use dialogue, but I would never, if someone that I may be interviewing, and following around, should say something, I would never quote as an old *New Yorker* profile might quote some fisherman for 8,000 words in a row. Never do I use direct quotations. I always take it out of the direct quotation and use it without quotations but always attribute. And very often, now, if I were interviewing Tom Wolfe, I would ask him what he *thought* in every situation where I might have asked him in the past what he did and said. I'm not so interested in what he did and said as I am interested in what he *thought*. And I would quote him in the way I was writing as that he *thought* something. Throughout *The Kingdom and the Power* I have people thinking things. And critics have said, "Now, how does Talese know that people are thinking that?" Talese just asked them what they were thinking. And you must know your characters well enough (that, of course, is important). Underlying that is great research, enough research to write almost a book about any one character that you're going into depth on. In the new book that I'm doing, I'm going to be using almost entirely interior monologue. No quotes. Scenes, and interior monologue.

Tom Wolfe: One example of the use of interior monologue that has intrigued me was in John Sack's book about Vietnam. Here was a man who followed this company through practically its whole tour of duty in Vietnam. He also came to the point where it became absolutely necessary to be able to tell what people were thinking, because so many soldiers when they go through a battle do it with absolutely stolid faces, and even by watching their faces and listening to what they have to say, you're not going to get what really goes on in a battle. What goes on in a battle is terror, mainly. I mean, if you've ever been in the presence of gunfire, the flashes and the sound doesn't really seem very real, and it all happens so fast, it's the terror that's the real thing. The reality of most police stories is the terror. And that doesn't come through in the account that you get. You have to project the terror into it. Sack started going around to each one of these soldiers after something would happen, and also asking them, as Gay was saying, "What were you thinking at that instant?" Now there is a valid criticism of this, which is simply the fact that it's very hard to remember what you were thinking thirty seconds ago really faithfully. But I think you can get an approximation of the mood, and I think it's justifiable to do it to at least try to get inside of the psyche somehow, and to be able to report on the interior of the skull in some way. The whole Freudian revolution is not about sex, it's about the effect of subjective reality on people's actions. And that's why I think it is a tremendous breakthrough to be able to have people writing in nonfiction to get into that. The other point that Gay just mentioned that I'd like to stress, too, is that in this kind of reporting you're really reporting scenes; that's what you're looking for constantly. You start following somebody or a group around, and you really have to end up staying with them for a day, sometimes weeks, sometimes months even. And you are waiting for things to happen in front of your eyes, because it's really the scene that brings the whole thing to life, that's where you get the dialogue. The old kind of reporting which I also went through ten years of you'd usually have only an hour to do something anyway, or maybe two hours, when you're on general assignments, you're going out to get something, so you're always going from the direct quote, What did you do at this point? and this kind of thing. And you are dependent upon that. And any time you asked a politican a question, you'd get this numbing response. The words start pouring out, but under the old system you're sort of duty bound to take them and you transfer these words from his desk back to your city desk, or from his desk back to a cable office, you're just a courier, that's all you are; you're not really reporting.

Gay Talese: Let me interject something. This form cannot succeed, I do not believe, unless the old style of reporting precedes it. I believe that the old style reporting has to be done too—I mean the constant interviewing of your subject or subjects, getting to know everything that you can about this person, so that later on when you follow them around, as Tom said, you wait like a fisherman for something to happen. You wait, sometime weeks, months, of waiting; months, for something to happen. When this thing does happen, you should be able to recognize the significance of it inasmuch as you know your character by that point. You couldn't just go out and be with your character, your theatrical director, your beautiful girl, your whatever it is you're writing about, unless you have begun with the direct interviewing approach. Interviewing from time of birth right through, and interviewing lots of other people who know your subject. And then having finished that, that work, the interviewing and understanding of your character, then you start. You start to follow the person around. And in the old form of magazine writing, they would have stopped at that point. They would have interviewed, asked the direct questions, throw it all together and do the piece. Well, that's where the old ended, and that's where now I would begin. With all that background just as an understanding of character, so that if something happened on the Broadway stage, I would know how that might have related to something in a person's career earlier or in childhood, or I would have an understanding of that.

When I was a newspaperman reporting was such as Tom mentioned—you go out, at two o'clock in the afternoon, you get your quotes or whatever it is of the alleged happening, most of which you didn't see, incidentally. The old journalism was never eye-witness, except in sports writing. I think a sportswriter was actually the only reporter who sees with his own eyes what he's reporting the next day in a newspaper. But most of us went out, and we got the police sergeant's version of the thing, together with the social worker's, or the bombardier's, or the press agent's or the PR man's. And in any case, we were not able to report how things changed, because the newspaper business is just a one-shot business.

Harold Hayes: I want to go back to something that Tom said, which I think is very important too, as I have observed it; and that is the importance of scene. Which I think also bears on Gay's point of research. Did not someone say that Character is action? Isn't that sort of a homily (sic) about fiction, that if you're trying to develop something dramatically, something has to happen to define character. The weak point in this kind of writing seems to me often comes when a writer knows the material that he wants to get out to the reader, but dramatically it's not working. He's telling the reader rather than having his material unfold, through some sequence of events. I can't agree that necessarily a magazine article is restricted to showing the kind of truth that many of these writers are after by this kind of total research. Of course it can only build to your picture. On the other hand, if you're fortunate, if you're where a scene occurs, and if you're deep enough into your story, it's entirely conceivable that you can get it within a day, and get it within two hours, if that magic thing happens before you. It certainly has happened to Gay, and it certainly has happened to Tom, and in a short time. So I would very much argue that. Certainly I would in terms of Norman Mailer.

Gay Talese: Now what Mailer does, that I'm not doing, is using himself as a character. The red balloon moving around. That's all right. I'm using a third person; I always try to use people.

Harold Hayes: That's for you. But, with the increased possibilities of nonfiction writing today, I think that Norman Mailer can decide, all right, I'll take five days in Chicago, and I will observe this as carefully as I can, and then with everything I have as a writer, I will try to tell this *my way*.

Gay Talese: You take on the moon reporting he did for *Life* a month ago. If you would have taken from that section of his coming book all that Mailer had written about himself, you would have no piece there, except some very good reporting about the technology, about science, insofar as the space program is concerned. But what he's doing is just writing from his own familiarity with his own past, beginning the moon thing with his relationship with Hemingway, and his stuff for *Harper's* about his four wives, and all the rednecks that his wife knew, and all that. That's wonderful, and it related very much to what he was covering, the steps of the Pentagon, and also the Chicago convention. But if you took Mailer's right to write about himself away from him, indeed, if Mailer tried to intrude into the skull, as Tom said, of his major characters—

Harold Hayes: That's essentially my point. Why should he? That's his great art. All I'm saying is that the range is broad enough to allow Norman Mailer to do something which absolutely nobody else can do.

Gay Talese: When he was writing shorter pieces for the *New Yorker*, you got the sense that Joe Liebling had established himself as sort of the fat man on the scene; it was, The Fat Man Goes to a Fight, The Fat Man Is in Parie Restaurants, or The Fat Joe Liebling is down in New Orleans with Huey Long. Liebling had established himself to a lesser degree than Mailer to be sure, established himself as a character so that he did not have to re-introduce himself every time he reported on an event, be it boxing or politics. Mailer does that now, and he has done it, through himself as a celebrity and himself as a superb writer, developed over the years, has introduced the public to *him*. Now he can ride on that; he can coast on that. He can assume a knowledge on the reader's part that I, for example, cannot; I must do the reporting, and that's why it takes me much more time than it would someone like Mailer.

Professor Robinson: But there is a relationship between you and Mailer, Gay, isn't there, insofar as you're both interested in the interior monologue. He's interested in his own inner monologue, which he can be an expert on, without the kind of profound research you have to do; you have to become an expert from the outside looking in. He's in a powerful position—already inside himself, and able to use himself as his own subject. A strong position, the position of the novelist, omniscient and omnipotent. But you both conceive a reality as inside basically—he inside himself, you inside your interviewees.

Harold Hayes: I think an interesting point as far as the two writers that are here today, is the question of impulse. What is it that gets them into a story, what is it causes them to start to see things their own way? With Tom, the thing that was absolutely fascinating for us at *Esquire,* was the point when he decided to write good stuff, but fairly conventional stuff. And suddenly, on a weekend, Tom discovered a voice for himself, absolutely unique, and it is now perhaps one of the most copied voices in all of magazine reporting. He's ruined a whole generation of journalists, I think.

Tom Wolfe: Well, I've written about the way this thing happened; I was doing a story about custom cars for *Esquire* and I went to California, did all the reporting, and I came back and I just got a total block on it.* And *Esquire* has many ingenious ways for making you either turn out some copy or relinquish your material; they told me that they had $10,000 worth of plates on the press and that if I didn't get the story in it would be down the drain. Ten thousand dollars seemed like the end of the world or something. Anyhow, I tried and tried to write this thing, but the subject was so new to me, the custom cars, I ran into a whole world I hadn't seen before, that I just couldn't do it. Finally, Byron Dobell who was Harold's second-in-command at that point, told me to just type up my notes and hand them in and they'd get a "competent" writer to write them up.

Harold Hayes: An old journalist?

Tom Wolfe: So one day about eight o'clock I started typing up the notes in a very straightforward way, but I did it as kind of a memo to Byron, whom I got to know pretty well in all the time he'd had to nag me to get the story in. I started off, writing a letter about what I had seen on the custom cars. My only intent was just to write down in black and white all of my notes. But I had them here in front of me, and I started to type "The first place that I saw custom cars was at ————," and that's the way this story actually begins. Well anyway, I ended up writing all night long, finally by about six in the morning, I had

---

* [Editor's note: See Tom Wolfe, "Introduction to *The Kandy-Kolored Tangerine-Flake Streamline Baby,*" page 29.]

typed up 48 pages of what in effect was a letter to Byron Dobell. At the end of that he just knocked the Dear Byron off and ran the letter. Well now the thing that this proved to me about style was, (a), that most people end up all of their lives doing their best writing in letters. Especially to a friend, or somebody you think understands you, and somebody you're not inhibited with, because you don't have all of those forty or fifty or seventy people looking over your shoulder that most of us feel like are there when we actually start writing for public consumption. We think that all of our professors, teachers, other writers, and all sorts of terrific people are looking on. (In fact, they're not; they're not ever looking.) But in a letter to a friend you just start letting it all roll out; you don't hold back the little random comments.

Of course the second time around it's a little hard to do this, because the second time around you're fooling yourself; you know, you're saying, well I'm going to write this as if I'm writing a letter to a friend, only you're really not. But nevertheless, you do find something, once you've done that. You start to see what your own voice is.

Gloria Steinem: An Interview

Question: Before *New York* magazine, did you work for news-papers?

Steinem: No, I never did. It's kind of hard for women to break into newspapers, and it's hard for me as an individual to work in a structure. So I started out freelancing in '62.

Question: Now that you have a name and a reputation, and you've done some things that might get you hired on a newspaper, could you, doing the kind of journalism you do, work on a newspaper?

Steinem: I don't think so.

Question: Why?

Steinem: Well, I shouldn't say that so quickly because I think in a position like that of Nicholas von Hoffman, for instance, I could—but as a columnist, not as a reporter. Partly, it's writerly conceit. It's be-cause you want to do your own thing your own way. And partly, it's because the who, what, where, why—in inverted pyramid form—is not one for writers; it's one for telegraph operators, which is why it was invented in the first place.

Question: Do you think newspapers are getting away from that, aside from the columns?

Steinem: Yes, I think they are, and I think it's unfortunate that the journalism schools continue to teach it. I've been talking lately to

The interview with Gloria Steinem, a founder and editor of *Ms.* magazine, appeared in *The Bulletin* of the American Society of Newspaper Editors, February, 1971.

students at a couple of journalism schools, and they feel—and they're right—that they're not learning what will be useful to them later. Journalism schools are really kind of bad, it seems to me, most of them. A way of getting money. The most it does for you is force you to practice to write stories. But, I was interested in this idea of the New Journalism, enough to do research on it, because people would ask me what it was and I really didn't know what it was. Really, what it is is the old journalism, because before the advent of the telegraph machine, news stories were done in essay form, or short story form, or some literary form. And, it was only with the telegraph machine— when it was necessary to train large numbers of people who weren't writers to gather log material from a big area and give it back to a big area, therefore, eliminate regionalisms—that they invented this inverted pyramid form so it could be cut off at any point and still make sense in one paragraph. It's not sacred at all. Unfortunately, in the meantime, it's become holy.

Question: Aren't we just as dependent upon the telegraph machine now? What with the terrible rush of stories that news editors are confronted with from all over the world, the efficiency of news gathering has certainly increased. Don't you think it's just as important now to have the who, what, where, when?

Steinem: But now we have writers out there, large numbers of very talented journalists. The '50's was really an age that produced enormous numbers of people talented in nonfiction writing—in the '60's too. So, I don't see why we should restrain them to this non-writers form.

Question: Do you know of any good journalism done in newspapers, besides the columnists whom you admire?

Steinem: I see individual pieces. For instance, every time I read a piece in *The New York Times*—and think this *can't* be *The New York Times*—it turns out to be Israel Shenker's. Now he's writing reports, but he's not writing them in the who-what-where form. I think there are a lot of people like that that you run into all over the country who are really good journalists.

Question: There are some who say that the best journalism today is in a magazine like *New York,* or between hard covers. Like the things written by Rachel Carson, Ralph Nader, Truman Capote, Norman Mailer. Would you agree that that kind of journalism ought to be done?

Steinem: Yes. Those stand out in our minds because one can explore in greater length, and they're good exposé journalists. The problem with adhering to form, plus being dependent on news releases and traditional sources, is much greater for daily newspaper writers. In *New York* magazine, and other places, we're self-indulgent. There's no question about that. At least we're honest. As Pete Hamill says, "If we fall on our ass, it's our ass." I mean, we say, "I think." We say, "We don't know," and we try to check what we present as facts, as fact. But, what's so insidious about *The New York Times* is that they would never say "We don't know" or "We're not sure."

Question: What would you like to see a daily newspaper become?

Steinem: I would like to see it broken down into community sections internally, so that you get the international news—hopefully no longer in the old inverted pyramid form—but with some kind of human mind's work trying to make sense of all this stuff, and questioning what the President says and not just reporting, not just accepting the State Department news releases. But then, inside the paper I'd like to see more community emphasis with people, reporters who live in the community and cover that exclusively, and who are visible to the community, so they have to be responsible. You know, they're living there, right? So even if they do something really inaccurate or opinionated, they're going to be told about it.

Question: Are you saying there shouldn't be opinion in the pieces written by individual reporters?

Steinem: No. I'm not saying that. I think you can only make sense of a situation by giving the human viewpoint, which is opinion. But if it's not reporting what really is, and reporting it accurately— what is really the trend in a general way—then it can be very destructive. If it's self-fulfilling prophecy, that's the problem.

Question: In reporting politics, the broad spectrum of politics, how does one take care to discern the beginning of a political movement as opposed to a small fad?

Steinem: I'm not sure. It's hard to explain, but I don't think it's a mysterious process. I just think it's the fact that our heads are the best computers ever made, and take in great amounts of information which we're not aware of, which is not necessarily information in a sense of facts and figures, but impressions of the characters of individuals and human reactions and how they're changing. We have to, at some point, trust the output of these computers, because what *The New York Times* and others do is insist on proving the output by long division, which is terribly time consuming. So, five years later you're saying what you knew damn well five years before. It was very true of the draft resistance movement. I was convinced that it was a very different kind of movement, much bigger than the Korean war, and, I gather, also bigger than the Second World War. I tried to sell that to every editor in New York City in the summer of '64 and '65. No one would believe it. An editor who hires a writer should hire him not because the writer is a writing machine, but because he trusts his judgment. Therefore, when the writer is out in the field—which is inevitably the case, since the editor is shut up in the office—the editor has to go with the writer's instincts. I think that's what's important about a magazine like *New York*. It's a writer's magazine, not an editor's magazine.

Question: Do you think that newspapers should become writer's newspapers?

Steinem: I think they really should trust their reporters much more, because the editors are locked up and reacting on the basis of their own experience, and not experiencing the field.

Question: The writing reporter usually thinks he needs more length then he gets now in most newspapers. But there are readers who simply want raw data. Would you prefer newspapers with, say, the formula that's used by *The Wall Street Journal*—three or four well-done, deep-feature pieces, and a lot of short stories—that kind of formula?

Steinem: I'm not sure. I hadn't really thought it out. I think most stories are too long, and the whole notion of the newspaper is old-fashioned. I mean, we take up enormous amounts of space with engagement and marriage announcements, which nobody wants to read. And, if indeed they must be there, they should be paid for. If they're there as news, then you should have the male's picture too, because otherwise it comes off like a meat market. Sports sections should be much, much smaller. We don't need editorials on the beauty of spring and other lyrical things that can better be left with magazines.

Obviously, until maybe five or six years ago, we never thought about reporting on the black community, or on the Mexican-American community. We were caught with absolutely no sources, no reporters. So, if we can just look at the whole community—the real community in terms of percentages and who makes up the community—and cover those areas, that's the first broad change to be made. Then, after that comes a decision about which story deserves an interpretative essay, because it's complex or important enough or maybe important in the future.

Question: One problem that the reporter runs into is his identification with the thing he's covering—getting so close to it that he may not be able to see it. Wouldn't that be a problem in personal journalism?

Steinem: People are always asking me about advocacy journalism, and I always used to react to it and explain it. And one day I figured, why am I reacting? I'm not the advocacy journalist any more than *The New York Times* is. I keep using *The Times*, but I mean convential newspapers advocate the status quo by the nature of their reporters who are white males, by the nature of their editors who are even more white male. They may send a woman or a black out to write about women and blacks, but the man who makes the decision is somebody else.

The biggest problem for me, personally, is not so much getting involved with something and advocating it, because I don't have any problems. For instance, with being an advocate of the United Farm Workers Union over the growers, when the growers are lying most of the time. I mean, it seems very clear to me where the needs are, where the priorities are. But the problem is personal when you write about someone and you know it's going to hurt that person—it's going to hurt the position of the movement, or him or her individually. Somebody told me I was afflicted with galloping kindness the other day, and that was my problem as a writer.

Question: There's one other problem: There are people who are not particularly eager to talk to you as a reporter, and see their names in print. How does a newspaperman overcome that problem?

Steinem: How you get around it is a problem we aren't up to yet. The power of the media in this country is so vastly overrated that I think, so far, it's all been healthy. To be confronted by people who really don't give a damn whether you write the story or not is good. It's had a very salutary effect on the magazines and newspapers that I know of. People have been burned so much in the past, by being misrepresented; if we look at the reasons for their reluctance and try to understand them, we're a lot better as journalists.

Question: Think of a case of misrepresentation, if you would.

Steinem: I can tell you the one that's closest to my heart, which is the women's liberation movement, which has been systematically ridiculed. It's been made to seem an upper middle-class white nut movement. For instance, one hears about bra burning all the time. The truth is, only one bra ever got burned. It was in Atlantic City in 1968; that wasn't even burned, because they couldn't get a fire permit. And yet it turned up in everybody's lead paragraph. We have enormous social myths: that this country is always right or that it has the right to interfere in the affairs of other countries; that black people and other minority groups are somehow different, or inferior, or limited or stereotyped; and that women are inferior. This is an age where myths are breaking down and, unfortunately, we're in the position to perpetuate them. So, we have to be very, very careful. We have to watch our adjectives, especially, and all our characterizations of people, and whenever they conform to popular stereotype, I think we ought to question them. It's true of everything, except white Protestant males, when you come right down to it.

Question: I wonder how you think you fare as a clinical, critical reporter, as a woman committed to the women's liberation movement, operating in a white male-dominated political world?

Steinem: Well, it's very simple. When I first started writing in '62 until '68, when *New York* magazine started, I wasn't allowed to write about politics or economics because that was for men—no matter how many ideas I submitted, and actually I was working in those fields. So, I was leading a very divided life. I was writing profiles of Paul Newman and working in political campaigns, and I had had more experience than men my age who were doing political work for papers. It's very rough. It's much rougher than I would have admitted at the time—and much more humiliating than I would have admitted at the time.

Question: What do you think of political writing as done by most newspapers these days?

Steinem: In general, I'd say when it's about the Federal Government, state government, traditional areas of politics, it's better, probably, than most other kinds of reporting—than social reporting, than reporting on minority groups—because it's something we all deal with every day and understand and see on television every day. We're in more trouble when we cover things that are stranger to us. But, having said that, I think the biggest internal problem is that the power is very seductive, and the reporters get next to it and they preserve their sources, and they preserve their relationships.

Question: Do you get the idea after a while that politics is to get people elected, and to establish liberal or conservative trends, and nothing else?

Steinem: Yes. Without affecting peoples lives. It's like the history books of the 18th century, which only recorded the activities of the top 2 per cent. We don't know what the rest of the folks were doing, for the most part.

Question: Is it maybe because that's changing, or because newspapers do a fairly decent job on politics, that President Nixon is shying away from the writing media and using television?

Steinem: Television is very valuable and can do a lot of things writing can't. The most important thing is that it can give us some idea of the man's character, not just the words written down, but how he says them, and his manner and the whole set of signals that we take in about an individual other than the verbal ones. That's terribly important. It could be the town meeting of the world, if it were used properly. Unfortunately, he as the President, and others, are in the position to control it. It seems to me if candidates—especially Presidential candidates—were forced to be on television for two hours straight, unedited, locked in a room together arguing, we would have at the end of that time a much better idea of the guy's character.

Question: One of the things you said recently is that Washington is not where things are happening.

Steinem: I think it might have been fair to say in the Roosevelt Administration that a lot that was going on in Washington was crucial to the country. But, I think now it's fairly clear, since you can hardly get anybody to go to Washington. That's no longer the case. I mean, nobody even wants to go there. Nothing much happens unless you form a grassroots constituency for it first. New York is very much where it happens—first and biggest, usually. I think it's easier for anybody here to get a picture of what's going to happen next year, than it is for people sitting in Washington.

Gay Talese:
An Interview

JOHN BRADY

At his high school in Ocean City, New Jersey, Gay Talese was an underachiever. Sixteen colleges turned him down before he finally got into the University of Alabama. After graduation in 1953, when he went looking for a reporting job in New York, six of the city's daily newspapers rejected him. Finally, he got a job with the *New York Times*—as a copy boy.

Today that ex-copy boy is one of the most respected and successful writers in America. Gay Talese at 40 has all of the accoutrements that accompany a bestselling author's fame and success: celebrated friends, *Who's Who* recognition, travel, TV appearances, two sports cars, a Cardin wardrobe, a beautiful wife and two lovely daughters in a handsomely furnished brownstone in Manhattan's upper East 60's.

How did it happen? Like most "overnight" success stories, this one goes back a few years.

By 1955 Talese had worked his way up to the status of reporter at the *Times*, where one of his peers called him "a reporter who can write and a writer who can report." He was already experimenting with what would later be called the New Journalism—highly interpretive reporting consisting of in-depth research, enlivened with plenty of

---

The Gay Talese interview was carried in two issues of *Writer's Digest*, January and February, 1973. John Brady teaches English at Indiana State University.

descriptive personal detail in a dramatic writing style: the techniques of fiction applied to the craft of nonfiction.

"Talese's work pre-dates all the other New Journalism," writes David McHam, professor of journalism at Baylor University.* "He was doing it back on the *Times,* as careful readers will remember. Many of the pieces were short, but they had the color, the flavor, the feel of something special in writing." During this period Talese was also collecting data for his now-classic chronicle of the *Times, The Kingdom and the Power.*

In 1961 Talese started freelancing articles for *Esquire,* where his byline appeared thirty times over a ten-year period. Most of these pieces were profiles of celebrities (many of them past their prime) such as Frank Sinatra, Joe Dimaggio, Peter O'Toole, Joe Louis, Floyd Patterson and George Plimpton. For a typical profile Talese devoted from four to twelve weeks of observation to his subject, absorbing moods, tensions, drama, conflict—finally writing as if from inside the mind of the person he was profiling.

One of Talese's most famous pieces for *Esquire* was a profile of the *New York Times* managing editor Clifton Daniel, which *Time* magazine called "the talk of the publishing world." This in turn led to three years of research on *The Kingdom and the Power,* during which time Talese interviewed hundreds of people, many of them on a dozen occasions. Written in the manner of a nonfiction novel, *Kingdom* became a Book-of-the-Month choice, and for six months of 1969 was a national bestseller.

An anthology of his earlier work, *Fame and Obscurity,* was published the following year. In addition to including his famous *Esquire* profiles, the book contains two of Talese's earlier books: *New York—A Serendipiter's Journey,* which depicts the obscure, anonymous, forgotten little people of a big city; and *The Bridge,* a human documentary about the people involved with the building of the Verrazano-Narrows Bridge.

One book that Talese had wanted to write since 1959, when he occasionally did a crime story for the *Times,* was the Mafia story. The project did not become possible until 1965, however, when he met—and eventually won the trust of—Bill Bonanno, the son of Mafia godfather Joseph "Joe Banannas" Bonanno. Said Talese: "I traveled with Bill. For awhile I was like a bodyguard, though I never carried a gun."

Over a period of six years, Bill Bonanno and other members of his family confided in Talese the intimate details of their lives: Bill's illegitimate son; his wife Rosalie's attempted suicide; and so on, in what eventually became the first inside nonfiction look at the Mafia—1971's bestselling *Honor Thy Father.*

---

* [Editor's Note: See David McHam, "The Authentic New Journalists," page 110.]

To date, more than 300,000 hardcover copies have been sold, including those sent to Literary Guild members; in March 1972 the paperback rights were sold to Fawcett for a record of $451,000. Why 451? "Because I wanted a thousand more than Mario [Puzo] got for *The Godfather*," says Talese, referring to their friendly rivalry with a smile.

I spoke with Talese in his comfortable, memorabilia-filled office/library/den on the ground floor of his Manhattan home on a Thursday summer morning. He is of medium build, with youthful, pointed features vaguely reminiscent of Dustin Hoffman or John Updike. He dressed casually, had a tennis-court tan, and was just getting started on the research for his new book, which concerns the sexual revolution in America—notably changes in middle class attitudes toward sexual permissiveness and different married life styles.

Talese had just spent several days at Sandstone (a California community whose occupants wear mostly no clothing), doing research in the nude. Now, back in Manhattan, he was managing a "massage parlor," gathering more data for the book. "I'd rather not talk about what I'm doing just yet, though," he told me. "It'll take years to do, and I'm not sure how it's going to turn out."

With that, he turned his phone over to his answering service, and, with the sounds of the city waking up in the background, we sat and talked over coffee and cake.

Brady: You mentioned in some remarks to another interviewer that you never use a tape recorder. Why don't you?

Talese: It would be, I feel, an intrusion. People would see the recorder and know that everything they are saying is going to be on record, and maybe they wouldn't be as frank or free with me as they would be if I were just there establishing personal communication without the presence of a third element: the recorder. I avoid using a recorder so that I can achieve a more direct communication with the individual I am trying to talk to.

Brady: How do you take notes then?

Talese: In the beginning I do not take notes. My purpose initially is to get to know the person, and to be able to have that person relax— and also for *me* to be able to relax. So the first few meetings will consist of my explaining what I have in mind—what my ambitions are for the article or the book that I'm going to be doing. It's more social than anything else. Since I take so long with the people I'm interviewing, I usually get to know the answers to questions that I'm asking through a process of knowing the people. I do occasionally take notes. The reason for the notetaking would probably be very specific information— a date, an address, or something that I would not want to try to remember.

Brady: When you are on a story and you haven't seen an event yourself—haven't been there to witness it—you interview witnesses. What happens when you get conflicting reports from witnesses to the same event? How do you go about reconstructing it?

Talese: I don't take chances in imagining, or in having someone else create fiction for me. I stay with what I can find out and believe to be as close to the truth as is possible. When it comes to reconstructing, if I have conflicting viewpoints on one point or another, I may just not even get into that area. You can stay within the information that you have available to you that is not disputed—you write within the area of what you have and you do not extend into areas that might be questionable.

Brady: With a book the length and depth of *Honor Thy Father*, how much of what you learned is left out?

Talese: That represents everything I got. I do not have in my head at this time marvelous untold anecdotes. I do not have any information that I didn't put right into the book. When the book first came out, I thought, "Well, I'll be subpoenaed." I wasn't, but if I were I'd have said: "Well, here's the information. Here it is—it costs ten dollars. You can get it for nothing if you call the publisher because you're a member of the court." And if criminal investigators wish to know what I know about the Mafia, there it is—it's all in the book.

I used to work for the *New York Times*, and one of my first assignments when I left sports reporting, when I went to cityside, was political reporting. I went to Albany in 1959. Governor Rockefeller was newly installed, and I got to know a political reporter who had been with the *Times* for twenty or thirty years. I noticed how the politicians in the state capitol of New York would give information to him. They all trusted him. This political reporter was obviously a popular man.

I found out later he was popular because he was a man who didn't tell all he knew: he was a man who could keep secrets. A man you could trust. And he died years later with some of the greatest untold political stories of his time. While his kind of reporting made him popular, and undoubtedly made his life easier in many ways, I'm not sure his kind of reporting was in the noblest tradition of journalism. I learned then, and I don't believe today, that I'm going to go to my grave with great untold stories. I can keep a secret. Let's get that: I *know* I can keep a secret. But I don't want things off the record. In *Honor Thy Father*, what I was told, what I could find out myself without being told—to the best of my abilities as a gatherer of information—is all there in the pages of this book. And that went with my other books and the many magazine pieces I did for *Esquire*. All of this represents the best of my ability in getting information, and I don't know of any great secrets that I am keeping.

There was one incident, I remember, with George Plimpton when I interviewed him years ago. This is back in 1963. Few people had heard of Plimpton then. He had not done his particular kind of research—playing along with teams, the Walter Mitty kind of research. He hadn't begun doing that on television. He had written a book called *Out of My League*. I don't think he'd even done *Paper Lion* yet when I interviewed him. But there was an incident that happened during his prep school days—I think it was at Phillips Exeter. He had gotten into some trouble there, and he asked me if I would keep it off the record, and I did, and I have. I never dealt with that subject because it was very painful to him, and to his father, as I recall. That sort of thing. I'm sure I could find something in the Joshua Logan profile like that—something to do with the death of Mr. Logan's father, circumstances around that which were not really so relevant to what I was doing. But I certainly respected those wishes, be they from Joshua Logan or from George Plimpton or from whoever. I do respect those things. But they are not really pertinent to what I am doing, anyway. I don't consider it a concession in any way.

Brady: Have you ever had a negative reaction to something you have written by someone you have written about? Any of the personalities you have profiled in *Esquire?* Any members of the *Times?*

Talese: Let's take *The Kingdom and the Power.* Yes, there are people on the *Times* who did not like that book one bit. To begin with, the book critic. I was a little hard on book critics. In *The Kingdom and the Power* I analyze the *New York Times Book Review,* as well as the role of the daily book critic—and not too flatteringly, I'm afraid. And I have been paying a small price for that since—in the reviews I have gotten from the *New York Times.*

There were some other editors who did not like the book, but this is understandable. It would have been a miracle if they all liked the book. It probably wouldn't have been a very good book if it had unified approval or praise from the many members of the hierarchy of the *Times.* But I don't believe that I lost a friend. I had many friends during my years with the *Times,* like the managing editor A. M. Rosenthal. Now, Rosenthal is dealt with very frankly in *The Kingdom and the Power.* There are things, I think, that Rosenthal did not find easy reading in that book, particularly about himself, but I tell you it never meant that he became angry at me. In fact, our friendship continued after the book was published. He's the person I was closest to when I was on the *Times.* I worked for him when he was the city editor, and I like him and admire him and I value his friendship. And when I was writing the book I thought, you know, maybe Abe Rosenthal would be incensed by this paragraph; or I might have thought "Here goes our friendship" after writing another sentence. But no. None of this happened.

Brady: What about the Frank Sinatra piece?

Talese: Frank Sinatra—and I get this secondhand from many sources—did not like the long profile I wrote about him. I don't know why he didn't like it. But there were scenes in the piece—there was a scene in a poolroom where Sinatra is getting into an argument with a young Los Angeles kid (actually he turned out to be a fiction writer) who was wearing a certain kind of boots that Sinatra didn't like. I described in this piece the tension in the poolroom as Sinatra, with some of his men around—Leo Durocher, a couple of others, Sinatra's publicity man—and all of these California-cool pool players were playing in The Daisey discotheque in Beverly Hills. I described this scene, which was very revealing of Sinatra and his impulsiveness. I know he didn't like that scene. And there were other things in the piece that I've been told he found offensive. They were not untrue —but he's a very touchy man, as you know, very sensitive, and I think that in certain areas I got pretty close and he found them uncomfortable, I believe. I'm not sure.

Brady: Some of these people find it uncomfortable or unflattering, but have any of them ever accused you of writing something that is untruthful?

Talese: No, I've never had a libel suit, never had any defamation of character action brought against me; nor have I even had any lawyers write me letters saying "What you wrote here, here and here in this paragraph or that book or this article is untrue." No, I've never had that. I am very careful with my facts. I try to be 100% accurate. I think that I am, but I'm not sure—maybe I'm not. But if there are mistakes, I haven't been told about them. And I am very careful.

Brady: What does the Mafia think of *Honor Thy Father?*

Talese: The Mafia doesn't "think"—at least not as a great harmonious body. The Mafia, as every other organization—legitimate or not— has varying opinions about just about everything, my book included. If the Mafia were in agreement on any one thing, there wouldn't be so much feuding and shooting between Mafia elements. Mafia gangs. There were some in the Mafia who didn't like my book, and some who did. I was writing about one Mafia family, one Mafia organization headed by Joseph Bonanno, a controversial person in the underworld through the 1960's. Many people disliked him, and there were those who would like to have seen Bonanno floating in the river. I was writing about him—but really writing about his son, Bill. I was writing about a father-son relationship. *Honor Thy Father* is an ironical title. When the son *does* honor his father, it costs him: He goes to jail.

Honor Thy Father is the story of a sad and somewhat complex father-son relationship in which the son aspires to be a big gangster like his father. His father was/is a very dynamic and dramatic man, an elegant man in many ways, and the son tried to emulate his father and failed. It's a book about failure, really—a book about how the second generation failed to match the sum of the strengths of the older generation. It's a story about generations.

Well, Bill Bonanno, when this book came out, I think, was—well, I know he read it four times, and each time he read it he got a different reading. I know this because I correspond with him. He's in jail now. He read the book, and at first I think he was a little offended, shocked and displeased because he doesn't come off as a heroic character. He is *not* a heroic character in this book. When the father, Joseph Bonanno, first read it he was infuriated because his son Bill had been as frank with me as he had. Much—most—of the information about their relationship naturally came from the son. I could not have built a bridge to Joseph Bonanno, the father. There was my own generation gap with the older man, and he—great Mafia leader that he was, Sicilian born—would never have talked to a newspaper man or to the writer of a book or to any outsider. Now, the son, who is my age and who was born in this country, does not have the Old World ideas that his father has, so it was not anywhere near as difficult for me to have a relationship with Bill as it would have been had I tried to have a relationship with his father, although I did meet the father. Through the son eventually I got to know Joseph Bonanno, was entertained at Joe Bonanno's winter home in Tucson, Arizona. I've had Joe Bonanno to dinner here in New York in my own home when he was living in the East, and through the Bonannos, of course, I got to know many of the bodyguards, many of the ranking Mafiosi and their organization, got to know their wives and children and the whole family structure that I wrote about in *Honor Thy Father*. And their reactions varied.

Some of the women that are portrayed in the book did not like what I wrote, and some of the women *did* like what I wrote. The results of their criticism have not been violent. Obviously, if they had been, I wouldn't be here. But I think in a way that the Mafia people were more broadminded about the way I wrote about them than some of the *New York Times* people were in response to *The Kingdom and the Power*. I think that journalists perhaps (and I should include myself) become, through years of writing about others and not being written about ourselves—maybe we become a bit thin-skinned, or unaccustomed I should say, to being written about objectively. I think this accounts for those journalists and editors who were offended by *The Kingdom and the Power;* I think it's just a case of their not being accustomed to being written about. Politicians, you know, are so accustomed to being written about they can take almost anything—most of them can. They are very thick-skinned, as are actors and playwrights and novelists. People in the arts have to be *willing* to accept incredible criticism from the press, from the critics—whereas the press does not have critics. It should. There should be on television, on the radio, a program dealing with the press. I don't mean "Meet the Press." I mean critics. There was for awhile on television, if I'm not mistaken—it might have been radio—a brief attempt by one of the major networks to have a press criticism show, but I don't think it went over well with the audience.

Brady: You started a thought a few minutes back about Bill Bonanno reading the book four times, and you said his first reading was not a very favorable one. How did he feel about it by the fourth?

Talese: As he read it more, the second and the third and the fourth time, he had varying reactions to it. It was truthful. It was not flattering. It was sensitive. The book did deal with him with understanding. It seemed to cope with the complexity of his own relationship with his own father. I believe that finally his conclusion about the book was that it was an honest piece of work. That's what he told me. He thought I brought it off.

Bill Bonanno is a remarkably honest person. If that were overheard by some prosecuting attorney for the government, he would be shocked by the remark I just made. But Bill Bonanno, I repeat, is a remarkably honest person about himself. If Bill Bonanno were a reporter and I the subject, I do not know if I would have been as candid, as open with him as he was with me. I do think that the book for him—the research, I should say—was almost therapeutic. He really wanted to talk about himself for the first time. And deeply. And he did.

Brady: Let me ask you a chicken-egg type question: Which came first, the story or the friendship?

Talese: First came the interest on my part, the curiosity on my part *about* the story. I knew the story before I even had it. I knew what the story was that I was looking for. I had never read a factual account of someone in the Mafia, particularly someone my own age. I was trying to write about the changing generations in the Mafia, about a Mafia son. I had no idea that I would find one, but I thought: There's a good story. Everyone's writing about these big guys with wide hats shooting it out on the sidewalks of Brooklyn. No one ever writes about their own internal world, their own families. And what about their sons? I mean, how do you get into the Mafia? And if you have a son, does he have to go into the Mafia if his father's in it? What are these young men like? Where is the younger Mafia generation going?

So it was one day in a courtroom in 1965 that I met Bill Bonanno, and one thing led to another. I got to know him, and eventually, in the course of five or six years I was able to write about him. It wasn't a matter of arranging things in an orderly way at first because as I said before, I do not take a note pad or tape recorder or anything like that. It's just a matter of being around and trying to be accepted, and that may take a year. I did with Bill Bonanno. So I didn't do *any* work. I mean, I was working the first year, but I had nothing to show for it after the year. But all that was instrumental in what I finally wrote.

Brady: Was there ever a point where you thought you might abandon the book?

Talese: Yes, about a year and a half after I met Bill for the first time. So that means sometime in late 1966 or early 1967 I did abandon the book. I did so because Bill and other people in the Mafia were having a shooting war and I couldn't reach anyone. The telephone numbers that I'd received, that I'd been able to collect from knowing Bill Bonanno and others—all these numbers were changed, and some of these people moved to different locations. I lost touch with everyone. They were in their own world at that time. They had no interest in what I was doing, so I lost touch with them. They simply disappeared.

I more or less abandoned the Mafia book, and didn't think I'd ever get back to it because I really felt that my main subject, Bill Bonanno, would be killed. In 1967 I was quite sure he was going to be killed. They tried. The Mafia group that was opposing the Bonanno group had tried in 1966, and almost succeeded in killing Bill Bonanno. He had been set up to be ambushed on a sidewalk in Brooklyn, and they came very close to doing it on this particular night. So I thought, well, they missed that night—but they weren't going to miss again. And I did give up the book. I started writing for *Esquire,* and one article I did was on the managing editor Clifton Daniel. This gave me the idea for another book—a book on the *New York Times.*

Brady: How did you get the idea for the *Esquire* article?

Talese: It was given to me by Harold Hayes, the editor of *Esquire.* Hayes, who's from North Carolina, thought that the idea of writing about an editor from North Carolina—Clifton Daniel—would be an interesting piece. And I'd worked at the *Times* before that. I did know Clifton Daniel a little bit, but I didn't know him well. I had very little dealings with him. But I did begin to research the Daniel piece, though, as I say, it was not my idea. But after I got into the magazine article, then I saw the relationship the managing editor had with the publisher's family (the Sulzberger family); the relationship the family had with other elements in the paper—the advertising department, the production department, as well as the Sunday department. So I saw for the first time, two years after I left the paper, what the *New York Times* was really like. In a way, I was like the journalist who was too close to the story to see it when I worked on the *Times;* and I, too, was unaccustomed to writing about newspapermen.

We who live in the world of the city room each day are dispatched by editors to go out to the world, the city, the sidewalks of the city, and write about what you are assigned to write about. And what you are *never* assigned to write about in the newspaper business are other newspapers. We on the *Times* would never have been dispatched to go downtown and write about Dorothy Schiff of the *New York Post,* or to go over to the other side of town to write about the managing editor of the *New York News,* or the editorial staff of the *News.* We would never see these individuals, influential and colorful as many of them are. We would never see them as subjects for news—except in times of strikes. When there was a newspaper strike, then you might do a very delicate profile on some labor leader, like the printers' leader Bertram Powers; or, on the closing of the *New York Herald Tribune,* there might be articles on the Reid family, or the Whitney family, or whoever is in charge. You know, on an occasion such as that. But as for charting out journalism as a source of news, as an area within which are interesting people to write about—newspapers do not do this.

When I first started to write the book on the *Times,* there were not that many *publishers* that were interested. I did not get a large amount of money to write that book. I asked for an $11,000 advance from one publisher—Farrar-Strauss, I think—and was turned down.

Brady: You were originally with Harper & Row, weren't you?

Talese: Yes, that's right. But they didn't think (and I think that other publishers would have been in agreement) that a book about a newspaper would be worth a lot of money. Therefore, a publisher couldn't give a large advance for the writing of the book. But that's where they were wrong. And most newspapers would have been equally wrong in underestimating the interest the public has in journalists, in owners of newspapers, in editors, in the whole world of the city room. It's a fascinating world. I knew it as that. I was always fascinated by the people who work in newspapers—and when I wrote about them, it became a bestseller.

Brady: It sold well and was a popular success. I've noticed in some of the reviews, though, that it took a lump here and there.

Talese: Oh! It took lumps all over the country.

Brady: I found the words "gossip" and "gossipy" used on several occasions. I have a quote here from a book called *The New Journalism,* by Michael Johnson, and he says: *"The Kingdom and the Power* as literary art is perhaps closer to Arthur Hailey's *Airport* or *Hotel* than to Capote's *In Cold Blood."* Now, how would you answer a remark such as this?

Talese: I think that Johnson's an idiot. That's how I'd answer that. This is reporting—this is not fiction that is trying to draw on a factual situation. It is fact reporting—and not only fact reporting, but reporting about the fact factory of journalism, where any little error that I made would have been exploited by the editors or critics who work for the *New York Times.* It's unlike Capote's *In Cold Blood,* where we were presented for the first time in detail with the incident of the murder in Kansas.

Now Capote could have made dozens of mistakes in his reporting there, and we in New York, Chicago, Los Angeles wouldn't have knowledge of these. I'm not saying he did, but I am saying that when you make a mistake about the *New York Times,* you have, first of all, five thousand people in that building on 43rd Street between Eighth Avenue and Broadway. You have five thousand people who have their own ideas of what the *Times* is like, who have their own ideas of what goes on in that building. And when you try to write, as I did, about that building, you are writing for a *very* tough audience and accuracy *really* is tested. And I did not have any charges of inaccuracy in that book. That's what I am most proud of in the writing of *The Kingdom and the Power.* I also think it's a damn beautifully written book. I'm not at all modest.

Brady: And with good reason. I'd like to get back to Sinatra a bit, and, for that matter, Joe DiMaggio. Sinatra is known as a man who is not very cooperative with journalists; and you say in your introduction to *Fame and Obscurity* that DiMaggio started to cooperate with you on the profile you wrote, then had a reversal.* When this happens —when you run into someone like Sinatra who is so insulated from journalists, or when you run into a reluctant subject like DiMaggio— how do you get in there close enough to do the story anyway?

Talese: Let's take the Sinatra one first, because we haven't dealt with DiMaggio yet. Sinatra was *surrounded* by people almost at all times, meaning I could not get close to him. But that was good. I was able to see him surrounded by people who were preventing me from getting close to him, and that was part of the story about Sinatra— that he's surrounded. Now all I had to do was get close to the people who were close to Sinatra and see what role they play in his life. Which I did. It was much more interesting to see Sinatra with his

* [Editor's note: See Gay Talese, "Author's Note to *Fame and Obscurity,"* page 35.]

retinue, with his various vassals and serfs and the whole order of subservient people encircling him. It was *fascinating* to see these people in operation when they went to Las Vegas, or when they went to a prize fight, or when they were going out to dinner in Beverly Hills. It's *marvellous* to be able to stand back and watch this whole scene.

Brady: You originally had an interview scheduled with him, didn't you?

Talese: I had had an interview scheduled with him, which had been arranged by his public relations man in Los Angeles. I flew from New York out to Los Angeles thinking I was going to get to spend time with Frank Sinatra and to interview him on the occasion of his fiftieth birthday—that was the news peg for the piece, I think. When I got out there, Frank Sinatra was not feeling well and everyone was very nervous—"everyone" meaning those people who worked for Sinatra, like the publicity man and a dozen other people who have various roles. And Sinatra had a cold. Because he had a cold he was very irritable. He also had two television shows to do. I was told that every time he had a cold he became extremely irritable, not only in ways you can imagine, but psychologically, because his voice was affected. He was not able to sing with the ease and perfection that he might otherwise be able to do. This was interesting. The cold affected not only him—it affected his whole group, his whole organization.

The people who were more or less employed by Sinatra numbered around, I think, 150 who might be part of his record company, his movie company, his airlines, his missile-parts company, his gardener, valet, chauffeur, tailor—all these people who made either all or part of their living off Frank Sinatra would be affected by his cold because he affected their income. His good will, as he dispensed it on that—or any—particular day was very much affected by how he felt.

Anyway, I wrote about this. The piece was called "Frank Sinatra Has a Cold," and there were parts in it he didn't like. I was never able to get an interview with him. I was never able to sit down alone with Frank Sinatra and say: Here is what I would like to know about such and such. Never! But this wasn't very important because if I *had* been able to sit with Frank Sinatra, this man who for thirty years had been in the public eye, and if I had been able to ask him questions, I don't think I could have asked him—nor do I think he could have answered—those questions in any way that would have been as revealing of himself as I was able to gather by staying a bit of a distance away, *observing* him and overhearing him and watching those around him react to him. All these inter-actions and counter-actions that I was able to observe during six weeks of travelling around more or less in his company were far better than being able to finally have an audience with him.

Brady: How were you able to follow him around, as you say, more or less in his company?

Talese: I became a part of his group, his entourage, because, as I said before, his publicity man had told *Esquire* that an interview could be arranged with me and Sinatra, and it was for that reason I went out to California to begin with. When Frank Sinatra had a cold, the interview was postponed till he got better. Now, while he was getting better—which took about a week or ten days—I was waiting for the signal from him or from one of his lieutenants that I could arrange to interview him. Well, it was during this six- or seven- or eight-day period that I was seeing a better story than an interview. I was seeing the reactions.

I was able to see the publicity man at work on other things having to do with Sinatra's life. I was able to learn a lot about the Hollywood press agent—that type, that high-priced, very successful, very nervous kind of man such as Frank Sinatra had hired. Many people like that in Hollywood. I was actually getting character: What is the press agent like? What does he do for relaxation? Whom is he answerable to beside his client? And who's answerable to him? You have this whole pecking order in the Hollywood publicity business.

There were also people in the record business. I was able to know something about records and juke boxes and big bands and arrangers and saxophone players—this whole group from the big band era that was part of the Sinatra out-of-the-Forties decade. I was able during this eight or ten-day delay to really get onto another story which was far better. And I was able to hang around because I had a reason for hanging around. I was there in the company because, "Well, when Frank gets better, he's gonna give this guy an interview." Meanwhile, I'm traveling with him. I'm going to recording sessions Frank Sinatra is having in various parts of Los Angeles. I was able later on to go to the Patterson-Clay fight in Las Vegas—paid my own way, bought my own ticket, but I travelled with the publicity man who was part of the group, you see, so I was able to witness scenes in the Las Vegas nightclub gambling parlors, was able to be part of the Sinatra group, and it was a marvellous experience.

Brady: What about someone like DiMaggio, who's more of a loner and doesn't have a platoon of people to insulate him from a writer?

Talese: He's very different. He dealt with me directly. The profile on Joe DiMaggio begins with me arriving at the DiMaggio seafood restaurant at Fisherman's Wharf. I had met DiMaggio before in New York at Yankee Stadium on Oldtimers Day. He had been one of the honored guests, and there were a lot of people in the locker room when I approached him and said I'd like to come out some day and talk to him. He said, "Yeah, yeah," probably just to dismiss me. But he *did* say, "Come on out," or "Get in touch with my brother Tom," his older brother who more or less runs the family's affairs. Well, about four months later when I knew I wanted to go out to San Francisco, I sent DiMaggio telegrams and they were not replied to. I called him up and couldn't reach him—but I was told the messages had been received, and he was in town. So the best thing to do was just go out there—which I did.

I showed up the next day at the restaurant and as I walked up I saw DiMaggio in the dining room alone. Just as a matter of formality, I asked someone in the outer room of the restaurant if Joe DiMaggio was there, expecting this man to say, "Yes, just a moment. Who's calling?" or "What is it you want?" But I was told, "No, he's not here," and I had actually caught a *glimpse* of DiMaggio. And then this dialogue began—this interesting scene which I wrote about in the article.

Brady: In that article you write of yourself from the third-person or objective point of view.

Talese: Right. I do that because I don't like first-person reporting. I believe that some of the density, some of the depth is lost if you do it first person. You see, if you start writing first person, you're going to have to stay with it. That means you yourself become the focal point of the piece, and everything reacts to your writing about yourself as a person who is going out and having things happen to him. Norman Mailer, for example, did it in going to the steps of the Pentagon—the piece he did for *Harper's* that later became a book. When Mailer writes about himself, he does well, he does beautifully. But we do not get depth, we do not get a sense of other people in great depth.

What I do is this: I go from person to person. I will be writing about, let us say, oh, in the Frank Sinatra piece, to get back to that for a moment—I'll be writing about Sinatra maybe in one scene, and then I'll shift and write about Sinatra's press agent, in this case James Mahoney, and I'll describe that morning in the publicity man's life—what the secretary looks like, a description of the interior of the office and the telephones ringing and overheard conversations. Then I may shift in the next scene to Mahoney getting into his convertible Mercedez Benz and driving to a recording session. Then maybe I'll shift the scene to Nelson Riddle and his orchestra. Riddle's been with Sinatra a long time. I'll give you something about the orchestra leader. I will have researched that, but I'm writing about him as a character.

So I'm shifting from the star of the piece to the publicity man to the orchestra leader, then maybe to some member of the Sinatra group. I wrote about a double. Sinatra was making a movie at the time, and there was a guy who looked something like Frank Sinatra and who was there to stand in his place under the hot lights to mark areas of the stage to help the cameramen get into focus. I remember I wrote about Sinatra's double in one scene. I'm like a director, and I shift my own particular focus, my own cameras, from one to the other to the other; eventually I have a whole gallery of people I'm writing about. And you can only do this with the third person. I find that I can then get into the people that I am writing about and I just shift. That's where my own subjectivity, or creativity, as you will, comes into play. I make the choice of where the camera is going to go. I decide who I will focus on, and the order of the focusing, too.

This gives me a lot of options. It allows me to be creative and yet factual. That's what I think is exciting about nonfiction these days. You can do all the novelist can do—you just have to do a *hell* of a lot of research. You have to know your people very, very well. And you have to be able to work within their words, and work within the framework of their lives. But if you dig deeply enough into their lives, you come up with so much that it gives a lot to work with, and you can still be creative and selective in what you choose to work with.

Brady: You originally were writing straight reportage. Then with the early magazine pieces, you seemed for awhile to be using a combination of reportage and this new type of journalism—using straight reportage along with devices of fiction.

Talese: Scene setting. Right. Dialogue and interior monologue, yes.

Brady: Now, in your most recent book, *Honor Thy Father*, there is very little reportage—it's almost exclusively the setting of scenes, establishing of character. Do you think, if you follow this transition, that eventually you'll become a fiction writer? Are you working your way out of nonfiction and into fiction?

Talese: No. I am working, in fact, deeper into nonfiction. You referred to *Honor Thy Father* as being not as much an example of reportage as the previous things you read. Well, I don't think that's true. This is really reporting, but it's the way it's written that makes it seem it's not reporting. I don't use direct quotations very much in *Honor Thy Father*. In case of dialogue I do, but I have gotten away from the direct quotation.

Brady: Why?

Talese: For a couple of reasons. Let's get to it first from the point of view of the people you are interviewing. People do not speak in sentences. So if you are going to quote them directly, word for word, accurately, verbatim—you are going to find that people are not going to seem articulate. If you quote accurately, you will find that it is difficult to communicate with your own reader what the person you are interviewing is trying to say. Almost without exception, you can say it better if you don't have to stay within the quotes that come out of this person's mouth. You can put it better. You can explain more what he's trying to say. You can do a better job of saying it in writing than he can by just talking off the cuff.

Of course, if you quote him directly, you shouldn't change the quote—although I know from my days as a newspaperman that when I and others would go out to cover a story, we'd all be quoting directly and I would see variations in the quotations. We would be out interviewing for, oh, some dock strike story, and we'd be listening to some labor leader. I would get what I thought was a word-for-word quote, and I'd look at the *Herald Tribune* or the *New York Post* or the *Daily News* the next day and I would see differences. Sometimes we even matched quotes after our assignments were over—we would go to a bar and go over things ourselves. Even then, I noticed there would be variations. Not intentional—no, we didn't change the meaning of the words out of the spokesman's mouth. Just a couple of words we changed here and there. I never did believe in that so-called *accurate* note-taking and quoting verbatim. It wasn't always that accurate. It wasn't like this tape recorder you have going every second, so there would be a lot of little changing around. Even within direct quotations by newspapermen.

Brady: And even when you were using direct quotations, you felt uncomfortable?

Talese: Sure, I missed a few words here and there. But now, why do we have to stick to this man's words? Why don't I just try to get most accurately as I can what he is trying to say, and put it in my own words, attributing it to him. Why do I have to stick to his particular vocabulary? Well, there *is* no reason, except we were taught —all of us who come out of journalism schools in the 1940's and 50's—the old formula reporting: the Old Journalism, if you will.

Why do we have to stick to other people's words? Particularly when we're the writers. Let's put the story in our own words—that's how we can communicate more fully and more accurately. At least, I can. That's why I got away from using direct quotes, although I always attribute material to the proper source. In a story I will say, well, in the case of yourself, John Brady said such and such— but I wouldn't put it in quotes. Or, earlier you relayed to me some thoughts you had while driving into New York this morning. Instead of putting that in quotes, I would say you were *thinking* such and such as you were driving over the Triboro Bridge. You were alone; you weren't *telling* anything to anyone. If I were reporting about your day, though, I would have you thinking that you were born and reared in Yonkers. I would write that, you see: John Brady though this as he was crossing the Triboro Bridge.

Now, when that's in print, someone could read it and say, "How in the hell does Gay Talese know that Brady was *thinking* this?" Well, obviously, because Brady *told* me that he was thinking about this. But if I put it in direct quotes, they wouldn't challenge me—although direct quotes oftentimes are inaccurate. Quotes are not always word for word what the person has said. In *Honor Thy Father* I got away from direct quotations because I could report and write more accurately what Bill Bonanno was telling me by using my own words than I could if I stuck with his words.

Finally, there's a point of style. This goes back to journalism, too. Sometimes you find reporters (I was among them) who would work so hard on the first paragraph, the lead of a story—they would work and work and polish and make it clear, and get right into the story. The second paragraph was usually a bit of an elaboration on what was said in the lead. And the third paragraph, inevitably, and sadly, was always a quotation. Simple formula reporting. It might be the third paragraph, or maybe the fourth—but you'd know there'd be a quote, and that's where the story got boring.

I found the story got boring because the writer stopped writing, the reporter stopped using his skill: he fell into the quote, the easy way out. Then he would start writing with these direct quotes through the body of the story, and it was boring. You were losing the interest of the reader. You were *not communicating*—which was why you went on the assignment in the first place: to tell the reader what happened. If you told it in your own words, I found, you couldn't stop working—you couldn't lay back and say, "I've got a direct quote and therefore I'll lay it on him." It's much more interesting to read if you put it in your own words. Well, I extended that to the book. The whole book is in my words—but it truly reflects the attitude of the people I am writing about, *more* accurately than if I'd had direct quotes.

Brady: All right, now what has to happen for you to decide to use quotations?

Talese: People have to say things in such an original way, a unique way that would be so peculiarly their own that it would reflect so much of what they are, their style of speech, that I wouldn't attempt to imitate it. I wouldn't use my own writing style, which is very formal. I do not use contractions, I do not use slang, I do not use informality in any way. It's a very simple, I hope, but formal style—and if I were writing about people who said things in such an original way, then I would go with the way they spoke. Obviously, if I'm writing an article about, oh, let's say the comedian Jonathan Winters, or the manager Casey Stengel—well, obviously, you'd have to use some of his language because that language would be so much a part of *him*.

Brady: You mentioned in a piece of writing once that you had reached a point now where you try to pick a subject's brain by asking the right question at the right time, and this gives you the thought processes of a character. Can you give me an example of this technique?

Talese: Take *Honor Thy Father*. I had been having difficulty in getting enough uninterrupted time with Bill Bonanno to deal with the whole section of his life that had to do with the attempt by other Mafia men to kill him. I knew, as I told you before, that there had been one attempt to kill him, and I knew that he didn't like to talk about this. Whenever I did try to approach the subject, someone else would enter the room, and he didn't want to be seen by bodyguards or other people telling me about the time when he was going to what was supposedly a peace meeting between these two rival Mafia factions where they were supposed to settle some problems that had threatened to start a Mafia war, and they tried to kill him in Brooklyn on a January night in 1966.

Well, about three years later, in 1969, I wanted to get him to tell me about this. What were the issues in the feud? Where did he park the car? How many blocks was it to walk from the parked car with his bodyguards to this particular relative's home where the rival Mafia group was supposed to also come and sit down at a table and discuss their differences? I wanted to know what Bill Bonanno was wearing, what he was thinking. I wanted to know so much about it, and I never could really sit with him because we were always interrupted.

I knew it would take a long time for him to do this, and I didn't want interruptions. I wanted to have him tell me about when he first heard the shots. You see, there were guns focused on him from the roofs of buildings along this street where he would have had to walk to get to the location where the meeting was to take place. I wanted to know about the first shots, I wanted to know what direction he ran. None of this did I know, nor did anyone else except him. He knew the streets of Brooklyn. I wanted to know if he ran south or southwest, what streets he passed, what he did after dodging these bullets. He made a phone call. Where did he make the phone call? I would then check and see if there was a phone booth in this place. Who did he call? What time was it? All these details, all this detail work—it was going on in his own mind, you see. It was a scene of action.

Well, years later I'm out there in San Jose, which is where Bill Bonanno moved after he left New York, and I heard that he was driving to Phoenix from San Francisco. That's a long automobile drive—that's about twelve hours. I overheard him talking to one of the bodyguards about going down with him. Bill had to see his father on some issue, and the bodyguard wasn't that enthusiastic about taking a twelve hour trip, although he would have. So I volunteered. "Look," I said, "if you want company, let me keep you company." He said, "Fine," because I had gotten to know him very well. During this trip I would have twelve hours without the phone ringing, without people being around—I would have him all by myself. So that trip was a very fortuitous journey. I was able to ride next to him in the car—he was driving—and I took notes, got all the detail work about his thought processes I mentioned before. Notes. Detail.

Now we were talking about direct quotations before. If you play this tape back, John, you will find my sentence structure is going to be very hard to understand if you are going to use direct quotations. If you quote me directly, some paragraphs will get a sense of what I am saying, but in others you will find that the sentence structure is somewhat reversed. *You* can understand me, but when you try to put this on the written page, I will not communicate well. That's why, if you were to do what I did—write a series of interviews for a magazine piece or a book—you would be wise to take the essence of what I am saying and put it in your own words. It will read better. As I was talking to you the last fifteen minutes I was aware of things I'd just said and the reversal of words.

Brady: You like it out in front of you where you can re-arrange things and make them more grammatically correct.

Talese: More grammatically correct and more sharply pointed up.

Brady: These are quickies. I'd like to get, if I can, a kind of gut reaction from you on these items.

Talese: OK.

Brady: Tom Wolfe.

Talese: I think he's terrific. I like him, I like his reporting, I like his originality, and he's a friend of mine, so what I say is not too objective. Forget that: he's really a rare talent.

Brady: Harold Hayes.

Talese: The greatest popular editor to my knowledge. A great man. He's been incredibly helpful to me. I trust him. I trust his judgment on writing as no other editor that I know.

Brady: Jimmy Breslin.

Talese: Breslin is certainly a talented and ambitious and hard-working—*really* hardworking—man. His style of writing is out of Jimmy Cannon, out of Runyon, and that's OK; I mean, it has its place. It's a good influence. I like Cannon.

Brady: Do you like Breslin? His writing?

Talese: It's not my style. I like Cannon. Cannon's not my style. Runyon is certainly not my style. My style is formal. I don't like the colloquial, I don't like the slang, I don't like the echo of the streets in writing. But when Breslin reports, you do get a sense that he was there, and he is hardworking. I tip my hat to any reporter who is hardworking, and that includes Breslin certainly, one of the hardest-working reporters that I think has been in journalism in New York in all the time that I've been here.

Brady: Playboy magazine.

Talese: Very influential publication. Probably the most influential publication of my lifetime. It has influenced middle America. It has recorded and been in the vanguard of change, sexually, in this country. It's a great barometer of public temperature of sexual beat. Hefner will probably go down in modern history as one of the most influential men of the 1960's and 70's in the whole country. Tremendous impact on American sexual habits; on the law, too, I believe.

Brady: What do you think of the writing that goes on there?

Talese: Not much for the writing. I don't read *Playboy*; I look at the pictures, like most people. I like the pictures. I love the great-looking women. I don't read Nabokov. If I'm going to read Nabokov, I'm not going to read *Playboy* to read him. Or Barth or Updike or whoever is in there. Even the interviews. *Playboy* supposedly does these great interviews—I don't like that kind of interviewing.

Brady: Do you like *this* kind of interviewing?

Talese: I don't mind doing it, but I'm not going to read it. When it comes to reading an interview, I want the whole thing. I want the writer to have worked on the piece. If they are going to do a piece on Vladimir Nabokov, well, I want the writer to have done all the research, read all the books, and gone, spent time with the old gent with his butterfly net—really give me the flavor of Nabokov and the sense of presence that a writer or an interviewer can sometimes bring. Oh, I suppose if I'm really interested in the subject—if it's some great sage of our time like Howard Cosell that *Playboy* is interviewing —then I might read it because I know Howard Cosell. I'm not likely to read those interviews otherwise.

Brady: Sportswriting today.

Talese: Well, I was a sportswriter and have opinions of sports-writing. There's some good stuff done by Larry Merchant of the *New York Post,* for example. I read him. And David Anderson of the *Times* is good.

Brady: I saw a blurb by you on the cover of Roger Kahn's book.

Talese: Oh, you are talking about books and sportswriting in general. Roger Kahn is wonderful, and *The Boys of Summer* is one of the best books I've read. Loved it.

Brady: Truman Capote.

Talese: Really a skilled reporter, a very fine reporter. And an awfully good writer.

Brady: Dwight Macdonald.

Talese: Not my favorite person. Pompous, argumentative without ever dealing with the issues that he raises all the time. No, not my favorite man. I think he's unfair, and I don't trust him.

Brady: If you hadn't become a writer, what would you be today?

Talese: Probably a director. A movie director. But I would probably want to write my own scripts.

Brady: Who are some of your favorite writers?

Talese: In fiction, *The French Lieutenant's Woman* was the best novel I've read in memory. John Fowles. A fantastic novel. Updike—a terrific writer who has ripped off some nonfiction in some of his novels, I've noticed. In his last book, *Rabbit Redux,* he writes about this middle-American character, Rabbit, on the day when men are landing on the moon. You get a sense of journalism, really. Updike gets the attention of the reader by giving him something the reader is familiar with, having lived through the day that Armstrong went onto the moon. In a previous book, *Couples,* you have the day Kennedy was shot; Updike has situations going on that day, and the reader again is riveted to the page because he is reliving a factual event—the death of the President.

Philip Roth's last book—*Our Gang,* or *Our Crowd,* or whatever the hell it was—was awful. It's like a long, long, long Russell Baker satire, not as good as Russell Baker does it. It was like, if you can imagine, an interminable Russell Baker column not done with Baker's skill. It was a bad book by Roth. But it was journalism—it was *bad* journalism. I think the novelists should stay out of journalism unless they know how to do it. Capote knows how to do it. Styron *knows* he can't do it and stays out of it. Mailer is into it, and is a good reporter, except he reports a bit too much on himself—but he does it with style and wit, and it's therefore justifiable. He has great humor, Mailer does.

Brady: What sort of people do you hang out with?

Talese: My friends are often people I admire professionally. Like David Halberstam. I admire him tremendously as a professional, and I am very close to him as a friend. There is A. E. Hotchner, who wrote a marvelous book on Hemingway—the best book that ever *will* be written on Hemingway is *Papa Hemingway,* by Hotchner. There have been a lot of attacks on that book, but that's the only really good book on Hemingway. Hotchner's a good friend of mine. He has a new novel coming out, *King of the Hill.* And Nick Pileggi is another writer I admire—he works for *New York* magazine.

Brady: He does quite a few pieces on the Mafia.

Talese: That's why I know how good he is. I've been checking on him.

Brady: What sort of work habits do you maintain as a writer?

Talese: When I'm researching, I don't have any habits; I'm out on the road a lot. When I'm at the writing stage, I work in the morning. I write from nine o'clock to one o'clock if I can get through that hour.

Brady: Every day of the week?

Talese: Yes, I *try* to work from nine to one. I'm not saying I *do* it. I try to stay alone during those hours—turn off the telephone, occupy a downstairs apartment in a brownstone. I try to make it through twelve or one o'clock. Then I have a light lunch and go play tennis with Hotchner or with other people, doubles or singles. I try to get back around five o'clock to do a little more work. It's never heavy work in the evening, in the early evening—it's going over what I've done and maybe rethinking a few things to be picked up the next morning at nine. I try not to read the newspapers in the morning. When I'm working, I don't want to see the paper; all I want is a cup of coffee and a glass of orange juice, in reverse order, and then I get to the typewriter. I don't eat much—a piece of coffee ring, a cup of coffee, and that's it. If I have a hearty breakfast, I can't write.

Brady: And your evenings are your own?

Talese: Yes.

Brady: Do you write in longhand or on the typewriter? Is there any particular pattern?

Talese: I used to use the typewriter when I was working on the newspaper. I can't anymore. I get into different routines. When I really do not know what I am saying, or how to say it, I'll open these Pentels, these colored Japanese pens, on yellow lined paper, and I'll start off with very tentative colors, very light colors: orange, yellow or tan. These pens come in eight or nine different colors. I'll just play around with how I could write.

When my thoughts are more formulated, and I have a sharper sense of trying to say it, I'll go into heavier colors: blues, greens, and eventually into black. When I am writing in black, which is the final version, I have written that sentence maybe twelve or fifteen or eighteen times. I have something that is really coming clear now. Then I go to the typewriter. But it is a stage of pale colors into the dark colors, onto the typewriter—retyping, retyping, retyping. Eventually it's there. I'll write a paragraph and it's final. When I finally settle for a page, it's pretty much as it will appear a year or two later in type. I write page by page.

Brady: Do you still use field glasses?

Talese: No. I did use field glasses when I was writing magazine pieces. The reason, to explain—well, I used to work in one of the apartments I used to live in. The apartment had a red, felt wall, and I used to tack the pages that I had done on this wall. I just finished telling you that I write page by page. When I was doing magazine pieces, I had a deadline, and since I rewrite each page so many times before I finally settle on that page, there is much rewriting and I tend to forget and am unable to see what I have written clearly. Literally, I was so familiar with each word, having pounded over it so many times on the typewriter, I couldn't see it and I had to back away from it.

I had a deadline. I couldn't just put something away for a month and reread it. I didn't have the time to be able to gain my sense of objectivity and removal by putting it away. I had to deal with it immediately. So the idea was: how could I *quickly* remove myself that distance? Instant distance is what I am probably trying to say. I came upon the idea of hanging these pages as I did them, almost like a clothesline, across the wall: one page after the other, strung from left to right—page one, two, three . . . all the way through to fifteen, sixteen pages of a magazine piece. I would put the lights on the desk on these pages, go across the other side of the room with field glasses, and focus on these pages. When I read these pages, they were so sharp—through the binoculars with the light from the desk focusing sharply on them across the room—that they almost looked as if they were in type, as if the whole thing was in the magazine. I am a very careful typist. My final draft is almost flawless typing. So, looking through the binoculars, it was not as if I had typed the article, but as if it were in type—you know, gone to the printers, and now there it was in final form on the glossy pages of the magazine. Believe me, it sounds insane, I know. But it worked for me. I was able to read it and see it with a kind of freshness that I was not able to see through my own eyes when I was at the typewriter at the desk with those pages.

Brady: At that point, do you trust your own judgment absolutely? Do you ever give it to someone to read before sending it off to an editor?

Talese: Yes, I do have Nan, my wife, who's a senior editor at Random House, read everything I write, and I trust her absolutely.

Brady: When was the last time you got a rejection slip?

Talese: I think probably in the 1950's when I first started writing. I had a great idea for an article, so I wrote a great memo—an outline. If you go to *Life* or *Esquire* and say, "I want to write an article," they say: "Let me see an outline." I had a *terrific* idea for an article on a sociologist who had made a study of locker rooms and athletes and the dating habits of athletes, a sociologist who had really gone into the world of high school sports. I wrote a marvelous outline about this man; I interviewed him and I had just enough to write an outline.

I sent it to *Life* magazine and they bought it. They gave me $750 and said, "Here it is, we commission the idea, do it as a piece for us." This was in 1959. I turned in the article and they rejected it. I kept the $750, but I would have gotten $1,500 if I'd done the whole thing. Then I sent the outline to *Sports Illustrated* and they thought it was a *terrific* outline, a great idea for an article, and they said, "We'll give you $2,000 if you do it right. Take a thousand now." But when they saw the article, they rejected it. Then I went to *Esquire* and gave them the outline, and they also commissioned me to do the piece. They gave me, I think a guarantee of $300-$400, and they rejected it. I put the article away. I've never drawn it out since. It's a great outline, and a lousy article. That was it—my last rejection. But I got well paid for that memo.

Brady: If you're going to be rejected, you might as well do it with style. Was there ever what you might call a low point in your career?

Talese: Yes. The lowpoint in my career as a newspaperman was in the early 1960's—1962, '63—when I was frustrated by what I was unable to do at the *New York Times*. I wanted freedom. I wanted to go around the country, to report and write about what I thought was important, interesting: a convention, the World Series, some revolt of farmers in Iowa, or whatever. I wanted to have some freedom to go places; I didn't want to be nailed down.

I think the *Herald Tribune* in its last years provided its reporters with tremendous freedom. A dying paper is a place where the troops, the members of the staff, have great amounts of fun, freedom. And I was seeing the freedom of the *Herald Tribune*—those reporters my own age going around and writing with freedom—while I on the *Times* was subjected to the scrutiny and the tough pencils of the copyreaders. I felt great frustration, and undoubtedly this led to my resignation.

I left the paper rather late. I was going to quit in 1962, but then Abe Rosenthal returned from Tokyo to become the city editor of the New York staff, and he convinced me to stay a couple of years longer. I should have quit in '62 or '63 instead of '65, and I *would* have quit if Rosenthal hadn't come back. I probably did a little better under Abe Rosenthal—but I guess I was ready to leave daily reporting at that time, and so I left.

Brady: You often write about certain themes—success, power, and sometimes failure . . .

Talese: Oftentimes failure.

Brady: . . . the effects that these things have upon people. Now that you are successful, how would you say that your own success has affected you?

Talese: It hasn't affected me at all, I think—but I might be the last person to know. Financially, it hasn't affected me at all because I don't have any great expensive tastes that are going to be fulfilled with a lot of money. As for my work habits, I'm a painfully slow writer. I take a long time to research a subject, and I have not changed, I don't think, a bit in the last four or five years insofar as the basic ambitions and goals go: to report and to write to the best of my ability. There is a new project, there's a book to be done, and I do it the best I can. I only do one thing at a time. I don't juggle, I don't do a lot of things; I don't have a novel in the works and a screenplay I'm writing for Paramount. I'm doing one thing. And while I'm writing, researching a book, I don't even want to do anything else.

Brady: Has your first name ever been an inconvenience to you as a writer?

Talese: In the early days, when I was getting bylines in the *Times,* people would confuse me for a girl, and I would get mail: Miss Gay Talese. And sometimes obscene phone calls at night, too. But as I came to be better known, and appeared on television, that stopped. Having the name Gay—which is my mother's idea of a great name— didn't bother me in Alabama, where it wasn't so uncommon. But now with Gay Liberation, well, it doesn't bother me, but I see my name all over the place.

Brady: How do you get people to talk about themselves so intimately? I am thinking, for example, of the information you had in your book on the lovemaking of Bill Bonanno and his wife. This is, I think, reporting at its most intimate level, and you obviously obtained this information. Just how do you get so close to get this?

Talese: You have to get close to the people so that they are willing to confide in you. We all want to talk about ourselves; we want to talk about ourselves with people we think will understand us. So the first thing is to understand that other person, to convince the other person you understand him: to establish a rapport. Once that is established, you really can delve and penetrate deeply. That's what happened with Bill Bonanno and myself, and also Bill's wife confided in me— found me, I think, a means of communication to her husband. She would be afraid to tell him things, so she would tell me, more or less wanting me to tell him. It was an interesting relationship we had going when I was doing the Mafia book.

I still see the people that I write about. My research doesn't really end with the end of a book. I might do another book on Bill Bonanno ten years from now, see what happens when he gets out of jail. He's in jail now on a credit card case I wrote about. I might write about him, write about his children when they are ten years older. I may go back some day and write another book on the *New York Times,* on Punch Sulzberger when he's sixty years old, maybe ten, twelve years from now.

Brady: Your books sound like children that you are fond of; you like to see them grow older.

Talese: Yes. I'm very interested in reporting change. That's what I would do—go back and take another look at the same place I'd once been.

Brady: You've been quoted as saying, "I think a writer can only write three good books in a lifetime." Where does that leave you?

Talese: Well, I've written two. I hope to write a third. If I don't write it this time, I'll have another chance, I think.

Brady: Could you tell me something about your childhood, your growing-up years. When did you first become aware of the desire to become a writer?

Talese: It was to become a journalist; that desire was when I was fourteen year old. My father used to read the *New York Times* every morning. It would be there and I would read it—the sports pages, I didn't read anything else. I had my favorite sportswriters on the *Times,* and I aspired to be like them. Being a sportswriter, I felt, in the small town that I came from on the southern shores of New Jersey, was the ultimate in good living: traveling, seeing games, being able to write freely (sportswriters are given more freedom than political reporters), and I thought it would be a lot of fun. I became a sportswriter for the local newspaper in Ocean City, reporting the high school news.

When I went to the University of Alabama, I became sports editor for the campus newspaper, and I also did some stringing for the Scripps Howard paper in Birmingham, the *Post Herald,* as a sportswriter. I did other things—some feature stories on non-sports personalities—but mostly sportswriting, and when I went to the *New York Times,* first as a copy boy, and later on got a job on staff, it was as a sportswriter for two years. Many writers—people who later on write books, novels, whatever—start off as sportswriters. Like James Reston. I think Hemingway did a lot of sports. Steinbeck. John Updike is capable—he did a marvelous profile on Ted Williams which you may have read. Well, I became a sportswriter, then became tired of it and wanted to do other things, and when I was about thirty years of age—29 I think it was— I went into general reporting.

Brady: Ultimately, how would you like to be remembered?

Talese: I take myself very seriously. I do not do anything quickly, do not take shortcuts. I'm not ashamed of anything that I've done with my work. I can go back now and read old clippings in the morgue of the *Times*—articles in these little folders, articles that I've written in 1958, '59, '60—and there's not one article that I could pick up as I leaf through my past and say, "Gee, I wish I'd done this better." Everything I wrote under those deadline conditions—maybe four or five or three hours to write a story—I did the best I could. I know I did the best I could. I take great satisfaction in that.

I'm also proud of the magazine pieces that I've written. *Fame and Obscurity:* I'm very pleased with that collection. And I'm not falsely modest, as you can probably gather. I do reread what I've written; I'm one of my biggest fans. I like what I've written. I like to go back and read sections from *The Kingdom and the Power.* I think that's a marvelous book, probably the most ambitious book I've ever done—it's much *tougher* than *Honor Thy Father. The Kingdom and the Power* was a tough book because you are writing about many people. You couldn't find a major personality in the *Times* because nobody dominates that paper, so the task of writing was that I had to develop a series of minor characters, including the publishers, the whole family that runs it. Nobody dominates the damn thing, this enormous empire, the *New York Times.* Nobody really controls it.

So I wasn't writing about a family, as I did in *Honor Thy Father.* There at least I had power, raw power; I could write about a man in charge. He might not have been in charge of his Mafia group for a long time, but at least for the time that I was writing about he was a man in power, clearly in power. Curiously, the title *The Kingdom and the Power* is almost a misnomer for the *Times* because there was power, but not in the hands of any one person or in any small group of people. It was diffuse power, power collectively, yes. The *Times* as an organization is immensely powerful, but to write about it, as I always do, from the point of view of people—to approach it as a people story—was difficult because I had to write about a series of people and their interrelationships, and build through these relationships, these large collective relationships, a sense of power—and the organization of that book was a very difficult bit of work.

Brady: You haven't nailed it down quite yet, though.

Talese: How I want to be remembered?

Brady: Yes.

Talese: I want to be respected. I have never won a prize.

Brady: At all? In all your years . . .

Talese: No. I never won a prize at *anything.* I never won a Pulitzer Prize. I though I had a chance this year with *Honor Thy Father.* I thought that was damn well deserving of the nonfiction reporting prize—I mean, that's a well-reported book, as was the other. I never won a prize from any journalism school. I never won a prize when they give out these Headliner Awards. I don't know what the names of the prizes are because I'm not familiar with them, having never won them. But now I don't give a *damn* about prizes.

I used to be, like when the Pulitzer Prizes were announced this past year. A friend of mine, David Halberstam, said, "You know, I have bad news for you. Did you hear the news about the Prizes?" I said no. "Well, you didn't win." I thought, well it never occurred to me that I would have been up for it, that I would have had a chance, because I don't think in terms of prizes. I've never won them, and I don't think that winning prizes now will make a bit of difference.

But I *would* like to be appreciated by the people I respect for being one hell of a good reporter and for writing very well. I'm not just satisfied being a reporter, because too often that doesn't mean writing. I think I can write as well as any novelist going today. I don't have great respect for the novel. I don't want to write the novel. You asked me that before.

I believe that reporting is an art form, can be an art form, and that people who really care about reporting are artists, can be artists as much as a novelist can be an artist. Take a person I admire very much, like Tom Wolfe, or like David Halberstam. They in nonfiction are as worthy of respect and have the possibility of displaying their talent as much as, say, Updike or Roth. Probably. And so I see reporting, fact writing, as an art form, and I'm pursuing it that way.

So I'd like to be remembered, I guess, as an artist, because that's what I think I am. I'm dealing with facts, I'm reporting; but I am *not* unambitious, and I am pushing this as much as I can in my own way to fulfilling an ambition that I have to be an artist. But I do not want to go the conventional way, and I agree with Tom Wolfe in this area: I don't think the novel is the form we have to strive for. It's fine for some people, and it's great when it works. But I think that reporting is the art form—or *can* be an art form—pursued by me or Halberstam or Wolfe or Breslin or whomever. Pete Hamill. Any of us that know one another's work. We want to pursue reporting as an art form. I think that is wonderful: the reporter as the artist. Wonderful.

The Authentic
New Journalists

DAVID McHAM

Lost in the hue and cry over activism in the news rooms, participatory journalism and pros and cons in definition of "new" journalism is the simple fact that change has been taking place in reporting and writing in this country in the last decade.

Those who spend a lifetime inside a newspaper office are sometimes the last to notice what evolution brings to their products. The pressures of other considerations do not allow for sufficient time to take full note of developments in related journalism, particularly in magazines and books.

The threat is what veteran news management personnel respond to most readily. Of late there has been a threat, as viewed from the eyes of the traditionalists. It is personified by men with long hair, sideburns and beards and women who'll come to the office in anything from hot pants to ponchos.

Not all these people, mostly young, wearing long hair or ponchos bring with them the taint of activism, although they seem fated by the "birds of the feather" adage. Perhaps there are just as many closely shorn and properly dressed young men and women in news rooms who have adopted something approaching the so-called activist approach.

David McHam's article appeared in the September, 1971, issue of *The Quill*. He is a professor of journalism at Baylor University.

The young ones may adopt the more participatory attitude out of naivete, poor training, improper motivation, inadequate guidance, lax newsroom discipline and/or a variety of other commissions and omissions.

Older ones reach a point of despair at what they see as inept traditional approaches, imperfect methods and, most serious, the inability—intentional or otherwise—of the press to respond to its readership as fairly and responsibly as it professes.

The tendency in this confusion of people, motives, situation and circumstance is to look for the easy and oversimplified explanation. And often that explanation goes something like this: "So this is the 'new' journalism we've been hearing about!"

But it is not. That is, there is something going on that has been called capital N, capital J New Journalism, but it is not necessarily activist or participatory and it is not necessarily practiced by untrained, inexperienced, undisciplined would-be journalists.

One of the difficulties associated with the development of New Journalism is that no one has written a handbook explaining what it is and how to go about it, although Tom Wolfe is working on a book about it he hopes to have out in the fall.

The present state of the art has come about informally, slowly and on a number of fronts. Word about it passes through conversation and discussion among writers and hopeful writers. But mostly New Journalism is discovered through reading and observation and learned by experience and hard work.

There is no such thing as the one example of New Journalism. What or who is included during discussion is determined by point of view. Few or many sources might be examined. Naturally the more writers, magazines and books listed the more difficult becomes the attempt to explain by example what it is.

New Journalism is not alien to newspapers and wire services. The story that won the Pulitzer Prize for Thomas Powers and Lucinda Franks of United Press International on Diana Oughton, the young radical who was killed in a Greenwich Village bomb factory, is an example. So too are many of the works of Hugh Mulligan and news-feature writers of The Associated Press. And newspapers abound with examples, some not so "new."

But magazines have been the best proponents of the trend and indeed they have had much to do with sponsorship of it through publication of articles that have been reported and written in what may be called the "new" approach.

Esquire was the first and has done more for the new approach than any other magazine. Selected articles from *Esquire* during the 1960s appear in a book, *Smiling through the Apocalypse.* Harold

Hayes, the editor of *Esquire,* edited the book and wrote an introduction in which he explained how the change took place at the magazine.*

Hayes said the attitude "took shape as we went along" and that "any point of view was welcome." Then he said, ". . . but we tended to avoid committing ourselves to doctrinaire programs even though advised on occasion that we might thereby serve better the interests of mankind."

That introduction by Hayes is a must for anyone attempting to get his bearings on the subject. He explains what the writers were trying to do in becoming "central to events." For instance he lists "freedom-riding down South, slogging through the Mekong Delta, marching on the Pentagon, backtracking Kansas killers, running from cops in Chicago and so on." He says that these writers were "keeping witness in the truest sense, and all readers were the richer for it."

There are so many outstanding examples in *Smiling through the Apocalypse* it is not fair to pick out one or two and ignore the others.

But one situation regarding *Esquire* stands out as a point of reference. It involves Tom Wolfe, who was commissioned to go to California "to take a look at the custom car world." What emerged as "The Kandy-Kolored Tangerine-Flake Streamline Baby" is the title story in Wolfe's first collection of his work. In the introduction he tells how he came to write the story in the way he did.**

"But at first I couldn't even write the story. I came back to New York and just sat around worrying over the thing. I had a lot of trouble analyzing exactly what I had on my hands. By this time *Esquire* practically had a gun at my head because they had a two-page-wide color picture for the story locked into the printing presses and no story. Finally I told Byron Dobell, the managing editor at *Esquire,* that I couldn't pull the thing together. O.K., he tells me, just type out my notes and send them over and he will get somebody else to write it. So about 8 o'clock that night I started typing the notes out in the form of a memorandum that began, 'Dear Byron.' I started typing away, starting right with the first time I saw any custom cars in California. I just started recording it all, and inside of a couple of hours, typing along like a madman, I could tell that something was beginning to happen. By midnight this memorandum to Byron was twenty pages long and I was still typing like a maniac. About 2 A.M. or something like that I turned on WABC, a radio station that plays rock and roll music all night long, and got a little more manic. I wrapped up the memorandum about 6:15 A.M., and by this time it was 49 pages long.

---

* [Editor's note: See Harold Hayes, "Introduction to *Smiling Through the Apocalypse: Esquire's History of the Sixties,*" page 54.]

** [Editor's note: See Tom Wolfe, "Introduction to *The Kandy-Kolored Tangerine-Flake Streamline Baby,*" page 29.]

I took it over to *Esquire* as soon as they opened up, about 9:30 A.M. About 4 P.M. I got a call from Byron Dobell. He told me they were striking out the 'Dear Byron' at the top of the memorandum and running the rest of it in the magazine. That was the story, 'The Kandy-Kolored Tangerine-Flake Streamline Baby.' "

What these articles such as Wolfe's and others do is to get into a subject in depth, to look at it with great detail, sometimes from more than one point of view and sometimes with penetrating insight into only one point of view. The mode gives the writer the opportunity to get into a subject, to move around inside it, to look it over and then give that information to the reader.

The articles are not preachy, they do not intend to have the only answer, they do not evaluate the material in terms of right and wrong. The information is there for the reader to look at, to mull over. In the end the reader can make his own decision about it.

Such an approach may not be new. If there is anything new at all it is the trend that has developed. But it is refreshing, especially from the reader's point of view, because he is able to read an article he can think about and discuss. If there is any participation at all in New Journalism it is that of the reader.

More than likely what the writer has failed to include becomes apparent and, at any rate, the reader isn't bamboozled. This is a change from the staid, strictly-structured, this-is-the-way-it-is method that may quote everyone accurately (if out of context), be balanced and be fair to everyone but the reader, who gets an unclear picture of what is actually going on.

Wolfe referred to this in his introduction to *The Kandy-Kolored Tangerine-Flake Streamline Baby* in explaining how he covered a Hot Rod & Custom Car show in New York for the *Herald Tribune*.

"I brought back exactly the kind of story any of the somnambulistic totem newspapers in America would have come up with. A totem newspaper is the kind people don't really buy to read but just to *have*, physically, because they know it supports their own outlook on life."

So there may be some activism in New Journalism, but if there is it is in opposition to the traditional method. And it is loyal opposition. The result is in the reader's favor, as Hayes said. Because of the type of writers attracted to New Journalism, magazines instead of newspapers present the best forum.

One such forum is *New York* magazine, which got on to the new concept back when it was the Sunday magazine in the *New York Herald Tribune*. Clay Felker and staff are doing it with a rarity among modern journalism, the successful, independent, weekly magazine that was started from scratch. Well, practically from scratch.

Tom Wolfe may have provided the turning point for *New York*. His "Radical Chic: That Party at Lenny's" appeared in the June 8, 1970, issue and seemed to provide a spark for the magazine. If all this seems to make Wolfe the father of New Journalism it is not intended to. Hayes and his staff must share in that title and Gay Talese has played an important part. Even Truman Capote and Norman Mailer can stand up for bows. But more on that later. Back to *New York*.

A look at almost any issue will bring forth examples. Two articles appearing in the May 3 issue will serve as cases in point.

Gail Sheehy covered and wrote interestingly about "The Putnam County Witch Trial," a controversy over the dismissal of an elementary school teacher at Mahopac Falls, New York. The article was written from the point of view of the teacher, Kathleen Marcato, and hence was more than a little sympathetic. While it wasn't advocacy, the article did tend to emphasize the incredulity in the situation.

A paragraph from the article points this out: "Her crime was the hanging of a poster on a public-school bulletin board as part of a Christmas display. It was flowered and carried the message: WAR IS NOT HEALTHY FOR CHILDREN AND OTHER LIVING THINGS."

In the same issue Robert Daley gave a vivid portrait of Frank Serpico in "Portrait of an Honest Cop: Target for Attack." What makes this story interesting besides the information contained in it is that *New York* magazine apparently found Frank Serpico, although he was there for anybody to find. Two weeks later Serpico was a guest on the Dick Cavett show and his appearance demonstrated that a writer is able to capture a situation and the personality of the participants better than a talk show host with the major participant there.

This was followed with stories devoted to Serpico in the May 31 issues of *Time* and *Newsweek*. *Newsweek* said: "The crusading cop came into the public spotlight earlier this month in a story in *New York* magazine. Soon after it appeared, the story's 41-year-old author, Robert Daley, the son of the *New York Times'* sports columnist Arthur Daley and himself a former *Times* correspondent, was appointed to the job of police press-relations director. And Serpico, after eleven years on the force, received the gold detective's shield signaling promotion from patrolman's rank."

Time recounted the story in great detail but without the incidents, the stories and the dialogue that made Daley's account stand out. *Time* also reprinted a picture from *New York* magazine, with credit.

The result of the *New York* story and surrounding publicity has been to focus attention on corruption within the New York City police department and helped spur what *Newsweek* called "the biggest crackdown on New York City police corruption since the Harry Gross bookmaking scandals of the 1950s."

The styles of the "witch trial" and "honest cop" stories were different, but they had things in common: they were well researched, imaginatively reported, they had as many facts as were consistent with the scope of the articles and through the presentation the reader got to know the principals involved. The stories were not necessarily, in the strictest sense, balanced, however, and persons with different points of view might even say they were not fair.

The May 24 issue of *New York* contained 10 letters in response to Miss Sheehy's article. The letter writers were complimentary, they were outraged in the teacher's behalf, they begged the inclusion of additional information and one was critical. The letter said: "It is true that most people held strong opinions on how the case should be resolved, but the difference between us and your reporter is that whichever way we feel, we are willing to respect the other view, believing that most people reached their decision after careful thought and investigation." Then later: "In the final analysis, what you have done is damn an entire community, create a sincere doubt about the accuracy of reporting on difficult or controversial issues and damage the reputation of many sincere people." The writer was a woman who lives in Mahopac, New York.

So, New Journalism can be controversial, as is proved by the recent state of affairs at *Harper's*. The best of New Journalism of late had been wrapped in the package edited by Willie Morris. Without getting into the difficulties Morris and *Harper's* had with each other, suffice it to say that Morris, David Halberstam, Larry L. King, Marshall Frady, John Corry, et al. were putting out a product that was an advocate of New Journalism's dream.

The coming-of-age article was one David Halberstam did on McGeorge Bundy in the July 1969 edition. The article gives through Bundy a comprehensive picture of the uses and abuses of political power during the Kennedy-Johnson years and especially details the evolution of the Vietnam war.

Eleven months later Morris' return to Yazoo presented an interesting example of reporting because it involved the soul-searching that few writers must encounter. Morris' earlier *North Toward Home* was another example in book form. His "Yazoo . . . notes on survival," now also out in book form, is so complete it can't help but be balanced. Fair? It is fair to anybody except the reader who approaches it with a preconceived view.

Larry L. King may have been the best showpiece of the *Harper's* of old. His five articles over the year and a half just ending were the kind that caused people who appreciate good writing to meet their friends with a "Did you see the Larry King story on thus and so?"

They were "Confessions of a White Racist" in January 1970, "Whatever Happened to Brother Dave?" in September 1970, "Blowing My Mind at Harvard" in October 1970, "The Old Man" in April 1971 and "The Road to Power in Congress" in June 1971. "Confessions," now in book form, explains growing up in white America in a personal, intimate, frank way that is as sobering as it is revealing. And anyone who can read "The Old Man' without getting a catch in the throat or a tear in the eye is a hard individual.

While the essay and first person approaches may be held in disdain by many New Journalists, Morris (in *North Toward Home*) and King (at *Harper's* and in his collection, . . . *And Other Dirty Stories*) carry off a mixture of the two in superior fashion. And both can report, as seen in "Yazoo" and in "Road to Power."

On the "About This Issue" page of the June *Harper's*, King discusses how he went about the task of reporting on the ascension of Hale Boggs as House majority leader and the defeat of Morris Udall. "A lot of cross-checking was necessary: sometimes I'd get a half-dozen versions of the same story or incident, and then have to winnow out something that was a little more than a committee truth. There was always the problem of each politician telling the story so that it would do him credit or show up a rival."

There again is another aspect of New Journalism and in the study of the subject discoveries are made in just such fashion. In all these examples there are aspects of what New Journalism is. But New Journalism is something else, too. It is personal in that it tells about people, who they are and what makes them tick.

Therefore in examining New Journalism it would be appropriate to look at it by looking at the individuals involved, the writers. But what writers to include? For academic purposes, let's include Truman Capote, Norman Mailer, Tom Wolfe and Gay Talese. That omits a lot of people. But these four offer variety, if not the full scope of the field.

Truman Capote? you say. And Norman Mailer? Why them? Here's why:

Everyone knew Capote was on to something because he told us he was. In the January 7, 1966, issue of *Life*, to use just one reference of many, Capote recounted how he spent six years unraveling a Kansas murder case. In explaining why he, a novelist, did it he said: "I went way out on a limb and risked six years of my life not to get rich but to invent a serious new art form.

"My theory, you see, is that you can take any subject and make it into a nonfiction novel. By that I don't mean a historical or documentary novel—those are popular and interesting but impure genres, with neither the persuasiveness of fact nor the poetic altitude of fiction.

Lots of friends I've told these ideas to accuse me of failure of imagination. Ha! I tell them *they're* the ones whose imaginations have failed, not me. What I've done is much harder than a conventional novel. You have to get away from your own particular vision of the world. Too many writers are mesmerized by their own navels."

To quote *Life*: "But, Capote believes, he could have written just as effective a nonfiction novel about a topic far more prosaic. 'I don't think crime is all that interesting a subject,' he says. 'What could be more cut and dried, really, than two ex-convicts who set out to rob a family and end up killing them? The important thing is the depth you can plunge to and height you can reach. The art form I've invented allows for great flexibility that way.' "

Capote's claims to a new art form—the nonfiction novel—aside, he did through intense interviewing and research recreate a story almost as though he were there. The strange thing is he did it without taking notes or using a tape recorder. The prediction by Capote and others that more and more novelists would turn to the journalistic style has failed to materialize. But a few have tried their hand and the idea remains an intriguing one.

Along with Capote, journalism's greatest steal from the literary world has been Norman Mailer. But since Mailer isn't the kind of guy that people are neutral about, some journalists are ready to give him back to the literati. Some of them don't want him either. New Journalism will take him. It is not a closed corporation. Mailer's contributions have been significant in that he has done at least a couple of things that nobody else has had the foresight—or maybe the talent—to do.

The best example is *The Armies of the Night*, which earned him a Pulitzer Prize. Once you get past Mailer's ego—which seems to be his greatest fault as a reporter—you realize that he has captured an historical event with great depth and insight. How else could anyone know what the October 1967 anti-Vietnam march on the Pentagon was all about and what it was like unless he had been there. Mailer was there and he takes the reader there with him in the book. And some of the time the personal references actually help to set the scene.

His *Miami and the Siege of Chicago* perhaps offers better examples of his intuitive reporting skill. His characterizations of Miami and Chicago are classic and he places the personalities there in such a way they tend to take on the character of the cities and the political conventions. Or maybe it's the other way around.

Overlooked by many was an earlier Mailer attempt at reporting on the 1960 Democratic convention in Los Angeles. That effort appeared as "Superman Comes to the Supermarket" in the November 1960 edition of *Esquire*. It is also the lead story in *Smiling through the Apocalypse*.

Mailer's *A Fire on the Moon* will have to await the test of history. Some critics loved it, but as many or more detested it. Again, the ego seems to be the flaw. His "The Prisoner of Sex" in the March *Harper's* did not have to wait as long for judgment, but even the immediate response was mixed.

If Capote and Mailer are the literary specimen of New Journalism, Talese and Wolfe are its shining lights. They are the ones who did it not just once, but over and over again. It would be difficult to select one over the other as the best individual example of New Journalism. Both have done well and they have done what they've done in slightly different ways.

Wolfe, because of his interest in the sociology of the 1960s, because of his incredibly fortunate timing, because of his unusual writing style and because he has emerged as the spokesman of New Journalism, has attracted the most attention.

His published books now number four. Three are collections including the recent *Radical Chic & Mau-Mauing the Flak Catchers*. The fourth is the highly interesting account of life with Ken Kesey and the Merry Pranksters. Wolfe's range has been great and it shows he is definitely not mesmerized by his own navel.

His article on "The New Journalism" in *The Bulletin* of the American Society of Newspaper Editors in September 1970 is the most definitive work to date on the subject. The article will appear in expanded form as an introduction to *The New Nonfiction*, an annotated anthology of New Journalism, to be published in the fall by Harper & Row.*

In the article he discussed " 'saturation reporting,' upon which so much of the New Journalism depends. For years the basic reporting technique has been the interview. You have a subject to write about, so you go interview the people who know about it, you write down their answers and then you recount what they said.

"Saturation reporting is much harder. You are after not just facts. The basic units of reporting are no longer who-what-when-where-how and why but whole scenes and stretches of dialogue. The New Journalism involves a depth of reporting and an attention to the most minute facts and details that most newspapermen, even the most experienced, have never dreamed of. To pull it off you casually have to stay with the people you are writing about for long stretches. You may have to stay with them days, weeks, even months—long enough so that you are actually there when revealing scenes take place in their lives. You have to constantly be on the alert for chance remarks, odd details, quirks, curios, anything that may serve to bring a scene alive

---

* [Editor's note: The book, published in 1973, is called *The New Journalism*.]

when you're writing. There is no formula for it. It never gets any easier just because you've done it before."

Talese's work pre-dates all the other New Journalism. He was doing it back on the *Times,* as careful readers will remember. Many of the pieces were short, but they had the color, the flavor, the feel of something special in writing. At that time he was also collecting information for *The Kingdom and the Power,* the story of the *New York Times.*

Talese's sixth book will also be out in the fall. His others were *New York: A Serendipiter's Journey, The Bridge, The Overreachers, Fame and Obscurity* and the book on the *Times. The Overreachers* is a collection and *Fame and Obscurity* is a collection that includes excerpts from his other books.

His individual works may stand out above anything anybody else has done in New Journalism, particularly his "Frank Sinatra Has a Cold" and "The Silent Season of a Hero," his story on Joe DiMaggio.

While Wolfe uses language flamboyantly, Talese relies on what he calls interior monologue. In a panel discussion in which he, Wolfe and Hayes participated at the Graduate School of Journalism at Columbia in the fall of 1969, Talese noted another difference in himself and Wolfe: *

"Here you have in Tom and myself two people about the same age, who in reporting have gone off in quite different directions, although admiring many of the same things, including my admiration for him. But Tom is interested in the new, the latest, the most current; Tom is way ahead in knowing these things, and relays them to those who read him, including myself. What is so contemporary, or what will be. I'm more interested in the old things, the Joshua Logan trying to make a comeback, the Joe DiMaggio becomes an old hero, how his life is, a Frank Sinatra, who seems to symbolize, at least to me, fame and how a man lives with it. I keep getting off the point. The point was to try to say something about how I got into New Journalism. Or old journalism. Parajournalism is Dwight MacDonald's description of it."

In explaining his use of interior monologue, Talese said he was trying to carry New Journalism further. "I rarely if ever will use a direct quotation any more. I'll use dialogue, but I would never, if someone that I may be interviewing, and following around, should say something, I would never quote as an old *New Yorker* profile might quote some fisherman for 8,000 words in a row. Never do I use direct quo-

---

* [Editor's note: See "The New Journalism: A Panel Discussion With Harold Hayes, Gay Talese, Tom Wolfe, and Professor L. W. Robinson," page 66.]

tations. I always take it out of the direct quotation and use it without quotations but always attribute. And very often, now, if I were interviewing Tom Wolfe, I would ask him what he thought in every situation where I might have asked him in the past what he did and said. I'm not so interested in what he did and said as I am interested in what he thought. And I would quote him in the way I was writing as that he thought something."

These remarks by Talese indicate that even before New Journalism is firmly identified subtle changes are taking place.

While the debate continues over objectivity vs. subjectivity, New Journalists are turning their attention to subjective reality. It is objectivity without passion, to paraphrase Wolfe. He put it this way:

"In most cases the new nonfiction is morally objective—in the sense that it allows the reader to make his own judgments, based on the experience the writer has enabled him to have. The experience is the important thing."

Whether activism in the newsroom is good or bad may not be answerable without the benefit of historical perspective. There's little doubt that it has forced change and much of the change has been for the good. But the excesses of the activists may in the end do more harm than good in insulating "the system" against change.

But one thing is certain. There is a great difference between the indulgences of a naive, immature reporter and the thorough, detailed reporting of the likes of a Gay Talese or a Tom Wolfe.

And that's the difference in activism and New Journalism.

Part Two

THE ARTICLE
AS ART

The Article
As Art

NORMAN PODHORETZ

Anyone who has given much attention to postwar American fiction is likely to have noticed a curious fact. Many of our serious novelists also turn out book reviews, critical pieces, articles about the contemporary world, memoirs, sketches—all of which are produced for magazines and which these writers undoubtedly value far lower than their stories and novels.

Indeed, some novelists (and this applies to many poets too) tend to express their contempt or disdain for discursive prose in the very act of writing it. You can hear a note of condescension toward the medium they happen to be working in at the moment; they seem to be announcing in the very construction of their sentences that they have no great use for the prosy requirements of the essay or the review, that they are only dropping in from Olympus for a brief, impatient visit. But just as often—and this is the curious fact I am referring to—the discursive writing of people who think of themselves primarily as novelists turns out to be more interesting, more lively, more penetrating, more intelligent, more forceful, more original—in short, *better*—than their fiction, which they and everyone else automatically treat with greater respect.

Norman Podhoretz is the editor of *Commentary*. His essay on the artistic possibilities of the magazine article appears in his book *Doings and Undoings*.

Two examples spring immediately to mind: the late Isaac Rosenfeld and the young Negro author, James Baldwin. Rosenfeld, who died of a heart attack in Chicago two years ago at the age of thirty-seven, was immensely gifted, possibly the most gifted writer to appear in America in the last few decades. Born of immigrant parents and raised in a Yiddish-speaking milieu, he came to own the English language by an act of absolute appropriation. He could make it do anything he wanted—sprout lush flora, like a tropical landscape, or walk in stately simplicity as though it had been designed only to express the basic emotions and the most direct and uncomplicated apprehensions of reality. Beyond that, however, he was intelligent and literate, endowed with wide curiosity and a frisky imagination. He was also prolific: for years his name was ubiquitous in the world of the little magazine, with a story here, a review there, an article yet somewhere else. Though he published only one novel, *A Passage from Home*, and a collection of short stories, *King Solomon's Mines*, he regarded himself and was regarded by others as essentially a novelist.

Yet the truth is that he never produced a piece of fiction which drew on the whole range of his talent and sensibility. You got the impression that in order to write a story, this man had to suppress half of what he knew and saw, that he was possessed of a mind and an eye and an imagination which could not get their full play in a dramatic narrative. Though banality of thought and falsity of feeling hardly ever entered his articles and reviews, his fiction frequently suffered from derivativeness, artificiality, and mere cleverness. You would scarcely have suspected even from his novel that Rosenfeld was more than a bright young man who had read Proust and Joyce and saw himself, like a thousand other bright young men, as a creature set apart by his artistic vocation. You would scarcely have suspected him capable of that marvelous posthumous piece published in *Commentary* called "Life in Chicago," in which the smell and feel of a city and its history are rendered to perfection, in which the meaning of that history is defined through a deliciously fanciful theory of the effect on a city of distance from the sea, in which the combination of love and repulsion that a "rootless" American intellectual invariably feels for his home town is superbly expressed, and in which everything—description, analysis, exhortation, and sheer kidding around—converges in the end on a declaration of faith in the supremacy of the arts and what they represent over the prevalent values of modern life. It is a declaration all the more moving for its directness and candor, and all the more powerful for coming from someone who knows that he is flying in the face of the contemporary spirit—but who also knows that a man at some point in his life has to stop agonizing over his apparent eccentricities and say, simply and without refinement or embellishment, "This is what I stand for."

This essay gives you more of Chicago, more of what it means to be an artist and an intellectual in America, and more of Rosenfeld himself than *A Passage from Home*, which, as it happens, is also about Chicago, the artist in America, and the soul of Isaac Rosenfeld.

The case of James Baldwin is no less striking. Baldwin has so far published three books—a collection of essays, *Notes of a Native Son*, and two novels, *Go Tell It on the Mountain* and *Giovanni's Room*. The essays in *Notes of a Native Son* all appeared originally in magazines; a couple of them are literary criticism, one is a movie review, and the others are memoirs relating to various aspects of a Negro's confrontation with the white world both in America and Europe. Taken together they make up the best book I have ever read about the American Negro, a book that conveys a phenomenally keen sense of the special quality of Negro experience today. What distinguishes these pieces, even apart from the clarity, subtlety, and vividness with which they are written, is Baldwin's complex conception of the Negro as a man who is simultaneously like unto all other men and yet profoundly, perhaps irrevocably, different. The nature of the sameness and the nature of the difference are the subject of the book, and he never allows himself to forget the one term while exploring the other.

But it is precisely the loss of complexity that characterizes his novels. *Go Tell It on the Mountain* is a fairly conventional first novel about a Negro boy in Harlem, and though the hero's milieu (especially the religious background of his life) is well delineated, you nevertheless feel that Baldwin is trying to persuade you that there is no real difference between the situation of John Grimes and that of any other sensitive American boy who is at odds with his environment. But there *is* a difference, and it is not merely one of degree—as any reader of *Notes of a Native Son* can tell you.

Similarly with *Giovanni's Room*, which though it does not deal with Negroes, exhibits the same slurring over of differences in relation to homosexuality. (The white homosexual in America is in the same boat as the oppressed Negro—they are both, as it were, "black" in the eyes of their culture.) Baldwin, in writing about a young American living in Paris who discovers that he is a homosexual, tries very hard to make it appear that a love affair between two men is spiritually and psychologically indistinguishable from a heterosexual romance—which strikes me as at worst an untruth and at best an oversimplification. Here again, then, we have a writer who seems able to produce fiction only at the expense of suppressing half of what he sees and knows, whose discursive prose is richer, more imaginative, and fundamentally more honest than his novels and stories. And with proper qualifications in each case, similar points might be made of James Agee, Mary

McCarthy, Elizabeth Hardwick, Randall Jarrell, Leslie Fiedler, and several others.

Now it can, of course, be said that these examples prove nothing —and would still prove nothing even if another twenty were added to them—except that some people are better essayists than novelists. And if I asked why a first-rate essayist should feel obliged to work so hard at turning out second-rate fiction, the answer would be that the novel is to us what drama was to the Elizabethans and lyric poetry to the Romantics, so that an ambitious writer today will naturally make his bid there. In every college in the country, and probably in most of the high schools too, there are kids who want to be novelists when they grow up—who are convinced that a novelist is the most glorious of all things to be, and who are often prepared to make sacrifices in pursuit of this vocation. The aura of sanctity that used to attach to the idea of a poet has now floated over to rest on the head of the novelist—a very congenial switch when we consider that Americans tend to regard poets as sissies and novelists as hard-drinking, hard-loving, hard-fighting men of the world. (Compare the public image of T. S. Eliot and Wallace Stevens to Hemingway's or Faulkner's and you see that the poets and novelists themselves seem driven to play true to type.)

But the prestige of the novel cannot account for the fact that so much good writing about precisely those experiences which are closest to the heart of life in America and which we would suppose to be the proper province of fiction—experiences involving the quest for self-definition in a society where a man's identity is not given and fixed by birth—has been done in our day not in novels but in discursive pieces of one kind or another.

Lionel Trilling made a similar observation in a review of David Riesman's *The Lonely Crowd:*

> People of literary inclinations . . . have a natural jealousy of sociology because it seems to be in process of taking over from literature one of literature's most characteristic functions, the investigation and criticism of morals and manners. Yet it is but fair to remark that sociology has pre-empted what literature has voluntarily surrendered.

Nor is it academic sociology alone that has "pre-empted what literature has voluntarily surrendered." The reportage done in magazines by professional journalists like Dwight Macdonald, Richard H. Rovere, and a good many others, has carried on a more exhaustive and more accomplished investigation of our morals and manners than the bulk of contemporary fiction.

The novel form is honored as never before, yet a feeling of dissatisfaction and impatience, irritation and boredom with contemporary serious fiction is very widespread. The general mood was well expressed by Leslie Fiedler who opened a fiction chronicle in *Partisan Review* not long ago with the complaint that the sight of a group of new novels stimulates in him "a desperate desire to sneak out to a movie. How respectable the form has become," he lamented, "how predictable!" Many other critics have tried to explain the low condition of current fiction by declaring that the novel is "dead," an exhausted genre like the epic and verse drama. But whether or not the novel is dead (and I myself don't believe that it is), one thing is certain: that a large class of readers, with or without benefit of theories about the rise and fall of literary forms, has found itself responding more enthusiastically to what is lamely called "nonfiction" (and especially to magazine articles and even book reviews) than to current fiction.

This is not, of course, a new observation. The popularity of "criticism"—a word often used as a catch-all term for any writing about literature or culture in general—has been deplored even more passionately than the dullness of postwar fiction and poetry, and has been taken as a sign of the sickness of our present condition. Some years ago, Randall Jarrell, in a famous article, christened this period, "The Age of Criticism," and complained that nowadays young men were taking to their typewriters not to compose poems but to analyze and explicate the poems of others. Personally, I have never been able to understand why Mr. Jarrell was so eager to have everyone writing poetry; we can, after all, take it pretty much for granted that any young man who has it in him to become a poet *will* become a poet, even in an "Age of Criticism." And I should have thought that the danger was not that the popularity of criticism would rob us of poets but that the prestige of the "creative" would rob us of good critics, who have always been rarer, even today, than good poets.

Writing in the heyday of piety toward the "divine faculty of imagination" that succeeded the great flowering of English poetry during the first half of the 19th century, Matthew Arnold provided the best possible retort to Mr. Jarrell:

> Everybody . . . would be willing to admit, as a general proposition, that the critical faculty is lower than the inventive. But is it true that criticism is really, in itself, a baneful and injurious employment; is it true that all time given to writing critiques on the works of others would be much better employed if it were given to original composition of whatever kind this may be? Is it true that Johnson had better have gone on producing more *Irenes* instead of writing his *Lives of the Poets*. . . ?

Arnold's allusion to the distinction between the "critical faculty" and the "inventive" is one that any modern reader would pass over with automatic assent, so accustomed have we all become to thinking in terms of two radically different categories of mind—the imaginative, which is the mind that creates, and the . . . well, there is not even an adequate word for the other kind of mind. "Critical" won't do because it has too restricted a reference; nor will "philosophical" quite serve. The fact is that our attitude reveals itself beautifully in this terminological difficulty: we call everything that is not fiction or poetry "nonfiction," as though whole ranges of human thought had only a negative existence. We would all admit, if pressed, that books like Freud's *The Interpretation of Dreams* or Tocqueville's *Democracy in America* are as much works of the imagination as *Ulysses* or *The Waste Land,* but we tend in the ordinary course of things to identify "imagination" and "creativity" exclusively with the arts and, where literature is concerned, with poetry, the novel, and the drama. This idea is a legacy of 19th-century aesthetic theory. Throughout the 18th century the word "imagination" (or its synonym, "fancy") was often used pejoratively and sometimes held to be the source of lies and the enemy of reason. Reason was considered the faculty for perceiving truth, and good poetry was regarded as one of its products.

"A poet is not to leave his reason, and blindly abandon himself to follow fancy," declared the critic Thomas Rymer, "for then his fancy might be monstrous, might be singular, and please no body's maggot but his own; but reason is to be his guide, reason is common to all people, and can never carry him from what is natural."

Even before Coleridge formulated his famous theory of the poetic imagination as the highest mode of apprehending reality and credited poetry with a truth superior to the truths of reason and science, early Romantics like William Blake were pushing toward a doctrine that would justify the claims of the poet against those of the "natural philosophers." By the age of Victoria, the Coleridgean view had swept all before it; nothing is more characteristic of the Victorians than the reverence they felt toward poets and poetry (a reverence, as Mr. Jarrell should have remembered, which led to the production of more bad verse than any other period has ever foisted upon the world). The poet was a saint and a sage: the robust-minded Keats became to the Victorians a delicate aesthete languishing away for the sake of beauty and killed by the cruel barbs of the critics, while Shelley—a man up to his neck in politics and causes—was thought of as the wholly spiritual Ariel. The wicked Lord Byron only added to the charm of these images, and the somber Wordsworth was well suited to the role of Olympian wise man.

One of the consequences of this conception of the poetic faculty was to foster the idea that poetry could be written only in a kind of fit of divine inspiration that had nothing to do with intelligence or consciousness or concern with what was going on in the world. And a plausible relation can be traced between that notion and the decline of poetry in the latter part of the 19th century. It was the novelists of Victorian England, who had not yet quite achieved the status of "creative" and "imaginative" writers and to whom the smell of vulgarity that had once been associated with the novel still clung—Dickens, George Eliot, Thackeray, James—who represent their age most vitally and powerfully. What strikes one today about Victorian fiction is the scope it provided for the exercise of intelligence, the testing of ideas in the medium of experience, the examination of major contemporary problems. The novel flourished partly because it was such a free, amorphous, sprawling form in which almost anything (except, of course, explicit discussion of sex) could go: there was no question of George Eliot's having to suppress half of what *she* knew and saw when she sat down to write fiction. And it flourished because it remained in touch with the world around it, while the poets were busy transcending the mundane and the prosaic.

By now we seem to have reached a point where the novel has taken over from poetry as the sanctified genre, and this has coincided (just as with poetry in the 19th century) with the aftermath of a great flowering. Proust, Joyce, Lawrence, Mann, Kafka, Hemingway, Faulkner are all behind us; in our eyes they have borne out the claims made for the "art of the novel" by Henry James and others, just as Wordsworth, Byron, Keats, and Shelley won the case for the superiority of the "poetic faculty" at the bar of Victorian judgment.

In a recent book called *The Living Novel* Granville Hicks, whose benign reviews in the *News Leader* have established him as the most promiscuous admirer of new writing since the days of Carl Van Doren, collected essays by ten well-known novelists aimed at refuting the charge that the novel is dead. Most of the essays are bad—bad thinking and bad writing—but they are interesting for what they reveal of the novelist's view of himself today. The dominant note is one of persecution. Mr. Hicks talks about the "enemies of the novel" and says that the novel has always had enemies. Almost all the contributors throw around words like "vision," "intensity," and, of course, "imagination" to distinguish the novel from other kinds of writing. There is a good deal of bitterness against the critics and a strong implication that they are resentful of "creativity." Saul Bellow (who has fared very well at the hands of the critics) says, for example:

> And so we are told by critics that the novel is dead. These people can't know what the imagination is nor what its powers are. I wish I could believe in their good-natured objectivity. But I can't. I should like to disregard them, but that is a little difficult because they have a great deal of power. . . . And they can be very distracting. But the deadly earnestness with which they lower the boom! On what? after all. On flowers. On mere flowers.

You can't blame Mr. Bellow for being irritated by people who insist that the novel is dead while he is trying to write novels, but it is worth noticing that he does not answer the charge by asserting that good novels are still being produced and then trying to prove it; instead he invokes the name of "imagination" in reverent accents and identifies it with novels (apparently whether they are good or bad), while criticism is a "boom" lowered in metaphorical confusion on the "flowers" around it. Now it would be hard to think of a more infelicitous image for a novel than a flower; novels, if you like, are trees, they are robust and sturdy, not at all delicate. Why should Mr. Bellow have seized on this inept image? Partly to arouse the reader's sense of pathos, I think, but also because the idea of flowers, with its associations of sweetness, fragility, and loveliness, confers an ethereal dignity on the novel.

The idea comes out of the same sort of thinking that was applied to poetry by many Victorians: poetry was delicate, transcendant, special, inspired—anything, in short, but the measured discourse of a keen human sensibility operating on a world of men. But a new element has been added to the Victorian view. Not only does "imagination" now sprout "flowers," and not only does it (as in Coleridge) represent the highest faculty of intellection; it has also become the principle of "life" itself, while mind and consciousness are now seen as having signed a pact with the Angel of Death. The novel is valuable, we gather from Mr. Bellow and some of his colleagues, because it is the only place left in our world where imagination and its correlatives—sensitivity, responsiveness, passion—still function. (The *reductio* of all this can be found in the "spontaneous bop prosody" of Jack Kerouac.) Mr. Hicks goes so far as to say that "there is no substitute now available for the novel, and those who talk about the death of the novel are talking about the death of the imagination."

I am not one of those who talk about the death of the novel, but I do think that it has fallen on bad days. I also think that the fault lies at least partly with these rarefied and incense-burning doctrines of the imagination, which have had the effect of surrendering the novel—to apply a remark of F. R. Leavis on Shelley's theory of inspiration—"to a sensibility that has no more dealings with intelligence than it can help." My own criticism of much contemporary fiction would be precisely that it lacks the only species of imagination worth mentioning—the kind that is vitalized by contact with a disciplined intelligence and a restless interest in the life of the times. And what the novel has abdicated has been taken over by discursive writers. Imagination has not died (how could it?) but it has gone into other channels; these channels are not by any means commensurate with the novel: they are, in fact, *channels* and not the sea. But there is living water in them nevertheless.

What I have in mind—and I cheerfully admit that the suggestion sounds preposterous—is *magazine articles.* I won't call them essays, even though to do so would make the point seem less disreputable and silly, because the type of thing I am referring to is not an essay in the old sense. Strictly speaking, the essay requires an audience that has no doubts about where the relevant subjects of discussion are to be found, and it is therefore written without any need to persuade the reader that he ought to concern himself with this particular question. The magazine article, as they say in the trade, always hangs on a peg; it takes off from an event in the news, a book recently published, a bill in Congress. And even then, with its relevance established in the most obvious way conceivable, it still has to sell itself to a reader who wants to be told why he should bother pushing his way through it when there are so many other claims on his attention. This is a tyrannical condition which can, of course, result in the reduction of all thought to the occasional and the newsworthy. But now and then a writer whose interests and talent go beyond the merely journalistic can be forced into very exciting pieces of work by the necessity to demonstrate the continuing importance of his special concerns by throwing them into the buzz and hum around him.

To my mind, the critical pieces of Lionel Trilling offer perhaps the best example we have of discursive writing that is not only rich in imagination but animated by an uncanny sensitivity to the life from which it springs. Trilling has spent most of his time analyzing books—often remote books—but who has told us more than he about the way we feel and think today? But for the purposes of detailed illustration, I would like to take a less well-known example, an article (published in *Commentary* in 1953) called "The 'Idealism' of Julius and Ethel Rosenberg" by the late Robert Warshow who, like Isaac Rosenfeld, died suddenly at thirty-seven just when his extraordinary powers were developing into full maturity, and who—unlike Rosenfeld —never wrote any fiction.

This article began as a review of the Rosenberg death-house letters which came out around the time the convicted couple went to their execution. Since Warshow was one of those who believed that the world-wide clamor against the death sentence was largely motivated not by compassion for the Rosenbergs or a desire to see justice done, but by political anti-Americanism of one shade or another, one might have expected the review to be a pronouncement on the Communist menace. And certainly the crudity and vulgarity of the Rosenberg letters provided enough opportunity for scoring points against them and the movement to which they gave their lives. But Warshow's imagination would not permit him to turn out a simple polemical tract: what he wanted was an insight into the soul of the

Rosenbergs, and it took a powerful act of imagination to find the soul of the Rosenbergs in the mass of depersonalized clichés that make up their correspondence. Considering the patent insincerity of their rhetoric, the temptation was great to deny them any human feelings at all. But again, Warshow's imagination would not allow him to fall into that trap. After quoting several particularly grotesque passages in which they discuss their children, Warshow comments:

> The fact that Julius Rosenberg can speak of a lack of toys as the "materials situation" does not in the least permit us to assume that he did not suffer for his children just as much as anyone else would have suffered. Nor does the impudence of Ethel's appeal to her "sister Americans"—whose lives she had been willing to put in danger—diminish in any way the reality of the "stab of longing for my boy." On the whole, the Rosenbergs in dealing with their children sound the authentic tone of parental love in the educated and conscientious middle class, facing each "problem" boldly and without displaying undue emotion, though "of course" not denying the existence of emotion either. . . . This is how we all deal with our children, and surely we are right to do so. If it happens that you must "prepare" the children for their parents' death in the electric chair instead of having their tonsils out, then doubtless something better is required. But what, for God's sake? Some unique inspiration, perhaps, and the truth. But we cannot blame the Rosenbergs for their failure to achieve an inspiration, and the commitment for which they died—and by which, we must assume, they somehow fulfilled themselves—was precisely that the truth was not to be spoken. Not spoken, not whispered, not approached in the merest hint.

Warshow goes on to show how the literal truth had ceased to exist for the Rosenbergs as a result of their commitment to Communism, and he connects this brilliantly with "the awkwardness and falsity of the Rosenbergs' relations to culture, to sports, and to themselves" that is evident in their letters:

> It is as if these two had no internal sense of their own being but could see themselves only from the outside, in whatever postures their "case" seemed to demand—as if, one might say, they were only the most devoted of their thousands of "sympathizers."
>
> . . . But it is important to observe the dimensions of their failure, how almost nothing really belonged to them, not even their own experience; they filled their lives with the second-hand, never so much as suspecting that anything else was possible. Communism itself—the vehicle of whatever self-realization they achieved —had disappeared for them, becoming only a word to be written in quotation marks as if it represented a hallucination. . . .

In the end, we discover that "they were equally incapable of truth and of falsehood. What they stood for was not Communism as a certain form of social organization, not progress as a belief in the possibility of human improvement, but only their own identity *as* Communists or 'progressives,' and they were perfectly 'sincere' in making use of whatever catchwords seemed at any moment to assert that identity. . . ." It is this, Warshow argues, that makes the Rosenbergs truly representative of the Communism of 1953. But his piece does not really close on a note of analysis or condemnation:

> The Rosenbergs thought and felt whatever their political commitment required them to think and feel. But if they had not had the political commitment could they have thought and felt at all?
>
> Well, we cannot dispose of them quite so easily. They did suffer, for themselves and for their children, and though they seem never to have questioned the necessity of their "martyrdom" or the absolute rightness of all they had ever done . . . , they wept like anyone else at the approach of death. . . .

I have quoted at length from this short article in order to let the grace and beauty of Warshow's style speak for themselves. It is a beauty that comes not from ornateness or self-conscious finesse, but from a remarkable fusion of feeling and intelligence: to follow this prose is to follow a language in which analysis cannot be distinguished from emotion. When the rhetoric surges ("But what, for God's sake?") it is not for the sake of sweeping the reader away, but in response to a simultaneous movement of the mind and the heart: the heart has discovered something and the mind springs like a panther to formulate its meaning.

A six-page review of a book in a monthly magazine; a discussion of a controversial political question almost completely forgotten only five years later—yet it turns out to be a piece of imaginative and creative writing as good as any we have seen in this gloomy period, a piece that is at once a moving expression of a man's ability to feel for two human beings who sacrificed themselves to a cause he hated and despised, a brilliant analysis of the Communist mentality, and a profound comment on the nature of sincerity. And the rest of Warshow's work—almost all of it as good as and better than the Rosenberg article—remains buried in magazines, mostly in the highly perishable form of movie reviews.*

Why should the magazine article, of all things, have become so important and fertile a genre in our day? Why have so many writers—both "critics" and professional journalists—found it possible to move

---

* Since this was written, Doubleday has brought out a collection of Warshow's pieces under the title *The Immediate Experience*.

around more freely and creatively within it than within fiction or poetry? No doubt it has something to do with the spiritual dislocations of the cold war period, but the essence of the answer, I think, lies in an analogy with architecture. It has often been pointed out that functionalism is more an idea than a reality: the products of functional architecture aren't purely functional at all, since they always contain "useless" elements that are there for aesthetic rather than practical reasons. Yet the fact remains that our sense of beauty today is intimately connected with the sense of usefulness: we consider a building beautiful when it seems to exist not for anyone to enjoy the sight of or to be impressed by, but solely and simply to be used. We think of those glass structures like Lever House in New York or the United Nations or the Manufacturers Trust Company building on Fifth Avenue as practical, in the sense that women call walking shoes practical; they have a kind of no-nonsense look about them, they seem to be stripped down to essentials, purged of all superfluous matter.

The same is true of the way we furnish our homes—Scandinavian efficiency is our idea of handsomeness; foam rubber rather than down our idea of comfort; stainless steel rather than silver our notion of elegant cutlery. I would suggest that we have all, writers and readers alike, come to feel temporarily uncomfortable with the traditional literary forms because they don't *seem* practical, designed for "use," whereas a magazine article by its nature satisfies that initial condition and so is free to assimilate as many "useless," "non-functional" elements as it pleases. It is free, in other words, to become a work of art.

This is not, of course, an ideal situation for literature to be in, but nothing can be gained from turning one's eyes away in horror. Certainly the rigid distinction between the creative and the critical has contributed to the growth of a feeling that the creative is "useless." Curiously enough, the very concept of imagination as a special faculty— and of novels and poetry as mysteriously unique species of discourse subject to strange laws of their own—itself implies that art is of no use to life in the world. What we need, it seems to me, is a return to the old idea of literature as a category that includes the best writing on any subject in any form. We need a return to this idea and we need it, I should add, most urgently of all for the sake of fiction and poetry.

The Article

BROCK BROWER

Of all extant literary forms, I'm afraid the general article asks the greatest general sufferance of us right at the moment, because it is concurrently in its dotage as journalism and in its nonage as literature. It is, in too many cases, simply senile—a reiterated banality wheezed to formulae for the engineered readerships of certain unreconstructed mass magazines ("What is a good article made of?" singsongs a wordsmith at her forge in *The Writer's Digest*. "STATISTICS, QUOTES, AND ANECDOTES!"). Yet it has proved itself, in some recent instances, to be a precocious instrument—a remarkably free engine for prose that such editors as Norman Podhoretz of *Commentary* and John Fischer of *Harper's* see as the most pertinent and immediate means of expression our culture can offer a writer. As a result, those of us who write it—and try to write it better than the newspapers are written—live in a din of huzzahs and alarums, and none of us knows exactly whether the article is ignominiously sinking, like the old *Collier's*, or emerging triumphant over itself, like a change in the language. The only thing that *is* certain is that it will not "survive"—in the sense that other troubled literary forms, such as the short story and the novel, are predicted to "survive" any current abatement of interest or debility of art—because there are enough of

---

Brock Brower's essay appears in *On Creative Writing*, edited by Paul Engle. He has written both fiction and nonfiction and is a former editor of *Esquire*.

us around who won't *let* it "survive." The article must now either go under along with all magazines that persist in believing some millions of readers can still be united by a single endocrinal response to "a sparkling lead," "a clear, lucid style," "universal reader appeal," et cetera, or become an entirely new and disturbing and quite different thing, put to broad general use much as Norman Mailer and James Baldwin have put it to more intensive personal use in their efforts to sear public awareness with their own convictions.

In other words, the impact of an article is coming to depend more and more upon the writer's individual intelligence and resolve, and less and less upon the corporate noodling of the journal in which it appears; and this shift proves out an interesting juggle that has occurred lately in the handling of our sense of reality. At about the same time that magazines began, I fear, to let reality slip, a number of fine writers—novelists, short story writers, some of the young and uncommitted—began desperately trying to close with reality. "Making a living is nothing; the great difficulty is making a point, making a difference—with words," Elizabeth Hardwick has summed up this impulsive search. These writers found that the point, the difference had to be made with more than fictions—that the "lies like truth" would no longer do for the Truth—and so they turned precipitously to the concreteness of fact. Or perhaps, in the end, Fact actually turned on them, like a cornered assassin, and almost defensively they reached for the first weapon at hand. The article, whatever else it may be, has always been bluntly at hand, if only because it has never been put by any definition out of reach.

It's important to understand how open and available a form it really is—much more so than the short story or novel—despite the false restrictions that popular journalism has imposed upon it. Of course, as long as only journalists wrote the article, it was bound to follow the journalistic crotchets—a "news peg to hang it on," "lots of quotes, high up in the story," "color," "the flavor of the man," and so on *ad nauseam*—but it was never bonded to journalism. In fact, by definition, the article is bonded to no one. The word itself (if a brief look into the N.E.D. can be excused here) comes from the Latin *articulus*, the diminutive of *artus*, or "joint." "*Articulus* in L. was extended from the joint, to the parts jointed on, limbs, members, 'joints' of the finger, etc; whence *transf.* to the component parts of discourses, writings, actions." An article then is "A literary composition forming materially part of a journal, magazine, encyclopaedia, or other collection, *but treating a specific topic distinctly and independently*." (Italics added.) It serves no genre, no subject matter, no periodical; it should never be written *for*—in that slavish sense— *The Saturday Evening Post, The New Yorker,* or any other master.

It should simply be "jointed on" its literary surroundings, as indeed the best articles always are, outlandish among the Contents.

Actually, there is only one specific obligation that touches the form of the article, and it derives from another branch of the above etymology. (Which is my only reason for quoting such wondrous and cumbersome stuff. Usually this is the kind of research a writer of an article does "to have the facts behind him"—and *leave* behind him.) From the same word *articulus* also comes the idea of breaking down a whole into its jointed parts, and treating each part carefully in sequence. For instance, in speaking—as so many of us were painfully taught to do—we *articulate*. "To express distinctly; to give utterance to. . . . To form or fit into a systematically interrelated whole." That is really all an article is obliged to do. It articulates any subject, person, or idea, and it may do so in any style that pleases the writer, so long as he does not fail to exercise at least two of his faculties: his own voice, so that his article will be distinct, and his own reason, so that his article will be independent.

Patently, neither of these faculties has ever been included in the basic equipage of a journalist, which may explain the vapidity of so much that has been published in magazines. Journalism is routinely voiceless, or whenever it gains a voice, it is a street voice, caterwauling for attention, not understanding. But far worse, journalism is routinely mindless. Its vaunted objectivity—its habit of piling the greater fact on top of the lesser fact, like Pelion on top of Ossa on top of a pebble—this is only an escape from the need to reason. When finally faced with a controversial point which demands some interpretation, the journalist is famous for the "Lib-Lab," i.e., "on the one hand, *this,* and on the other hand, *that,*" but neither hand is his. The easy generalization ("the greatest living . . . single most . . . best known . . . fastest rising . . . nonesuch on the immediate horizon") and the endless qualifier ("perhaps") are the two stylistic counterweights with which the journalist maintains his own commitment, and hence his own existence, at constant zero. The total impression is at last one of immobility, as if words indeed made no point, no difference, and the writing strikes us as literally inarticulate—that is, random, disconnected, *disjointed.*

The obvious effect of this practice on our sense of reality is to sap it, and for some time this seemed to be the deliberate case with many magazines. However, nothing can remain unreal for very long and still circulate, so that something of a panic has finally overtaken these magazines, and happily just at the moment when some of the better writers have independently hit upon their own means of articulating reality. In several cases—still far too few—there have been some most fortunate meetings of minds, and the article has begun to appear with both a voice and an independence within it. Put another way, the facts, which would have only been gathered and sieved by a journalist, have been enclosed within a single intelligence, and a mind has set to work, making independent observations that are far more capacitous than those of the tape recorder or the TV camera.

Actually, this is not a new thing, but only a resurrected approach; in fact, one of the best examples of this kind of writing in American letters is an article from *The Southern Literary Messenger*, April, 1836. It appeals to me especially because it shows, long before twentieth-century journalism elaborated itself into a huge staff operation with its own infernal technology, how far superior the work of a single good mind really is.

The subject of this article is what must have been one of the first computers. Or rather, it purported to be such. The machine was an Automaton Chess-Player, displayed by a German named Johann Nepomuk Maelzel, and it played chess against the local human competition (just as IBM7090 has been partially programmed to do) through a dummy seated at a chest, on which were a chessboard and six differently tapered candles. The chest was full of machinery—supposedly—and the dummy, called the Turk, was run by the machinery—supposedly. People had their doubts, of course, though they were allowed in a limited way to examine the mechanism before the Turk started his chess game. But the man who settled those doubts—and proved that a human being *had* to be inside the machine, even if he were a midget—was a writer of occasional articles named Edgar Allan Poe.

Now the remarkable thing about Poe's article, entitled "Maelzel's Chess-Player," is that he disproved the reality of the mechanism—dismantled it and looked inward at its chicane vitals—by simply reasoning it onto the logical scrap heap. He never had to go near the Chess-Player to demolish it. He never got "behind the scenes," or talked intimately with members of the Maelzel household, or met the midget in a bar and got him drunk. He merely observed, reasoned, and concluded. "Ratiocination," Poe was later to call this exercise of intelligence. He even managed by ratiocination to show that the man inside the Chess-Player had to be right-handed—a conclusion that follows irrefutably from the fact that the Turk plays a left-handed game. Poe adduced sixteen other refutations altogether, but two should suffice here to show the style of mind that he brought to bear upon just such a critical question of reality.

> 3. The Automaton does not invariably win the game. Were the machine a pure machine this would not be the case—it would always win. The *principle* being discovered by which a machine can be made to *play* a game of chess, an extension of the same

principle would enable it to *win* a game–a farther extension would enable it to *win all* games—that is, to beat any possible game of an antagonist. A little consideration will convince anyone that the difficulty of making a machine beat all games, is not in the least degree greater, as regards the principle of the operations necessary, than that of making it beat a single game. If then we regard the Chess-Player as a machine, we must suppose, (what is highly improbable,) that its inventor preferred leaving it incomplete to perfecting it—a supposition rendered still more absurd, when we reflect that the leaving it incomplete would afford an argument against the possibility of its being a pure machine—the very argument we now adduce.

4. When the situation of the game is difficult or complex, we never perceive the Turk either shake his head or roll his eyes. It is only when his next move is obvious, or when the game is so circumstanced that to a man in the Automaton's place there would be no necessity for reflection. Now these peculiar movements of the head and eyes are movements customary with persons engaged in meditations, and the ingenious Baron Kempelen would have adapted these movements (were the machine a pure machine) to occasions proper to their display—that is, to occasions of complexity. But the reverse is seen to be the case, and this reverse applies precisely to our supposition of a man in the interior. When engaged in meditation about the game, he has no time to think of setting in motion the mechanism of the Automaton by which are moved the head and the eyes. When the game, however, is obvious, he has time to look about him, and accordingly, we see the head shake and the eyes roll.

In these passages, the *style* of the intelligence is inimitable, but the *role* of the intelligence emphatically is not. In fact, it is precisely the role that every writer engaging reality must set for his own reason to play—first confrontory, then encompassing, and finally critical. Yet, under the circumstances that usually attend the writing of an article, it is the hardest role to assign independent reason. It is so easily usurped by the "actual assignment—what we want you to do with this one," the pressure of time, the ephemera around the subject, et cetera. The great usurper once was the magazine itself with its Draconic point of view, but this is not now so important as the bad habits this usurpation bred. It is so easy to quote, generalize, qualify, extrapolate *neutrally* around a subject—*Let the reader draw his own conclusions*—instead of facing it directly as something that must be plumbed by a dropline of pure thought.

In writing articles, I've always tried in some way to drop such a line—except when I've been dragooned into assignments that have turned out hopeless and ashen—and I find I'm most comfortable making the effort when I can draw as near as possible to Poe's exercise of pure mind. That is, I prefer to try to imbue an entire matter with an impersonal intelligence which infuses everything like a sudden freshness in the whole air than to set upon a subject with a rush of personality which bestirs everything like too sharp an individual breeze. I suspect this approach (that is, Poe's) is probably best for anybody initially attempting an article—unless he has a Nobel Prize, or expects one soon—but it certainly isn't, by any means, the only style the mind can assume. Much that has been achieved recently with expository prose has been exactly opposite in nature: highly personal, and as far removed from Poe's ratiocination as his terrors are from our own. But this still doesn't change the essential role that reason plays, for these must inevitably be the same force of intelligence in, say, one of James Baldwin's refutations as there is in one of Poe's.

> The American Negro has the great advantage of having never believed the collection of myths to which white Americans cling: that their ancestors were all freedom-loving heroes, that they were born in the greatest country the world has ever seen, or the Americans are invincible in battle and wise in peace, that Americans have always dealt honorably with Mexicans and Indians and all other neighbors or inferiors, that American men are the world's most direct and virile, that American women are pure. Negroes know far more about white Americans than that; it can almost be said, in fact, that they know about white Americans what parents— or, anyway, mothers—know about their children, and that they very often regard white Americans that way. And perhaps this attitude, held in spite of what they know and have endured, helps to explain why Negroes, on the whole, and until lately, have allowed themselves to feel so little hatred. The tendency has really been, insofar as this was possible, to dismiss white people as the slightly mad victims of their own brainwashing. One watched the lives they led. One could not be fooled about that; one watched the things they did and the excuses that they gave themselves, and if a white man was really in trouble, deep trouble, it was to the Negro's door that he came. And one felt that if one had had that white man's wordly advantages, one would never have become as bewildered and as joyless and as thoughtlessly cruel as he. The Negro came to the white man for a roof or for five dollars or for a letter to the judge; the white man came to the Negro for love. But he was not often able to give what he came seeking. The price was too high; he had too much to lose. And the Negro knew this, too. When one knows this about a man, it is impossible for one to hate him, but unless he becomes a man—becomes equal—it is also impossible for one to love him. Ultimately, one tends to avoid him, for the universal characteristic of children is to assume that they have a monopoly on trouble, and therefore a monopoly on *you*.

(Ask any Negro what he knows about the white people with whom
he works. And then ask the white people with whom he works
what they know about *him*.)

Nothing could conflict more with the immaculately analytic tone
of Poe than this homiletic style of Baldwin's, but despite the difference
of a century in moral feeling, there is still the same basic probity in
both men. Like Poe, Baldwin is also looking closely to see why "the
head shakes and the eyes roll." It is the same intrusive act of mind,
a stealing inside all reality's dumb shows to find out how false or true
the machinery within actually is, whether it is "operating" an automaton
or a white man or a Negro or a President or a revolution.

On a practical working level, there are numerous thoughts about
writing an article that follow from this insistence upon independent
probity, but basically they all come down to the hard fact that if a
writer expects to maintain this independence, he must do everything
for himself. If a single good mind is to encompass a matter, then other
minds become superfluous. The writer himself, for instance, is always
his own best researcher, despite what other adjunctive intelligences
may contribute, and the rule is that the research is only done when
the writer "meets himself coming back the other way," i.e., when
among all possible informants, the writer becomes, at least for the
moment, the best informed.

Similarly, all the interviewing must be done by the writer himself,
live—that is, without the excuse of a tape recorder to let him off
listening and responding—and all his efforts should be bent upon
staging in his own head a kind of symposium attended by his various
interviewees. Through him, without ever meeting, they "discuss" the
subject. He does not run around collecting opinions, like a pollster.
He actively seeks to create a dialogue among people who really only
converse through him, and his advantage is that to him each can
speak freely, where they might argue with, or shy from, or disdain one
another face to face.

And finally, only the writer himself can assume the full burden
of knowledge. Behind even the most personal prose, there is always
some privacy, or privacies, kept inviolate; there is always information
"on the record" and information "off the record." In fact, it is
positively the sign of mindless journalistic technology at work when
the written instrument exhausts the "available facts." Any writer who
is no such technocrat inevitably begins with a much deeper knowledge
of his subject than he can possibly put on paper, and the rule is that
no writer should set down a word on paper until he knows what he
must also leave unsaid.

These are some few of the demands made upon the writer when
reason is given its proper role, but they are all made, of course,

prior to the actual writing of the article. This is only preparation, and there is still the need to find a voice. That challenge—to discover a voice that will summon reality like a flourish from the horn of Roland—is the hardest to meet in any prose, and it is remarkable how large a success the article has had recently in discovering a variety of such voices. The explanation, of course, is that there has been a heavy borrowing from the house of fiction.

Actually, this is exactly as it should be, though this transposition seems often strangely inhibited. In the past, there existed a much closer tie between expository prose and narrative prose. To return to Poe for a moment, the prose that appears in "Maelzel's Chess-Player" is precisely the prose that he puts in the mouth of his great detective, M. Dupin. "But Truth is often, and in very great degree, the aim of the tale," he wrote in a famous review of Hawthorne's short stories. "Some of the finest tales are tales of ratiocination." As his own indeed proved to be. Even his literary criticism has this same ratiocinative tone as if he only required the one voice to swiftly subsume all forms. The same is true of Melville, whose reportage and fiction (and often their mixture) are given utterance in a single voice that stands reality on its ear. Such descriptions as he offers in *The Encantadas,* or *Enchanted Isles,* where "No voice, no low, no howl is heard; the chief sound of life here is a hiss," are enough to buckle our senses.

> . . . behold these really wondrous tortoises—none of your school-boy mud-turtles—but black as widow's weeds, heavy as chests of plate, with vast shells medallioned and orbed like shields, and dented and blistered like shields that have breasted a battle, shaggy, too, here and there, with dark green moss, and slimy with the spray of the sea. These mystic creatures, suddenly translated by night from unutterable solitudes to our peopled deck, affected me in a manner not easy to unfold. They seemed newly crawled forth from beneath the foundations of the world. Yea, they seemed the identical tortoises whereon the Hindoo plants this total sphere. With a lantern I inspected them more closely. Such worshipful venerableness of aspect! Such furry greenness mantling the rude peelings and healing the fissures of their shattered shells. I no more saw three tortoises. They expanded—became transfigured. I seemed to see three Roman Coliseums in magnificent decay.

Yet these tortoises are not what he "imagined" in fiction, but actual beings he "saw" on board ship, and indeed "next evening, strange to say, I sat down with my shipmates, and made a merry repast from the tortoise steaks and tortoise stews." There is no real discrepancy, for Melville's voice is a master instrument, tuned to mundanity as well as dream, and not a vulnerable lute that must be held safely aloof from the vibrations of reality.

Since the nineteenth century, this magisterial range of voice through any number of forms, particularly the article, has been sorely missed, but suddenly—out of a hunger for impressions that only an extreme sense of isolation could have bred—writers have begun again to attempt it. Nelson Algren writes a travel book that carries him out of his destitute fantasy of Chicago into the real world where he must bring whole nationalities, the Spanish, the French, the English, the Irish, the Turks, around the corner of South Street into his own blind pig. Truman Capote turns profilist, then chronicler of the Moscow *Porgy and Bess* tour, and finally detective, as he offers the police an important clue in a Kansas murder case, the latest grotesque he has chosen from the things of reality to transform directly into an exquisite bibelot of prose. Norman Mailer unleashes a diurnal attack against the culture that has pruned him of his goodly limbs and left him a stark and leafless trunk—a "success"—and out of this shock tactic, out of even the magazine deadline itself, he begins to find his way back from "prophecy" to the novel once more. "The drama of real life will not let down the prose writer," Miss Hardwick comments. "Life inspires. The confession, the revelation, are not reporting, not even journalism. Real life is treated *as if it* were fiction. The concreteness of fact is made suggestive, shadowy, symbolical. The vividly experiencing 'I' begins his search for his art in the newspapers."

And ends by publishing it in the magazines.

So the voice carries over from its beginnings in fiction, and sustains itself at the pitch of real life, perhaps even gains strength, as has certainly been the case with James Baldwin. More than any other writer, Baldwin has achieved his individual voice through the article form. He has even made the article assignment—that purchase order from a magazine for prose on an out-of-stock topic—into an iron link between event and personal vision. In his fiction, this voice has often seemed constricted, even *falsetto*, but set free to find its own natural limits—a liberty which the article form could indulge— it reached a lambency in prose that threw the black sufferings of his people into terrible relief against the white world. At the same time, no writer has set "the vividly experiencing 'I'" to face greater intrinsic peril, simply because every real event for Baldwin seems to catch at some thread in the worn, tacky, durable fabric of his being. He pulls at the thread himself, just a loose end, and then suddenly there is no knowing where the ravel will end or lead us. "On the 19th of December, in 1949, when I had been living in Paris for a little over a year, I was arrested as a receiver of stolen goods and spent eight days in prison," he begins an article for *Commentary*, "Equal in Paris," which I have included in its entirety at the end of this chapter.

The stolen goods were only a *drap de lit*, the "theft" only a misunderstanding; the event at bottom was insignificant. But it pulls from Baldwin a thread of existence that supports an awful burden of culture and race and alienation. Yet it never breaks, only delicately shines.

> One had, in short, to come into contact with an alien culture in order to understand that a culture was not a community basket-weaving project, nor yet an act of God; was something neither desirable nor undesirable in itself, being inevitable, being nothing more or less than the recorded and visible effects on a body of people of the vicissitudes with which they had been forced to deal. And their great men are revealed as simply another of these vicissitudes, even if, quite against their will, the brief battle of their great men with them has left them richer.

Am I saying then that only the displaced voice from fiction has sufficient resolve to force a personal articulation of reality upon the article form? Not at all. It is simply that of late the best voices have come over, impassioned or hortatory or simply bully, from fiction, and the writer of an article might better listen to them first if he wishes to find his own voice at all. Obviously no writer need master the short story before trying his hand at an article, but at the same time no writer should ignore the fictional techniques that have so strengthened the embodiment of fact in prose and made it "suggestive, shadowy, symbolical." What the novelists know naturally, the rest of us must learn at our pain.

In my own case, since I invariably keep at an impersonal distance from my subject, my strongest efforts in this area have been bent upon turning fact into imagery in an article. Faced with the usual Augean stable of data, I do not try to sweep it clean—as a journalist would in his Herculean labors—but rather to pick out the most redolent facts and deliberately hoard them for the aura of the stable. That is, I select facts not only as a rationalist, trying to bring an abstract line of reasoning to a conclusion, but also as an imagist, seeking to broach reality for a pattern. It is hard to pick much of an example from what has been a very broadly scattered exercise, but in an article on psychoanalysis, I tried to sum up its early history, while bodying forth the aura of the actual practice, in the following manner:

> That first couch was of horsehair. Pyramided high with pillows. *Berggasse 19, Wien IX.* ("After the—well, later when the Professor is no longer with us," the porter said one day to the poet H.D. on her way to her fifty-five-minute "hour," "they will call it Freudgasse." They never did.) For some of his taller patients, it was almost too short, and their feet under the couch rug nearly touched the glowing porcelain stove set narrowly in the corner. From the other corner, behind the couch's hard, slightly elevated headpiece,

came the cigar smoke and the fatherly voice. "Today we have tunneled very deep. You have discovered for yourself what I discovered for the race." Around him, the sublimations of a frustrated archaeologist: Greek amphorae, Assyrian and Egyptian statuettes, and other tiny, ancient totems, set all in a row. And over the couch—on the wall usually reserved nowadays for the stark probe of a favored pair of analytical eyes—a large steel engraving of the Temple of Arnak, for this was the only consulting room in the history of psychoanalysis where it was not possible to hang on that wall an honorific portrait of an analyst's chosen St. Analyst.

I wanted to begin with the facts at a particular point in time, but I also wanted these same facts to form an image of reality that would give back a semblance of life, of moment to the prose. My own voice, I'm afraid, is factual, not personal, and I depend much more upon a kind of factual density than upon any vision to help me articulate reality. But this is only one other writer's way of struggling for voice, not the lone arduous path to the one true expository style, and the eventual point is that many voices have lifted themselves above the jibber of mere fact to confound directly the reality behind it.

In fact, one of the best is also one of the most prosaic, that of George Orwell. In a way, Orwell preceded all of us into reality. His prose—which is as spare as experience itself really is—seems to have an absolute correspondence with his moment, his existence; his voice is so quietly suasive that reading him is like joining him. His articles don't end; rather, *he* departs, and leaves behind him both a sense of truth and a sense of embarrassment. In his famous article on "Shooting an Elephant," he ends by telling us:

> Afterwards, of course, there were endless discussions about the shooting of the elephant. The owner was furious, but he was only an Indian and could do nothing. Besides, legally I had done the right thing, for a mad elephant has to be killed, like a mad dog, if its owner fails to control it. Among the Europeans opinion was divided. The older men said I was right, the younger men said it was a damn shame to shoot an elephant for killing a coolie, because an elephant was worth more than any damn Coringhee coolie. And afterwards I was very glad that the coolie had been killed; it put me legally in the right and gave me a sufficient pretext for shooting the elephant. I often wondered whether any of the others grasped that I had done it solely to avoid looking a fool.

Orwell has already told us his pathetic reasons for having to shoot the elephant, even as he lies down in the road to do it, but this last is still a shock, the kind of humbling shock that a work of fiction can never bring home. It is, finally, too real.

Orwell, of course, wrote fiction, but in the end he is the strongest argument for the future of the article, for it was in this form that he expressed his best thinking in his most characteristic voice. He could not have told of "A Hanging" or "How the Poor Die" or " 'Such, Such Were the Joys . . .' " without the excuse that journalism offered him (though it was not journalism that he wrote). Fiction helped him find a voice, but it was a voice unnatural to fiction. It had to be heeded elsewhere.

It is quite possible that things have now gone even farther, and fiction itself has become unnatural to the voices *we* heed. In that sense, Baldwin has, much like Orwell, found a more proper form, and it could happen that the next generation of writers in America will not need to "come over" from fiction, but will only look back on it nostalgically as a point of departure. If this is anything like the case, the article obviously will flourish, and might attain the kind of excellence that existed in English prose during the eighteenth century.

But if anything like this *is* to happen, the reasons for writing about reality will have to attain to something like Orwell's humility in truth, for these is no gainsaying the disappointment and denial that will be let loose. "Go, go, go, said the bird:" in T. S. Eliot's poem, "human kind/Cannot bear very much reality." Few, including most magazine publishers, have any real desire to test the machinery inside, or to discovery whether these be automata or men that play the great chess game in the world. Few even wish to be articulate. It is over this guise of indifference—which is really the universal wish to "avoid looking the fool"—that voice and reason will have to triumph. The dead language of journalism has kept the article a corporate instrument in America far too long, but if it can finally achieve the sanctions which so naturally attend fiction, it will emerge as the one form with enough space to contain the risks of actual existence—the only form in which a man has enough room to shoot an elephant and admit his shame and folly.

How Else Can
a Novelist Say It?

HERBERT GOLD

It is not quite a revolutionary turn in behavior for the novelist to take pen in hand and heart in mouth in order to issue a direct communiqué from the battlefield of his life, without the intermediaries of invented character and story. The novelist, in the grand and non-specialized tradition, has often been as much *writer* as novelist. Dostoevsky filled a newspaper column with his tics, fulminations, speculations, passions; Balzac, Stendhal, and Dickens sometimes preached their sermons directly to audiences; Tolstoy, who is a better model of the literary saint than Flaubert, consecrated a large part of his life to analysis and comment, the point of which might be summarized with the title of one of his books, *What Can a Man Do?* In fact, the limiting of the novelist's attack to the cautious secreting of masterpieces—like the silkworm in its cocoon—is a phenomenon of special times and schools. There were specific causes for this rule. There are compelling reasons for breaking it now.

In a recent times there has been a revival of the direct and personal essay, attempting to name a truth about the world, by writers whose "normal" mask is that of story-teller. An audience willing to

"How Else Can a Novelist Say It?" appeared as the introduction to *First Person Singular: Essays for the Sixties*, edited by Herbert Gold. Gold's novels include *The Optimist, Therefore Be Bold, Salt,* and *Fathers.* His most recent book, *My Last Two Thousand Years,* is described as a memoir.

listen to them, wanting to find some truths, has also appeared out of the somewhere of America. James Baldwin on middle-class housing in Harlem, Saul Bellow on Khrushchev, Truman Capote on an American traveling theater, George P. Elliott on the isolation of California from the rest of the world, Norman Mailer on himself as a hipster, Warren Miller on Cuba, Mary McCarthy on Venice, on painting, Harvey Swados on the airline pilot as a sporty organization man, and many others have rediscovered something which a short recent tradition of novelists since Flaubert seemed to have given up. This is the joy of speaking out straight the work of a mind.

There had been a pious renunciation for reasons other than purity and piety, I believe. There was a high motivation in passivity and self-denigration. The novelist took on the philistine view of his role—he was a minor, albeit a romantic figure; he could attain to "fame, riches, and the love of beautiful women," but not give evidence like the scientist toward a vision of reality. In a period of increasing specialization, and impressed by the corroborating prevalence of the notion of the artist as a man apart, addicted to his holy madness and irresponsibility, writers of fiction had seemed willing to leave philosophy to the philosophers, preaching to the preachers, and commentary to the commentators, many of whom express the act of thinking by looking thoughtful. This division of labor was not always the rule. It seemed to be for a long time. Specialization was accepted at a high penalty to both writers and audiences.

Why a change now?

A shift away from the art-for-art's-sake aesthetic has certainly been encouraged by some sharp commercial reasons, but also, I believe, it reflects an important shift in our states of mind in this time of special urgency and perpetual emergency. Let us dispose of the commercial encouragements at once: Magazines will print "articles." Quick money there. A thirst for vivid and accurate writing has paralleled, let us say, the American middle-aged spread of junior colleges and adult education. Editors encourage novelists not to waste their talent in doing the major labor of their lives; they are asked to have their say, please, for immediate returns. Also, in some cases, there is a haste to bring mere face and opinion to the view of the public. The novelist is a fretful man who responds to seduction—like other men. A novel is a complex, artful way to say "Look at me!" while saying many more important things. The commitment involved in a noisy polemic is much narrower, the investment of character much less, and the reward in brief applause sometimes dizzying. Writers have no immunity against the temptation to display themselves like movie stars in a society which is avid to find new celebrities to devour. Many dangers here.

But the best of these novelists' essays—let us now frankly use that fine old word, which means roughly "a try"—is not merely a disguised fan interview in which the writer tells an as-told-to story to himself. This self-display is a symptom of hysteria, with the writer flying about in diminishing circles, divebombing the public with raw chunks of heart, until he disappears up his own soul. Something is expressed, but little is communicated.

The novelist-essayist, as I conceive him at his best, responds to a combative assertion that life is both terrible and full of delights, that the truth is both a joy and essential to the limited survival which we are allowed, that every man has an obligation to meet the facts of his time as directly as his powers permit. Having no power corrupts; a rational argument in the daylight is one way of asserting powers and possibilities.

It might be argued that the concentration camps and the atomic bomb are the cause of the revival of the serious essay by novelists. Of course, that would be simplistic; catastrophe is not a recent invention. Before these most total events, there was the War of 1914-1918, the convulsions to the East, the disasters in Spain and elsewhere. No one can record the specific date on which writers as a class suddenly cried out in chorus, "Enough of this timid abstention!" and began scribbling their moral and political views. But there has been a change from the time when novelists wrote their novels and an occasional review or a bit of fretful literary criticism, accepting politely the division of labor. The primitive need of the writer—to know, to master, to tell —has recaptured his intentions about himself. Along with speaking his mind by writing stories and novels, he has begun to speak his mind by speaking his mind. Some, like D. H. Lawrence, go on riding their obsessions and stomp over their audiences with a clatter of opinions about sex and politics. Some, like the contemporary writers already mentioned—and others come to mind at once—take the world curiously for what it is and make their passionate, delighted, or reforming projections of it. George Orwell has certainly been the most recent master in this vocation.

The long fantasy of permanent social security in an ivory tower has ended for most writers. For the best of them, of course, like James Joyce, this nonexistent dwelling was always firmly rooted on solid soil, with a winding stairway leading out into the city. Even dream towers cannot float in mere air.

As soon as the artificial isolation of the artist is broken down, the natural need to speak out in the man of ideas asserts itself again. The writer considers the world as the worm wriggles—with his entire body. Why stop this productive convulsion? No individual can escape the troubles of the world by armoring himself with silence and exile unless he is cunning enough to return to speech and fruitful connection with others.

The times are difficult, true. It is also true that the times have always been difficult. Even blind Homer would not have been Homer without the itch of unresolved doubt about the sense of our lives together on earth. (The hero, De Gaulle wrote in his memoirs, is always a natural melancholic. The writer, he might have added, is a man looking for ways to frustrate his natural melancholia.) But perhaps the times now are more than difficult, they are desperate. The novelist who once, to take a parody example, wrote from a comfortable weekend house near London, within earshot of the friendly crack of croquet balls on a lawn outside, now writes from within a buzz of implication: How long are we here? What about our children? Why do marriage and diplomacy and alcohol and money not perform their traditional soothing labor? Where is the work we like, the challenge we seek, the satisfying fulfillment in actions which can use us fully without destroying civilization?

Some of these questions have always played a part in the urge to invent stories. The lessons have been present and, if not solved, at least dramatized. The intelligent reader has always been purged of his congested desires by the experience contained within a work of art, however bemused he was by form and style. But now, in immediate need, many novelists no longer want to leave to others the formal judging and measuring of experience. The others just don't think well enough. Perhaps the novelists don't either. Nevertheless they travel the world, they read and study; most important, they are bitten by moral and metaphysical yearning. They have the vocation to pursue reality. They are not satisfied (few Americans are) by the answers washing over our heads in a flood of print. Therefore they are learning to speak out. In the United States they usually do this without official affiliation to party, doctrine, or church, although some of them occasionally take their supper at the White House of their choice.

What effect does this revived activity have on the reader? Well, at the very least, he is likely to find in the novelist's essay a superior variety of journalism, performed by a writer with a sense of pace and rhythm in prose and a vivid mission in his sense of life. Even when the novelist chops out a silly and self-important slice of punditry, he is likely to season it pungently. At his best, the novelist more than most people treasures his experience and husbands his memories; he keeps the doors and windows to feeling open late into his age; he keeps the fireplace burning. Reader and writer together may rediscover in the essay the grand truths customarily drowned in a ruck of informational, speed-reading and speed-writing prose. The form of the personal essay demands risks and commitments never possible in its surrogates, the "fact piece" on one side and the inside-dope novel on the other.

What is the effect on the writer's art as novelist? This, when all is said, is still his primary concern. The chances are that he has always hectored the world in his notebooks and kept journals of travels, reading, conversation, and ideas. But the responsibility for these notes is very different when they feed explicit conclusions in argumentative prose. The dialogue is actual, not imaginary. The writer is committed to reasoning out his questions and answers. Certainly no pat argument can ever be made to the questions, What should a man do? Why are we here? How do we meet love and reconcile with death? But each man must, in one way or another, reconcile with these general questions which are implicit in every day's portion of experience. The writer, emerging from the privacy of his philosophical journal and the disguises of his fiction, commits himself to both rigor and risks in facing the world directly. Intelligence does not have to be contraband goods in the offshore islands of fiction.

The result, going full circle, might finally be to bring back into fiction the full weight and suppleness of the writer's original motivation. At his origins, the story-teller stood before the fire as singer, historian, philosopher, priest, mourner. Civilization gave him a peculiar sense of his limits, and lately held him in thrall with the notion of "objectivity" or of being an "entertainer." This is not the same thing as disciplining a gift. Now some writers, the best of them, are once again using both the story and the essay to tell the most that they can tell about all that they know. Artificial barriers of form have gone down. An article is really an essay, just as a story, too, is really a try at mastery of the sense of human life on earth.

Introduction to SMILING THROUGH THE APOCALYPSE: ESQUIRE'S HISTORY OF THE SIXTIES

HAROLD HAYES

Decades seldom start on schedule. The Thirties began in '29 with the Depression; the Forties with World War II in '41; the Fifties with the election of Dwight Eisenhower in '52; and the Sixties ten months after the turn of the year when, in his television debate with Jack Kennedy, Richard Nixon's face signaled defeat. But for politicians and journalists, the first day of a decade opens a new epoch, ready or not, and *Esquire* reacted accordingly. In our January 1960 issue, the first paragraph of the lead article (by Arthur Schlesinger Jr.) read:

"At periodic moments in our history, our country has paused on the threshold of a new epoch in our national life, unable for a moment to open the door, but aware that it must advance if it is to preserve its natural vitality and identity. One feels that we are approaching such a moment now—that the mood which had dominated the nation for a decade is beginning to seem thin and irrelevant; that it no longer interprets our desires and needs as a people, that new forms, new energies, new values are straining for expression and release. The Eisenhower epoch—the present period of passivity and acquiescence in our national life—is drawing to a close."

Part prophecy, part wishful thinking. That January issue was

Smiling Through the Apocalypse is a collection of *Esquire* articles from the decade of the 1960s. The book was edited by Harold Hayes, then the editor of the magazine, and published in 1969.

published on December 14, having been assembled back in September of 1959. Actually, on Friday, January 1, 1960, no door opened. Khrushchev declared he would disarm Russia unilaterally, the French issued a one-franc coin worth twenty cents and N.A.S.A. announced plans to cut back space costs. If there were new energies and new values straining for release, most Americans were unaware of them. Rather, life seemed monotonously predictable. The average American was white, prosperous and torpid; a second car and a swimming pool were facts of his life, a new vacation home an immediate possibility. Though there was still plenty to fear from the Russians—perhaps a bomb shelter would prove a wiser investment than a beach house— the mood was benign. Of course the Negro was restless, and many people were distressed by news pictures of police dogs breaking up demonstrations in Alabama. But that was largely a regional problem; elsewhere, America was an ongoing enterprise. There was no war, the economy was sound (unemployment practically nonexistent) and our democratic institutions, God's church among them, were invulnerable. Arthur Schlesinger was right, however: The Fifties *were* drawing to a close. *Smiling Through the Apocalypse: Esquire's History of the Sixties,* is an account of what happened next.

A magazine is a promise, sometimes fulfilled, sometimes not. Responding to events of the day, it seeks to offer a bit more perspective than the shifting realities reported in the daily press, though the permanence of its views is only slightly less subject to change. Between the morning papers and the Cronkite show, there is often very little to add but—and this is the redeeming strength of all magazines today —attitude. The magazine engages its reader and holds him because it shares with him a certain point of view.

To land on the moon is to make news which transcends form: the faster the word gets out, the better. But once established, the fact moves from the simple to the complex, begging interpretation of a thousand varieties. A magazine's promise is the delivery, on a fixed schedule, of its own version of the world, its special attitude toward the reader.

The present-day attitude of *Esquire* was formed out of a reaction to the banality of the Fifties. From the raspberry to the hoax, in words and/or pictures (curiously the pictures always provoked the greatest outrage, especially George Lois's covers) and occasionally with some loss of dignity, the idea was to suggest alternate possibilities to a monolithic view. And how monolithic it was! The passivity of the Fifties was shared by garage mechanics and college presidents.

At *Esquire* our attitude took shape as we went along, stumbling past our traditional boundaries of fashion, leisure, entertainment and literature onto the more forbidding ground of politics, sociology, science and even, occasionally, religion. Any point of view was welcome as long as the writer was sufficiently skillful to carry it off, but we tended to avoid committing ourselves to doctrinaire programs even though advised on occasion that we might thereby serve better the interests of mankind. None of the programs available would permit us consistently to keep our lines open to the reader, so we stayed loose.

But despite this calloused lack of commitment—or perhaps because of it—we began to form the habit of searching for the right questions. If two superpowers have superbombs, how does one protect itself from the other? Should churches practice segregation? Should Arthur Miller be jailed for refusing to name those of his friends who were Communist? Was reverence due cherished institutions of American life, or irreverence? What evil lurked in the heart of Eisenhower, what virtue in the heart of Alger Hiss?

Raising such questions in the capacity of surrogate readers, we then moved as editors to find the appropriate writers, often the unexpected ones, to answer them. But the attitude, now roughly shaping, would become refined through more complicated means: the precise phrasing of titles—

"JOE," SAID MARILYN MONROE,
JUST BACK FROM KOREA,
"YOU NEVER HEARD SUCH CHEERING."
"YES I HAVE,"
JOE DIMAGGIO ANSWERED

—the toning and sharpening "house copy," those introductory copy blocks and captions accompanying visual features; and sometimes—increasingly more often—planning features executed exclusively by the editors to remind readers that we were ever mindful of where their interests lay (the rococo phase of this cycle occurring well into the Sixties with a two-page list entitled "The 100 Best People in the World").

And always, always pounding away on the Idea, ten a week from each staff editor until he either mutinied, buckled or broke through to some dazzlingly fresh concept which gained for the magazine another inch of new ground.

Few magazines have successfully defined their own attitude, and *Esquire* is no exception. For a while we called ours an effort toward a rational view, then satire and then irony. But only humor—of a most complex, often unfunny sort—is sufficiently flexible to cover the larger part of our effort, from black wit to custard-pie burlesque. Against the aridity of the national landscape of the late Fifties we offered to our readers in our better moments the promise of outright laughter; by the end of the Sixties the best we could provide was a bleak grin.

Arriving slightly behind schedule, Jack Kennedy opened the door to an epoch releasing new energies indeed, though it is now clear that many of his constituents missed the point of his coming. What Kennedy wanted was the acceptance of conventional liberal measures to ensure minimum creature comforts, freedom and security; what the country wanted was to be like Jack—young, rich, powerful and attractive. Backing up, like electric currents in a cloudless sky, those new energies collected around him until the terrible spark of his assassination set them loose, traumatizing the country more than any event in recent memory.

"The Rise and Fall of Charisma," Part I of this book, traces through the Sixties the pathetic parabola of the Kennedy spirit, concluding with the Chicago Convention of 1968. But the Kennedy chronicle, like some medieval legend, seems endless. *The Last Kennedy*, a 1968 portrait of Edward by Burton Hersh, was turned in only days before the assassination of Robert and hastily revised to allow for this latest misfortune to strike the President's survivors. In the light of Edward Kennedy's disastrous experience in the Chappaquiddick affair of 1969, Hersh's appraisal appears now slightly out of chronology (and context). But here it stands. Although we are told the House of Kennedy at last has fallen, it will be seen that the theme of this section argues the decline of the Kennedy ideal began even before the President's death. The Hersh piece, like others throughout the book which may seem inconsistent in view of our later knowledge of events, is without further revision because it reflects our impressions of the moment. (At the end of each article is the date of its publication in *Esquire*, serving as a guide for the reader to his own memories of that moment.)

"The Grass Roots of 'Now,'" Part II, derives from the section preceding it. As Arthur Schlesinger had predicted, new forms and new values would come along with the new energies, and in *Esquire's* view the forms tended to define the values. Thus more than a casual interest was expressed by our editors and writers in the diversions of the period—from baton-twirling schools to Las Vegas casinos. No longer was there an archetypal American; standing in his place, self-absorbed and passionate to the point of militancy, was a cluster of groups, some of them harsh and disquieting.

So were some of their new values, six of which underline parts of this book:

Power is an absolute, like truth or justice. (Part I, "The Rise and Fall of Charisma")

Public image is more important than measurable achievement. (Part III, "Egos, Superegos and Ids")

The government lies. (Part V, Section 1, "The Credibility Gap")
Youth is incorruptible. (Part V, Section 2, "The Generation Gap")
Minority rights are secured more effectively by intimidation than by legislation or Christian example. (Part V, Section 3, "The Color Gap")
Patriotism is an irrelevant reason for going to war. (Part VI, "Living Up to Our Commitment in Vietnam")

But sentiments changed even more swiftly than values, and in 1964, midway through the period, two young editors named Robert Benton and David Newman stood back from the moment and cataloged with striking economy "The New Sentimentality," epiphenomenal moods of the day which rejected old illusions and appealed only to contemporary life "as it has to do with you, really just you, not what you were told or taught, but what goes on in your head, *really*, and in your heart, *really*." * As a sort of way station along our seven-staged descent, "The New Sentimentality" stands alone as Part IV.

Only in Part IV, however, are value judgments themselves the subject of our attention. As this is a book about life in the Sixties, it is mostly concerned with the infinite variety of the odd and dissimilar: styles, conspiracies, education, sex, war, cars, establishments,** fads, drugs, Pepsi-Cola contests, murders, sports, riots and fashions. And with people of all kinds: winners, losers, clowns, revolutionaries, fools, mothers, actors, segregationists, topless waitresses, soldiers, villains, fighters, martyrs, hippies, yippies and L.B.J.

But the writer is the only hero.

"If any man have an ear," wrote St. John regarding a terminal point for readers of a wider audience than *Esquire's*, "let him hear." In the apocalyptic Sixties the message came through clearly, for writers were everywhere, sending back the word. "Creative Agonies," Part VII of this informal history, is concerned with the private lives of our writer kings.

It is doubtful whether even so egocentric an author as Ernest Hemingway saw himself as central to events as have some of the writers through these years, freedom-riding down South, slogging through the

---

* A fitting exegesis of the intentions of the same authors when they went on from *Esquire* to write the original screenplay of *Bonnie and Clyde*, a masterpiece of the Sixties.

** More than our share of them, perhaps: establishments on Wall Street, in the art world, the Washington press corps, the literary world, even a baseball establishment. In our pages, conspiracy lovers were fair game—until the Sixties turned around on us. See "The American Establishment" and "An Appreciation of the Nonmilitary Functions of War" in Part V. The former, published in 1962, spoofs the notion that there is an establishment; the latter, published in 1967, spoofs the notion that there is not.

Mekong Delta, marching on the Pentagon, backtracking Kansas killers, running from cops in Chicago and so on—keeping witness in the truest sense, and all readers were the richer for it. So were writers, by the way, some of them now millionaires whose celebrity had become international but troublesome. Because instant communication allowed the possibility of instant success, writers and readers by mid-decade looked expectantly toward the coronation of the Writer of the Year. Saul Bellow, '65, *Herzog;* Truman Capote, '66, *In Cold Blood;* William Styron, '67, *The Confessions of Nat Turner;* Norman Mailer, '68, *The Armies of the Night;* Philip Roth, '69, *Portnoy's Complaint.* But sudden though it was, modern fame could pass quickly. Last year's writer found himself working under an excruciating pressure imposed by the mass reader's perfidy. Despite the unprecedented wealth and glory paid out by the Sixties for higher achievement, the time warp ultimately conspired against him. Talent got him there but publicity would have to keep him alive. Like everyone else, he too wanted to be young, rich, powerful and attractive. A prominent symptom of his unstrung condition was the emergence of his claims to new literary forms—the "nonfiction novel," "history as literature and literature as history," the "New Journalism." While identifying characteristics of at least two of these forms may be traced back to articles appearing first in this magazine, the claim was misleading. Demands of the language remain constant, and varieties in technique are relative matters, drawing from old sources. Separating the spurious from the authentic in most activities through this decade is a task continuing over into the future. But there can be no doubt that ours was a time uniquely blessed with an extraordinary abundance of writing talent, men of great originality and style exquisitely sensitive to the nature of change going on about them.

Most are present in this collection, a number of them having earlier established their reputations independently of *Esquire.* But a few of them first reached a national audience through this magazine and have continued throughout most of the period to identify their principal efforts with ours. These are Gay Talese, Tom Wolfe, Jack Richardson, Garry Wills,* and Martin Mayer; and, among our by-lined editors, Robert Benton, David Newman, Robert Brown, John Berendt and Alice Glaser.

Ironically, many of the better novelists weren't writing much fiction, perhaps because social disintegration forced the writer to view himself as his own protagonist; perhaps, as has been remarked elsewhere, because the times were too stimulating for the interior vision

---

* For the record, William F. Buckley, Jr. sent over Garry Wills who had published, and continues to, in the *National Review.* But as Mr. Buckley would be the first to acknowledge, the editorial intentions of the two periodicals are so dissimilar as to allow the claim, on behalf of *Esquire's* readers at least, to stand.

to contain. Although there is no fiction included in this selection, *Esquire* published throughout the Sixties a number of outstanding stories, even serializing through one hectic season the chapters of a Norman Mailer novel turned out to monthly deadline. Possibly the quality of the fiction was superior to that of the nonfiction, the insights more lasting and—as our fiction department insists even to this day—more meaningful a way to view the period. Possibly. But in the Sixties, events seemed to move too swiftly to allow the osmotic process of art to keep abreast, and when we found a good novelist we immediately sought to seduce him with the sweet mysteries of current events.

Even so, for the very best of our writers, no single event yielded a key to the decade. There was too much going on—a fire in the street, a fight at the corner, a burglary in the house next door. The last two articles of our book—the *mano a mano* between William F. Buckley, Jr. and Gore Vidal—are as appropriate a conclusion to the Sixties as any other, yielding as they do almost no direct information on the changing times other than by suggesting indirectly—through the bitterness, jealousy, ambition and despair of two of our most eloquent sensibilities—the character of America's collective confusion.

Introduction to
WRITERS AND ISSUES

THEODORE SOLOTAROFF

Writers and Issues is a collection of topical essays. Since such writing is addressed to the issues of its time and place, and therefore can date quickly, I have limited my selection to the decade of the 1960s. But there is another reason for doing so. The Sixties already loom as that distinctive period we call an epoch. It can be said to have begun with the Democratic convention of 1960, which as Norman Mailer foresaw in his essay "Superman Comes to the Supermarket" marked the changing of the generations, the entry of an uncertain but dynamic element into the psychic life of the nation, and the advent, in the person and aura of John F. Kennedy, of a new political style. Kennedy was to campaign on the slogan "Let's get this country moving again"—that is to say, out of the doldrums of the closing years of the Eisenhower administration. In retrospect, this appeal has come to have a deep, Sophoclean irony. For since 1960, the nation has not stopped moving. But the momentum and direction of events has grown steadily more uncontrollable, the atmosphere more and more turbulent. The motion of change has been less like that of a journey than of a whirlwind, in which many of the agents and agencies of change, such as President

Writers and Issues was published in 1969. Theodore Solotaroff is the editor of *American Review* (formerly *New American Review*) and the author of *The Red Hot Vacuum,* a collection of essays and reviews dealing with contemporary writing.

Kennedy or the civil rights movement, have themselves fallen or been swept aside.

This stirring up of things also makes the Sixties a quintessentially modern decade. More than a hundred years ago, Marx and Engels characterized the modern era as follows:

> as uninterrupted disturbance of all social conditions, everlasting uncertainty and agitation . . . All that is solid melts into the air, all that is holy is profaned, and man is at last compelled to face with sober senses his real condition of life and his relations with his kind.

Viewing the extreme degree of conflict and instability, of factionalism and sacrilege that has characterized the recent years, one is tempted to say, *Plus ça change, plus c'est la même chose.* But some decades are more "modern" than others and the Sixties have probably been the most cataclysmic decade in American history since that of the Civil War. There have been wars since then, but none as bitterly unpopular, divisive, or faith-shaking as the one in Vietnam. There have also been serious social conflicts since America's first full confrontation with the evil of racism, but none so rife with violence, hatred, and terror as its second. In the wake of these two traumas, the one intricately and ominously reinforcing the other, has come a vast sense of doubt— sometimes expressed as active opposition, sometimes as passive indifference—about what used to be called, more or less honorifically, the American way of life. Though focused and energized by the issues of militarism and racism, this doubt spreads throughout the America that is being transformed by the economic and social pressures of the mass society, by its modes of communication, its technology, and its ideology. At the same time, the growth of politically radical ideas and behavior, often more anarchist than Marxist, along with the extension of liberal reforms in such areas as civil rights and censorship, and the spread of a more libertarian ethos in the realm of manners and morals, have fostered a potent reaction among those Americans who view the ramifying crisis of change in such terms as "law and order" and "public decency." As Philip Roth remarks in "Writing American Fiction," ". . . though one may refer to a 'problem' as being controversial, one does not usually speak of a state of civilization as being controversial . . ." Yet this is precisely the case today. There seems to be no important area of our national life—whether foreign policy or public welfare, family authority or community control, the city environment or the rural one, the elementary school or the university campus, the literary arts or the pop music scene—that does not bristle with the live issues of public concern.

As one would expect, this situation has had a strong effect on

American writing. Just as the decade of the Sixties can be said to have a characteristic "feel" of turbulence to it, so it can be said to have fostered a characteristic tone of expression: one that emphasizes immediacy, relevance, involvement, or, in the idiom of the day, "being where it's at," "telling it like it is." This influence can be seen in fiction, poetry, theater, as well as films and popular music, but is most widely visible in the field of magazine journalism, where it finds its most natural home. Mailer's essay on the nomination of John F. Kennedy has proved to be a harbinger in this respect as well, initiating as it did the vogue of personal journalism, or reportage, that was to burgeon in the ensuing years, as it always has in times of strife, when literary men are drawn toward the drama of events and issues and to the human burden of their meaning.

This attraction to the topical also stems from a less overt but possibly more general recognition: that we are entering a new age of mankind, symbolized by the Apollo flights but apparent in all walks of life. Thus the only historical term that seems to have much utility is the prefix "post-" which we apply to once stable terms—"Christian," "Western," "capitalist," "colonial," indeed to the term "modern" itself —to try to pin down where we are. In his essay "The Sealed Treasure," Saul Bellow characterizes the public mood as an "unbearable excitement caused by the greatness of the change." One symptom of this excitement is our obsession with contemporaneity. Just as "post-" is our chief reference word to history, so our chief reference to reality seems to be the word "now." In our curiosity and uncertainty, we study the trends, fashions, and fads of the moment as the Greek seers studied the entrails of a goat. Everyone wishes to keep up, especially the literate, college-educated audience which has grown in such great numbers in the past decade.

All of which has created a widespread and wide-open market for topical writing. From *The New Yorker* to the *East Village Other*, from *The American Scholar* to *Playboy*, magazines have been busily "making the scene." Novelists and social scientists, students and housewives, congressmen and hippies have been pressed into the service of journalism to describe, interpret, and argue about our days and ways. One result of this unremitting flow of information and opinion has been a marked gain in the level of public consciousness. Thanks in part to topical journalism we are much better "tuned-in" to the issues of our age than we were a decade ago. At the same time, it seems to me true that the proliferation of news about the new, accompanied by the steady barrage of contemporary events and images disseminated by TV and films, often has the effect of overloading the circuits of awareness by which we try to understand and orient ourselves to the world. The literate mind today is likely to find itself reeling from the competition of views, attitudes, and sheer phenomena to which it is exposed. For example, though I tend to believe what I read in both the *New York Times* and the *Village Voice*, it's sometimes hard to believe that they're published on the same planet, much less in the same city.

As an editor of several periodicals during the past decade, I have found it useful to discriminate among three kinds of topical writing. It should be kept in mind that the field of topical writing is very fluid and any such classifications will leak a great deal. The first kind I call "the tendentious statement." This is often found at the extremes of the political spectrum where the colors of truth tend to be black and white. The tendentious statement is written mainly to express and inculcate an attitude: it says that such and such—student protest, Malcolm X, the use of nudity in the theater—is to be viewed, understood, and judged this way rather than that. Details and examples, the stuff and test of reality, are chosen and shaped to follow the line of conviction and as such are often slanted to do so. The tone of the writing is typically aggressive, since this, too, has been conditioned by the pressure of the writer's opinion. As a result, he does not talk to his readers so much as at them. His singlemindedness can be valuable in cutting through the cant of an opposing position, but at the same time, is likely to generate its own. The tendentious statement is commonly the work of the doctrinaire, the sectarian, the true believer, and even when written with the courage and passion of his conviction, it runs the risk of preaching only to the already converted.

The second kind of topical writing is the "serviceable report." This is the staple of magazine journalism, particularly of those journals that occupy the middle ground. Its purpose is to provide coverage of some prominent question, event, or figure. As such it seeks to be informative rather than opinionated, its evidence is balanced rather than weighted, its tone is neutral rather than partisan. Because the standards of magazine journalism have risen in the past decade, the serviceable report may be quite sophisticated in its diction and references, its cleverness and candor, its show of personality. Indeed, under the aegis of magaines such as *Esquire, Playboy, New York*, a mode of topical writing has flourished known as "the new journalism," which specializes in cleverness, candor, and personality. Nonetheless, the serviceable report tends to be bound by a journal's requirements of space, approach, tone, and reader interest and by the writer's own economy of energy, which prompts him to go no more deeply into a question than he can handle smoothly and efficiently. The effect is to stay on the surface of the subject, to straddle its issues ("on the one hand . . . on the other"), to withhold complexity and commitment. If the usual trouble with the tendentious statement is that it is narrrow, the trouble with the serviceable report is that it is superficial.

The third category of topical writing I think of as the "necessary inquiry." It is more rarely found than the other two kinds, though it, too has increased in frequency in the past decade, fostered by the same conditions that have enabled them to thrive but that operate at a deeper level. As the phrase implies, the necessary inquiry is one that the writer, quite literally, has to write, or what comes to the same thing, has been saving up to write. Occasionally, an editor may offer an assignment that prompts it, but, once underway, the essay is not written to his specifications but to those that arise from the confrontation of the writer and the issue, and from the inquiry that he is conducting with himself. Thus such essays are typically personal, idiosyncratic, searching, unexpected, urgent. They eschew the narrow and the superficial approach; while they are fully informed, to the point of overflow, they are willing to go off the deep end, for their purpose is to touch bottom. The prevailing effect is that of a fullness of awareness placed in a fresh and significant perspective.

Obviously, there are no ready-made prescriptions of approach that create this kind of essay. It may be as subjective and impressionistic as Keith Botsford's "Youngers and Olders," an examination of the generation gap by a man whose girl friend is nearly half his age, or as rooted in the writer's imagination as Ralph Ellison's "Tell It Like It Is, Baby," in which he explores the American nightmare of race relations by describing one of his own dreams. On the other hand, such an essay may be as objective and reasoned as Nathan Glazer's "Student Politics in a Democratic Society" or as George P. Elliott's argument "Against Pornography." It may employ the narrative immediacy of George Dennison's description of the "two Americas" he found confronting each other at the Pentagon demonstration, or it may combine the hard data of political science and sociology with the truths drawn from personal experience, as does James Q. Wilson's corrective "Guide to Reagan Country." It may argue its case with the historian's circumspectness, like Jane Jacob's chronicle of "the victory over vitality" in modern city planning, or with the partisan spiritedness of Alice Walker's defense of the civil rights movement, or with the tensions of advocacy and criticism found in Eric Bentley's view of what it means to be alienated today. The necessary inquiry may be a chapter from a book (Ronald Steel's *The Accidental Empire*), or a book review (I. F. Stone's "The Pilgrimage of Malcolm X"), or the spin-off from a book (William Styron's "This Quiet Dust").

But whatever the form, the technique, the tone, the occasion, the common factor is a live, pressing relation between the writer and the issue, which makes him as much a witness of it as a commentator. We sense the man in the writer speaking to us, a citizen of our turbulent place and time who is laboring to set one part of it straight in his mind and in ours. Rather than adding to the clamor of current discussion, he cuts through it, clears the air, and fills the space with consciousness. Because his inquiry is vital to him, it becomes indispensable to us.

Part Three

FACT IN THE FICTION VOID

The Newspaper as Literature/ Literature as Leadership

SEYMOUR KRIM

To My Fellow Wordmen:

On Oct. 30, 1966 (but it could have been tomorrow), the late *New York World Journal Tribune* carried a page-one story by Jimmy Breslin from Fairfield, California, that told of the arrival at the Travis Air Force Base of four dead Marines from Vietnam. Breslin gave a closeup of exactly what happened as the four aluminum boxes were lifted off the transport plane that brought them in and were taken by covered truck to a mortuary on the air force base. He told how the cold northern California nightwind spun the tags on the metal coffins, how they were trucked in darkness behind the terminal where 165 new soldiers were about to fly off to the same place from where the bodies had come, and how the human remains of these dead Marines—called "H.R." in military shorthand—were gingerly handled by the embarrassed personnel in the mortuary:

> "Lift easy," one of them said. "Yeah, lift very easy," another one said. . . . The airmen brought the other three cases in and now the four dead Marines were side by side on the wooden rack. "There is nothing inside these boxes, just human remains," one of the airmen said. "Inside they got a rest for the head and then just an empty box," another one said.

Seymour Krim has worked on newspapers and magazines and is the author of *Views of a Near-Sighted Cannoner* and editor of two anthologies, *Manhattan: Stories of a Great City* and *The Beats*. His article, published in 1967, is reprinted in a collection called *Shake it for the World, Smartass*.

Breslin tells us that on each aluminum box was stenciled, "RE-TURN TO USAF MORTUARY TSN RVN," and in the last paragraph of his 1800-word story he explains that this "meant when the bodies of the four Marines were taken out of the cases, the cases should be put on a plane and returned to Tan Son Nhut in the Republic of Vietnam, so that the cases could be used again."

In that flat, open, deceptive (Gertrude Stein and Ernest Heming-way are stretched out in those "cases," repetitively tolled three times along with the dead Marines) and yet completely practical tone of voice, Breslin gave a picture of contemporary reality that went beyond the particular Sunday story he had written. By sticking entirely to the facts and selecting them with a prose artist's touch—the art in Breslin's shrewd hands being to underplay details packed with emotional conse-quence and by flattening them allow their intrinsic value to float clear—he forced his readers to experience larger meanings than the return of four men, or parts of them, from Vietnam. The simple details them-selves, without any evidence of strain on Breslin's part (naturalness is his big trump card as a persuader), became symbolic of the techno-logical impersonality demanded by war in the 60s; of how men who were alive 24 hours before on distant soil became converted into neatly packaged meat sent home in the wink of a mechanical eye; of how the quick utilitarian techniques for transporting and disposing of this meat becomes the foreground of a story about death today and makes the luxury of sentiment ridiculous; of how the living try to adjust to the rapid businesslike logistics of human annihilation and the only act of baffled mourning allowed them is to handle a sealed aluminum box gently.

For all they knew there could be dirty underwear in it, so weird, abstract, numbing to the emotions and mind is the way boisterous young bucks fly out from this West Coast terminal and quickly fly back as souls of aluminum.

All this and more can be legitimately read into Breslin's story, and yet he did not have time to calculate all the echoes set up by what he had written; working under a deadline for a daily paper, with his piece due in New York by roughly 5 p.m. on Saturday evening (Oct. 29th) at the latest, he had to write as well as he possibly could about an event dissolving in front of his eyes—like a sharpshooter on the run. (Actually, I heard later from Dick Schaap that Breslin had tried this particular story before and been dissatisfied with it; this was his second run on it, according to Schaap; but since every story a good newspaper-man writes is different, like a jazzman cutting several versions of the same tune out of an excess of spirit, it is not unfair to the existential reality of this story's composition to see it as a totally fresh shot out of Breslin's typewriter.)

The details enumerated earlier, with the actual names of the personnel on the air force base to be spelled correctly, the right numbers on the transport plane and the insignia on the mortuary to be set down so accurately that they could stand up in a court of law, constituted his materials. With this data plus the intake of his senses he had to build a story with a purpose and build it quickly; unlike a "pure" fiction writer he could not convert the four dead Marines into 24 to dramatize the scene—although an air force major in the story is actually quoted as saying that there were three separate shipments of aluminum boxes that day—nor could he alter the shape of the terminal or the number of planes parked out in front ready to fly newcomers to the combat area. (For the record there were two commercial airliners supplied by TWA and Pan American ready to do this unpublicized chore, with a third air force transport plane assigned to carry the equipment.)

But within the circumscribed reality of this particular story, without violating facts that could be checked by others and would be hotly scrutinized by those who had actually been on the air force base that night, Breslin had to write, rewrite, twist, carve his piece. If he wrote it in a West Coast motel room after covering the story, as is likely, he probably had no more than three hours to do approximately 10 wide-margin double-spaced pages. (Most metropolitan newspapermen triple-space on four stapled sheets of copy with carbons in between known as "books"; the triple-spacing is to allow for editing and the extra sheets go to various desks; Breslin's double-spacing on one single piece of copy paper at a time indicates the weight he can throw around any New York newspaper office except the *Times*.) Typing in clean bursts with an aggressiveness and intensity that doesn't appear in the copy, surrounded by hot, visibly smoking coffee, smoldering cigarettes, his $7\frac{1}{2}''$ x 5" wire-ringed National notebook and a nearby telephone which he might have used half a dozen times to fill in tiny chinks of information—Breslin has the personal style of a boom-boom MGM supernewspaperman but each of these props is active in itself or tends to create a rhythm of action—he had to see into this story with his own experience-cum-feelers and find the precise way for rendering a new event that had never crossed his consciousness before in all its fine relationships. Each story is totally new to the newspaperman or truthteller-on-the-run, even if he has taken a quick bite out of it before; each time he "covers" or "goes out on the street" he is faced with unique combinations of history, large or small, and the only way he can confront an event that he can't wholly anticipate or control is by his technique and finally his depth of perception.

Breslin's depth as a writer (and he can also be shallow and obvious) reveals itself in the quiet line-by-line way in which he places the significant small detail and the entirely believable, telling quote—

"We don't pick them up like freight," one of the defensive airmen tells him in the mortuary that "had white walls and no windows and a heavy air conditioning unit hanging from the ceiling." (Notice how he relies on the "and" to both keep his sentence moving and deal out the necessary facts without pausing; the device can get mechanical—and when a Breslin story fails it can be flatter than stale beer—but what Gertrude Stein and Hemingway never realized was how handy their simplified English would become for journalists who cram sentences to the teeth with fact and are always looking for the most painless way to do the job.)

As a columnist, Breslin is permitted to use the "I" whenever he wants since the very idea of having a column is based upon owning a big "I"; but his best or at least most serious stories direct attention to the scene itself—four dead Marines, a Greenwich Village firehouse that lost half a dozen men in a building cavein, the night at the New York Hilton when Rockefeller heard that he'd won the Governorship for the third time; the more important the event, the less Breslin will inject himself, although he has written totally knockout *New York Magazine* feature stories in the first person that gain their freshness from his willingness to bat out the literal truth about his drinking, rages, tyranny over neighbors-wife-and-family, bad debts, etc. These stories almost never fail to entertain because they shout with honesty of emotion and are never selfconscious. Breslin inherits the oldfashioned newspaper code of suspicion for intellectuals and intellectuality—which has been melting in the last several years with his support of liberal and vaguely avantgarde causes—but the virtue of his show-me-I'm-from-Queens stance, at least in the firstperson pieces, is that it keeps him earthy, tangible, solid and finally modest in a way that a writer who took his mortal being more heavily could not be. Breslin's comparative spiritual modesty as well as his narrowmindedness and occasional noisy rant seems the direct result of his Irish Catholic upbringing, which puts an unquestioned God cleanly above man and permits Breslin to be easy in print about himself because he is not trying to save the world.

From his point of view it would probably be blasphemous and even more important—to that knowing street-urchin eye—inexpressibly stupid.

But if this 37-year-old Babe Ruth, Jr., of the cityroom is ultimately easier to take and "puts a cheaper price on his ass" (to Pete Hamill the key to snapping newspaper prose) than other firstperson blabbers whose confessions appear in Important Books, there is nothing shy about the writing ego that went into "4 Bodies At Midnight," the headline for his dead Marine story. Here, disdaining to use the first person because it would have shown a lack of "class" (to which Breslin is as sensitive as Frank Sinatra—both gangster buffs), he had to project his feelings through the dead kids and the situation itself and did not let himself offer an opinion. In other words, he had to write a *short story* as formal as the kind taught in any fiction class, except his was about people with actual dogtag numbers and a real place still doing its ugly work today. By an unexpected evolution—or is it a revolution?—the American realistic short story from Stephen Crane to post-John O'Hara has now been inherited by the imaginative newspaperman, like Breslin, and all the independent probing of reality that the best native literary artists of the past have achieved can now be tried by a creative reporter without undue sweat.

Not only is there no longer any pretense involved (pretense in the sense that so-called "fine" writing was once a world apart, in a BOOK, while newspaper prose was supposed "to line somebody's birdcage" in Hamill's words), there is a definite advantage to the newspaperman in recreating reality if he uses every conceivable literary avenue open to him; for his job, depending on the intensity of his sense of mission, is to penetrate ever more deeply into the truth of every story—and this can only be done if he has the instruments of language, narrative know-how, character-development, etc., that until now have always been associated with fiction. ("Every technique of fiction is now available to us," Tom Wolfe said recently. And if Breslin is currently the Kid Ruth of the New Journalism, Wolfe is certainly its ultra flashy-smooth Ted Williams. Wolfe goes on to say: "Stream-of-consciousness and subjective truth is the next breakthrough. Gay Talese's article in *Esquire* in 1962, 'Joe Louis At 50,' is a classic in this direction; Truman Capote, who in my opinion is not a firstrate writer, was only doing in *In Cold Blood* what Talese had done six or seven years before.")

Perhaps there was a time, really, truly, down in the belly, when fiction in America shed more light on the outlook of a generation than nonfiction; but today the application of fictional and avantgarde prose techniques to the actual scene before us seems much more crucially necessary. When Breslin wrote his story about the silent flight of four statistics from Asia to California he was telling us things about the America that each of us must confront on our own—this real-unreal country and each of our lives in it being bound up with a strange war, monsterlike technology, guilt over the death of these four young guys, secret happiness that we escaped their fate, bewilderment toward the future. He was reporting to us from the outer perimeter of our own coolly murderous time, expanding through the clarity of his writing skill our knowledge of what is *actually going on* in places we can't possibly get to but which all add up to our sense of fateful identity as a people.

If for some reason he had written this same story as a fictional sketch—changing names, location, inflating or "working up" the tone while he disguised the specifics as so many unimaginative novelists do for no significant purpose except selfprotection—would he have achieved anything more? The question, admittedly loaded, answers itself. Not only with this kind of story would he have added nothing to the central mood that justly shakes up the reader after finishing it, fictionalizing what was as rich as fiction in his mind to begin with would have disgraced the reality of what he saw. The punch of his story lies in its actuality; although Breslin has a reputation in New York newspaper circles of occasionally "piping" or making up quotes that fit a situation or clinch a scene, this can only be done in small part and in itself is sometimes an act of courage. To put quotes in the mouths of living people is a more audacious act of the imagination than to invent words for people who have never existed, especially when the writer knows these quotes will be read by the participants and he will be judged for it.

Breslin's story *gains* its impact precisely because it is not made up; it can be checked; and it was written out of that dual responsibility which rides the writer-reporter as it doesn't the totally free "creative writer," namely factual justice to his material and yet equal pride in the literary possibilities offered by his imagination. He is playing the most potentially dangerous game of all, writing about real, observable, aftermathridden life situations; and yet—to the extent that he is a writer equal in skill and ambition to the best novelists—he has to invest this living material with every bit of his artistic sense, his concern for language, mood, nuance, insight, suspense, moral value. And if he is a genuine firstrate writer, on a par with any who have put their signature on this ruptured time, he has to illuminate the material with his own needlesharp angle of vision—"material" which is people who are very much alive, nameable, often prominent, people whom he will meet again as a vulnerable man himself caught up in the crosscurrents of contemporary U.S. life.

The reporter-writer does not have the freedom that the oldfashioned novelist or shortstory writer had and still has. He is hemmed in by his awareness of the living characters who make up the cast of each new story. If he wants to satirize them, make them pathetic, select a fact or describe a gesture that will perhaps show them up as frauds he has to be aware (and is soon made aware!) that there will be a kickback right in the psychic breadbasket. There is a resiliency between what he writes and the public, and if he takes risks either imaginative or moral he does not do it in a vacuum or in the eye of posterity; he is bound to be reacted to with a bang in the present. This means that in the case of a Breslin, Tom Wolfe, Pete Hamill—as well as Murray Kempton and Ralph J. Gleason, the two older pillars of the New Journalism—the literary imagination that each possesses is not allowed the freewheeling of a writer who is not called daily to the bar of justice for his work.

Breslin's artistic imagination in the dead Marine story had to function within the framework of the air base, the number of caskets, the name of the community that houses the base, all the tough facts that constitute the skeleton of every reporter's story; in addition, he had to cope with the intangible human element that hangs over every scrap of type that appears in a newspaper with a byline attached to it. Will he get punched in the mouth after the story appears? Has he wounded someone unintentionally or seriously fucked them up? Is there a possibility of inaccuracy that will backfire and embarrass not only himself and his newspaper but the precarious balance of the event involved? Within this network running from potential anxiety to real outward danger to hard-headed responsibility for the factual truth, Breslin or any feeling newspaperman tries his creative chutzpah to its limit in order to extract the most he possibly can from a fleeting set of circumstances that will never come again.

Until quite recently it was customarily thought that the place for high imagination in contemporary prosewriting was in fiction—but is this the kind of writing that is most significant today for the helplessly involved reader who is in a state of flux trying to relate his life to the world? When Establishment book critics say that there are no major novelists of the American 60s comparable to the Hemingway-Fitzgerald-Wolfe-Faulkner combine, they mean that none stand as solid and sharply cut against the waving backdrop of the shapeless age we inhabit. But these men, in spite of the bookish glamor attached to their names, were in the most radical sense *reporters* whose subjectmatter and vision was too hot or subtle or complicated or violent or lyrical or intractable or challenging for the massmedia of their period. They had to make up their own stories, based on what they observed and felt, and publish them as loners who leanly stood for personal integrity and subjective truth in opposition to the superficial "objective" journalism of their day. The exclusion of the deeper half of reality of oldtime journalism was very much at the bottom of the mystique of the American Novel as it has been sentimentalized in our time—that only in this medium could the real down-and-dirty story of the country and the nature of its people be told. If you were a prosewriter, there was almost a necessity to work in the form of fiction 20 or 30 years ago because only through it could you "tell" more than you could in journalism; by inventing characters with madeup names, put in imagined situations, you could reveal more about being a modern American than in any other way.

But why should the necessities of the 20s, 30s and 40s (although the fictional necessity was already fading by the end of the war) be right for today? The talk in New York about newspapermen like Breslin, Wolfe, Hamill, the perennial Kempton, Ralph J. Gleason of the San Francisco *Chronicle,* and after that journalists who write for weekly or monthly publications like Nat Hentoff, Jack Newfield ("The immediacy of TV has created the opening for this kind of writing"), John Wilcock, Allen Katzman, Richard Goldstein, Gay Talese, Barbara Long, Michael C. D. Macdonald, Gail Sheehy, Brian O'Doherty, Paul Krassner, Sid Bernard, Gene Lees, Lawrence Lipton, Saul Maloff, Jack Kroll, Warren Hincle, Roger Kahn, Albert Goldman, etc., is where the immediate interest and excitement lies. The freshness of these writers, first the daily newspapermen, then the weekly journalists, then the monthly essayists and social observers—include here half-time novelists like Paul Goodman, Harvey Swados, Mailer, Susan Sontag, John Clellon Holmes—is that they are using the eyes and ears that American novelists used 30 years ago upon a uniformly fantastic public reality that millions of people must cope with daily. A current of appreciation flows between their audience and what they have to say; they are "needed" in an acute, shit-cutting way that novelists no longer seem to be, if only because of the time-gap between real action out on the streets and fiction; it is only when the novelists gives us a deeper vision of this evidence before our eyes—like Heller with *Catch-22* or Selby with *Last Exit to Brooklyn*—that the naked individual imagination seems as pertinent as it once was, because it extends our understanding.

With present law what it is, Selby and Heller would have been jailed or murdered by their unforgiving subjects if they wrote their true names and deeds in the same way that they fictionalized them. And John Barth might be expelled from the human race (or at least his university professorship) for his view of it. But in 1967 that is the only practical justification for "fictionalizing"—if it says something that can't possibly be said otherwise. And with the accelerating frankness and freedom of expression that journalists demand today—they are perhaps the most disciplined literary rebels of our time because of their mature sense of fact, the moral radar because they are situated out in front and become the altered senses for the rest of us—how much *has* to be fictionalized? Reality itself has become so extravagant in its contradictions, absurdities, violence, speed of change, science-fictional technology, weirdness and constant unfamiliarity, that just to match what is with accuracy takes the conscientious reporter into the realms of the Unknown—into what used to be called "the world of the imagination."

And yet THAT is the wild world we all live in today when we just try to play it straight.

If living itself often seems more and more like a nonstop LSD trip—"illogical, surrealistic, and mad" as the 50-year-old Ralph Gleason keeps saying in his nuttily misnamed "On The Town" column in the San Francisco *Chronicle*—what fertile new truths can most fiction writers tell us about a reality that has far outraced them at their own game? How can they compete with the absurd and startling authorship of each new hour? It becomes a diminished echo, the average serious good novel today; but the average sharp piece of New Journalism can at present never become an echo because it keeps moving into this new universe of unreality and exposing it with the zest that Sinclair Lewis once used to tear the hide off Main Street. A new generation of authority-suspicious newspapermen can only take so much repression and traditional burying of what they know to be true before ripping up clichés in the face of a new scene; no one is in the professional position to see and communicate as much as the daily reporter, and yet up to now he has been handcuffed by the much-used and abused journalistic slogan, "good taste," which until the 60s left the most alive writing in a U.S. newspaper story on the copydesk floor. If I am covering a story about a Washington politician found dead in a screw-a-minute 43d St. hotel with a spade hooker, and I want to write about it truthfully, I have to mention details that would have offended my mother and father (dead these 35 years) because emotionally they couldn't handle this information. Newspapers, geared to the broadest readership of all publications, use to cater to people like my mother and father and yours, and such stories—prostitution, miscegenation, homosexuality, suicide, psychosis among well-known people, etc.—were edited or whitewashed so that the middleclass public could continue its hypocritical idealism in spite of facts which were quite different.

Then, during the first 40 years of this century in America, it was only a minority of the fiction writers, playwrights (practically none before O'Neill) and poets among the users of words who broke this conspiracy of public lying and attempted to show things for what they were. There was a pragmatic reason for our Stephen Cranes, Dreisers, O'Neills, Djuna Barneses, Faulkners, Hemingways. They were necessary if one wanted to know how creatures like oneself actually lived, suffered and died. Hollywood, slick magazines, radio—as well as newspapers—demanded by their cynical manufacture of safe good cheer, Protestant wish-fulfillment and the cleaning-up of evidence that a few brave maniacs of hairy expression take up the burden for all.

But this neat division between purity and compromise doesn't exist any longer—obviously. The current generation brought up under the huge umbrella of the massmedia doesn't despise the sellout aspects of the bigtime action as we 40-and-over puritans did because of our conditioning. As McLuhan suggests, the massmedia are an extension of the rock generation's nervous system—newspapers, movies, TV, radio, records, tapes, every device of communication which reaches millions of people—and it is inconceivable that they are going to romanticize (as we did) the power of a "fine" novel that sells 1500 copies in the wake of the communications hurricane on which they were suckled. No, they want to make it in the public media that this country since World War II has revved up to such a colossal pitch; but they want to do it on the terms that the former generation once thought of only for poetry, novels and serious plays—with total integrity; and right now a struggle for power is going on between the technicians who invented and the advertisers who capitalized on these octopal massmediums and the young visionaries (who might have been novelists 30 years ago) presently using them as hotlines of communication. But it is still the Word, written, spoken, sung, the very Word that has been the most significant instrument for men throughout history, it is that Word as conveyor of reality which is at the heart of this tug of war and through which a new and broader conception of literature is being shaped.

Does the book-reverencing literary critic or any other stubborn protector of the unsacred past realize that Lord Buckley, Lennie Bruce and Mort Sahl, Joan Baez, Buffie St. Marie and Bob Dylan, users of pop forms like nightclub comedy and folkrock preaching, have cut into the serious American literary man's ground by using the massmedia to make knifing comment of needed immediacy?

And does the Harvard doctor of letters recognize that a Jimmy Breslin or Pete Hamill, two cocky Irish parochial-school boys off the greater New York streets, are using that traditional literary doormat, the newspaper, to get to reality-through-language much more quickly than is done through books?

Sure they do; but they don't know quite how to handle it.

As you doubtless know, Matthew Arnold called 19th-century journalism "literature [written] in a hurry," a famous phrase that until now has reflected the sense of utilitarianism and literary inferiority felt by most journalists when they compared themselves to "writers." In Manhattan newspaper (and weekly magazine) shops you'll find veterans who spit on their work and automatically say that the importance of today's newspaper is to provide the wrapper for a smelly flounder tomorrow. The movie-portraits are for real, folks: no one is more snottily and superficially cynical about both reality and writing than the old-time, ex-alcoholic, security-obsessed newspaper grandad whom you'll run into on the overnight rewrite desk of a New York paper. He drools about Mencken or Hemingway or James Gould Cozzens, but it never crosses his mind that he could have done comparable work within the limits of his own job; from his point of view newspapering is merely Grinding It Out under the humbling restrictions of time, space, subject-matter and childishly basic English; he thinks newspaper work "ruins your prose" and any idea that every story—even an obituary—can be interpreted, shaded, significantly woven, carrying a human center and an implicit judgment on experience, has long since been shut out in the empty night of unthought while grandad figures out new ways to pad the overtime sheet.

But this hard-guy-with-soul-of-mush attitude, this fatalistic accept-ance and sneering embrace of the Grub Street rhythm of newspapering, is the dying style of a generation who looked at literature through the intimidated eyes of being "hacks," as they saw themselves, or "clerks of fact" as Pete Hamill has beautifully but it; selfmocking errand boys without a grain of conviction, carrying into print the latest fart of some celebrity of politics, entertainment or high (low) finance and being embittered because the Name was up there in lights that they helped plug in while they were condemned to doing white collar porter work in the cityroom. Traditionally, the average cityside newspaperman was a machine, a phone-bully, a sidewalk-buttonholer, a privacy-invader, a freebie-collector and not a writer at all—he had a formula for processing his information (much of it dumped on him by publicity men) and was not encouraged to depart from it. It is no wonder at all that the combination of what he saw—and the reporter has entré into every doorway of life without exception if he chooses to use it—coupled with the injunction not to express it produced that style of the Big Sneer which gave him his uniqueness as an American type. But underneath the cocked fedora and the rest of the so-called glamor crust you could find a man who thought of himself as a failure by the worldly standards pounded into his being by his work—money, achievement and status.

Newspaper offices were known in the trade as being comfortable, in-the-know flophouses where losers came to trickle out their lives; alcoholics floated on the assurance of seniority granted them by the once-righteous power of the American Newspaper Guild and those who weren't alcoholics floated just the same, notching up Army-style credits and cautious little nesteggs against the last winter of enfeeblement and the final smirk. The idea that they might be frontrunners snaring and interpreting reality as it broke before their eyes would have been a joke to the majority of these putdown experts who envied the stars on the world stage that they covered, but never conceived that they them-selves were in the position to make history and not merely record it.

But this lock on the imagination of the old cigar-chewing bigots—and their young imitators who snipe and curse at easy targets to prove that they are really in The Business—in no way deterred the balling sense of opportunity felt by a nuclear-goosed generation of newcomers now in their 30s (Breslin, Wolfe, Hamill, Gay Talese, Alfred G. Arono-witz, Dick Schaap, Eliot Fremont-Smith, Larry Merchant, Kenneth Gross, Vincent Canby, Mike Royko, Nicholas von Hoffman, etc.) and the two intransigent standouts 49 and 50 respectively (Murray Kempton and Ralph J. Gleason) who realized in differing ways what could be done within the dulling graveyard of a newspaper. Certainly there had been great inspirations in the profession only recently dead or played out: Heywood Broun (admired by Gleason), Westbrook Pegler (ditto for Kempton, Hamill and Wolfe in spite of W.P.'s politics), H. L. Mencken ("a favorite," Wolfe), Damon Runyon, Jimmy Cannon and even Walter Winchell (the last two hugely appreciated by Hamill for their language and Cannon in particular for his jazzy literary flair). But most of these older writers, however superpro in the daily journalism of their day, hit their high moments with the "crusading" approach that has been the essence of the American newspaper religion since Lincoln Steffens. If the large majority of professional reporters and editors of news have developed a protective sneer to cope with the stuffed urinal of human avarice, weakness and folly into which they've been dunked, the minority of newsmen whose names stand out from the past have always had their moral indignation heightened and made sharply eloquent by what they've been exposed to.

It commands one's respect, this unique kind of moral courage, and it is central to the oldfashioned idea of the press as watchdog to the community—more often a capped-tooth watchdog, unfortunately—but it is not at the heart of the style that lies waiting for the total reporters of the immediate future. This new style or revolution in reportorial values—which can be seen in varying part in Breslin (the novelistic fullness of his recreation of reality); Wolfe (the rhythmic montage of disjointed contemporary phenomena); Hamill (sophisticated realism which brings an urban snarl to bear on the absurdity of what he covers); Kempton (an elegance of mind and irony trained on the soiled collar of events); Gleason (his unkidding notion that the world today is insane and his enthusiastic tubthumping for popular avantgardists who can cut a path to the future)—goes far beyond the public role of pointing a finger at specific fraud or deceit, which has usually been the American journalist's finest hour from Steffens to Pegler. It rather points the finger at Self (both the writer's and the reader's) in relation to the World Out There; it concerns the *whole man*—the acting out in print, as Hamill intuitively senses on certain stories, of the subjective being as it collides with objective happenings. A good example would be the vulgarity and possibly the evil of Johnson's 1966 Asian tour as seen through Hamill's personal eyes (". . . a non-event") and then communicated to a public of half a million or more people through the *New York Post*. If the New Journalist is the outrider for news of reality itself—since we live in an age where the interaction between public events and private response is becoming the whole mortal show for everyone, the anonymous as well as the notorious, all of whom live under the threat of each new day's surprises—then it should be clear why the specific villain-baiting of a Pegler or, occasionally, Kempton is a cowboy-and-Indians game compared to the infinity of inner and outer space that the newspaperman has now inherited. When the New Journalist goes out to cover a story today he is handling nothing less than the time in which he lives; no matter how trivial his story, if his frame of reference is broad as well as acute, he can bring to bear upon it his own fate as a riddled modern man and relate it to the similarly riddled lives of his readers. It is no longer the mere formal outlines of an experience that we expect from a Beslin, Wolfe or Hamill, but its entire quality, overtones and undertones, in a word the "saturation reporting" (Wolfe's phrase) that we used to get from novelists but now need daily to understand the untrustworthy world in which our own small destinies are being negotiated.

This need to know our fate may be more intense than ever before— the "officialese" of which Orwell contemptuously spoke has grown thicker and demands immediate translation if men's minds are not to be permanently blown by impenetrable doubletalk—but the literary elite in this country has long shied away from American journalism in its crass or bulldog-edition actuality. Truman Capote, upon the publication of *In Cold Blood*, took great strenuous pains to distinguish what he was doing (and did very fastidiously well) from what the unelegant New Journalists were attempting to do every day on cheaper paper; their stuff was "just journalism," while his was "Art," dig?

But was it art in the most profound sense, which entails great risk, a new point of view, and above all the conviction to change the world to your way of seeing?

With the division of literary labor between the truckdrivers and the high princes of words—so common in our country for the last 25 or 30 years—the university, the abstract novel (Barth, Hawkes, Sontag, etc.) and literary theory have claimed the more refined or at least better-trained minds while it has been left to the guy next door to wade into the enormous literary problem of trying to tell the whole truth in the newspapers. Wolfe, 36 is a Yale Ph.D. in American Studies—true; but Breslin, Hamill and Gleason never graduated from college (Hamill, the 32-year-old whizkid, never even finished highschool) and Kempton apprenticed for what is currently the most mandarin style in daily journalism by being a grubby assistant labor reporter. These men learned by writing under the pinched code, the brutal deadlines and the unflinching pragmatism that characterizes all newspaper work; now— suddenly—the literary doors of their profession have been kicked wider open than at any time in the past and they have been catapulted into becoming spokesmen whose role and responsibility to truth has grown enormously. It is not unfair to say that as writers they are more pertinent to this time of permanent crisis than eight- or nine-tenths of the straight literary figures who read them regularly every afternoon and then patronize them in the evening over cocktails.

And yet—if one could undo years of aloofness, fear, luxurious introspection, sheltered alienation, university tenure, all the proud and wanly smiling snobbery that went with being a Serious American Writer of this period just ending—what better place for truly significant prose than the daily newspaper? Why shouldn't it seem the most logical place in the world for writers who teethed on fictional naturalism-realism to test their concepts of reality upon alive characters and report their findings to a huge captive audience that has to listen merely to get the news? More than that, the journalistic stakes are a thousand times greater than in the past because of the immediate reverberation of an original statement today: if Harrison Salisbury shook up the Washington power machine with his *Times* reports of the U.S. bombing of Hanoi, and William Manchester threw a gritty bomb into national Democratic politics with his imaginative and yet factual portrait of *The Death of a President,* consider the power that our most eminent prosewriters could finally wield in their own country by being the most sensitive conductors for news, the transmitters of verbal reality for the nation.

Power is not to be despised in a culture that uses it like America; and writers, too long the weak and easily seduced stepsisters of the national family, are not to be condemned for craving it; when H. L. Mencken said of this country and Poe, "They let him die like a cat up an alley," he was merely concretizing the hatred that literary artists have always felt in this society toward a citizenry that has found them ornamental rather than basic. But what could possibly be more basic than this generation's Poes and Melvilles (or Ray Bradburys and Saul Bellows) applying their vision of existence to news as it breaks, reading individual values into what is now a mechanical UPI report, interviewing Johnson as candidly as Brady photographed Lincoln, finally breaking out of the profound isolation of their heads and gambling their point of view on its involvement with events? News has *become* reality for millions in this Age of Journalism; but what if this reality—a mine disaster, a nuclear test under the Atlantic, the death of Anne Sheridan, a Harlem riot—were to be both accurately and originally reported at the very moment that it happened (not three months later in *Esquire*) by an Ellison or Kerouac or Jean Stafford?

Suppose, in other words, that our very understanding of what is news was to be overturned by coverage that made uncommon human sense as well as giving the facts, and that our information was no longer flat and closed but fully dimensional and open—as open and revealing and meaningful as the writer could make it by pouring his spirit into a union with the event? Have you ever stopped to think what could happen to the programmed newspaper reader if the finest literary talent was used to illuminate even the most perfunctory one-paragraph auto accident out on the street, how the closed or small mind would be jolted by a recognition of the mutual dependence of all our beings if a writer who cared interposed the warm hands of his typewriter between the cold statistic and fact-numbed heads?

The "symbolic action" that literary artists have frustratedly contented themselves with in a book would take a radical turn into monumental real action if they could dominate the sources of news, not only in the press, but in the fields of spoken literature as well—radio and TV. To be novelistically engaged with one's time in the manner of the early Malraux, Koestler and Camus is an undeniably great modern primitive example; but now there is a real chance that the masses' version of truth, of what is, of reality itself, can be revolutionized if men and women of proven artistic vision step down from their rickety subjective towers of private being into the communal ego-socialism of daily journalism. The artificial split between literature and journalism has never seemed more beside the point as the human race staggers into the last third of the 20th century not really knowing if it will survive or what kind of freaky mutation it will become. If such encompassing selfdoubt has eaten into the race, isn't it inevitable that it has affected literature as well, that the so-called transiency of journalism is no greater than the seeming irrelevance of most literature today? The step from a Jimmy Breslin "up" to Robert Lowell is no longer the giant step that it might once have been when newspapermen stood in awe of honest-to-gawd writers; the best of the New Journalists are already writers equal in their way to any of their generation; but the step from Robert Lowell "down" to a Jimmy Breslin has implications that go beyond writing to the possibility of the artist affecting the reaction to events themselves by shaping the significance of daily reality with his own hand. Since the New Journalists have gone like pilgrims to literature to learn the techniques for being faithful to all that they alone are in a postion to see, and sweat daily to give added dimension, nuance, perspective and insight to their stories, let once-mighty literature swallow its whitefaced pride and give its mythic propensity to journalism—the *de facto* literature of our time.

If this seems like a special curving of the truth, consider the fact that at least 30 underground weekly and biweekly newspapers— from such respectable rebels as *The Village Voice* and the Los Angeles *Free Press* to the latest *Rat* and *Oracle*—have sprung up like bayonets in the last 10 (especially the last five) years out of the same soil that once produced little magazines. Why have they replaced their toy tiger literary counterparts, or if not entirely replaced them at least been the strongest force for "new," "different," "anti-Establishment" writing in the last decade? Because (in essence) it is only by usurping the public sources of news or actuality itself—and newspapers more than any other publications have always been the official version of reality, the standard of sanity, the middleclass scale of justice—that fedup young writer-journalists can advance a totally liberated view of the contemporary scene which challenges the entire range of assumed belief. A strictly imaginative work, with no literal frame of reference outside the author's mind, can be evaded today by a defensive reader who claims it has no relevance for him; but how can any reader evade a typical L.A. *Free Press* story about two cops who were found stashing marijuana for themselves which they had confiscated from some young hippies during a bust?

If the 20s were the supreme time of technical experimentation and overthrow in literature, the 60s are the comparably radical decade for the revolution in human values and the breakout in personal lifestyle; it is no longer the pure "literary" expression of the private mind that grabs most of us, but rather the outspoken public declaration of the most hidden energies of individual being that have been crouching in the shadowed doorways of our society. Artists, and especially literary artists, have in the American past been the belligerent walking illustrations of a totally free individualism because they would have suffocated without it; now an entire generation of longhaired Flower Children (to use one of their fast-changing names) has taken over what were essentially the antiauthority attitudes of bohemia and the artist; and the significant word-artist himself—with exceptions like Allen Ginsberg, Mailer, Bobby Dylan, bruised but embracing Jewish sprinters who can identify more easily with change than their more stolid gentile brethren—has stood uncomfortably tight in the face of the very journalistic-pop forms where he is most vitally needed.

For the last two centuries the "artist" has been the martyred holy man of secular life (Van Gogh's ear, Nietzsche's insanity, Rimbaud's cancer, Kafka's tortured mental maze, Melville's polar isolation, the list of hell's angels is endless) whose vision of perfection ate into existence long after he was wiped out of the race as a blot on his generation. This was the reverse fairytale formula, that the genuine artist be despised or misunderstood during his lifetime and then haunt men forever from the untouchable penthouse of his grave. Anyone who presumed to be an artist took ironic comfort from the grotesque set of groundrules laid down over the last 150 or so years and prepared himself for misery with his work as his only blessing. The contemporary artist knew too much about the lives of his bitched breed in the past to expect anything different for himself; "silence, exile and cunning," as defiant Jimmy Joyce put it, were his strategems, his work was the goal, and death was his friend because they lived on such close bedroom terms until the work was done. This, in a bitter nutshell, was the diagram of most outstanding literary artists' earthly existences.

But the world has changed and the diagram must change also.

The lonely dedication of the artist pursuing his chimera no longer impresses us the same way it once did; it is a still-shot from the past, as out of style as a silent movie; mankind's survival itself, mentally as well as bodily, morally as well as materially, hopefully as well as horribly, seems much more crucial as we survey the climate of emergency that clobbers each heart and soul alive right now. The "heroic" suffering and victimization that once distinguished the artist's life has now become the property of everyman-everywoman in this bleak Beckett playlet called Existence, 67. The neurotic torments that once clung to the artist as to a lover are now democratically spread among the race at large. In other words, the artist's lot has now become the human predicament, they are one, and any artist worth the name must now attempt to solve the riddle of the world because there is no longer any other theme worthy of him. But if his torment is now shared by mankind at large, his imagination and the ability to make it tangible are still his alone until every human alive learns the trick of converting pain into fame; and they have not yet been used upon the mass-communication techniques (journalism in all its forms) that dominate this period as he has formerly used them on traditional stuff like clay, canvas and book.

Art, the most independently truthful form of human expression, was not made to hang on a wall or hide in a page but rather to show duller eyes a more radical and truer version of the life slipping through each generation's hands. For it to speak today—rather than be spoken about and not experienced at full volume—it has ready and waiting for it the outlets of press and electronic journalism; and on the reading-listening-looking end it has for the first time in history a mass audience of millions of individuals milling about in noisy desperation, confused, nihilistic, disgusted with political leadership, laughing at formal religion, looking for jet-age prophets from Tim Leary to Bobby Kennedy who will lead them to the promised land.

But modern literature and art has always been both more truthful and more accurate in its views of the contemporary crisis than any charismatic personality who flits across the headlines.

It has been the most penetrating and significant use of the imagination known to us.

Isn't the time ready for its potential to explode into the center of society via the journalism that has become literature for the majority, so that the human animal may finally know what the "landmine" (the word is Isaac Babel's) of great writing can do when it is hooked up to presidents, governments, prices, power, murder and every variety of antiparadise that clubs us daily? What is art for, from Shakespeare to Terry Southern, if not to transform the world by example? And if Camus is coming to be recognized as much as a spiritual leader as a rare, exalted writer, why can't we begin to see that the word-artist in action in this time *is* the new spiritual leader by virtue of the technological wings that carry what he says?

Jimmy Breslin, cute anti-intellectual that he can be, nevertheless once wrote a disgusted *WJT* column about the misuse and abuse of language by a machine politician who had the indifferent arrogance to run for office when he could barely speak intelligibly. Norman Mailer wrote an equivalent piece about the prose of LBJ. What they were saying is that language is the clearest indication of being in this time and that they as writers were by their own words superior to the individuals they were writing about. But the implications extend beyond Breslin, Mailer or any single individual; what it seems to mean practically speaking is that articulate leadership has been thrust upon the writer in the authority-empty vacuum of this period; and the most effective way for it to reveal itself is in the mirror of the daily press where the intelligence and sensibility of the writer-artist can carve the very news of the world each day into a revelation that will in turn *act* upon history instead of merely reflect it. What else but actuality itself—and what is "news" in our time but actuality compressed to a boil?—is worthy of the revolutionary insight that the literary artist has always lined his work with but until now has never had the chance to impose upon the literalness of events? It is no longer just a technical literary question of "fiction" vs. "nonfiction"; the essential issue that creative writers are now faced with is whether the literary-artistic imagination is to be effective in creating a new view of reality that does not shrink the potentialities of being alive in the 20th century or whether it is to be wasted on a pen-pusher's slavish copying of a life which is no longer tolerable according to the deepest needs of men.

If writers of the highest rank were to invade journalism as did E. E. Cummings, James Agee and Albert Camus—and if multimedia journalists are in fact the current "arbiters of reality" (the phrase was first used by a reporter on *The New York Times* about his own paper)—then it is inevitable that the original point of view of the creative writer trained upon people and events in the news has to open new possibilities in every newspaper reader's concept of the real and hence in himself. We writers, in other words, now have the long-sought-for opportunity to basically influence men's conception of the present and therefore the immediate future on a *mass scale* if we are not too proud or frail to enter into the race for moral and ideological power through our daily work in the massmedia. If we show our gossamer stuff in the day-to-day terms that the majority of people understand—pitting our skill and insight and freshness of seeing against the raw acts of this time that make up the news and undermining today's brute reality by our verbal projection of a greater one—there is nothing that can stop our long-postponed hunger for ultimate justice and beauty here and now from becoming a radical force in the life-game. If you agree with me that art is the only untainted vision of truth that can be made demonstrable to all, and if we demonstrate it upon the daily happenings of this time in the journalistic forms that capsulize authenticity for the terse minds of modern men, how can we dodge the fact that we have an alchemic dream within our grasp—the transmutation of base everyday matter into the poem of life?

We may well be on the doorstep of that necessary leap into the future when the world itself is literally governed by art, or truth made manifest, because there is nowhere else to turn and everywhere to go.

Sincerely,
Seymour Krim

Truman Capote: An Interview

GEORGE PLIMPTON

Why did you select the particular subject matter of murder; had you previously been interested in crime?

Not really, no. During the last years I've learned a good deal about crime, and the origins of the homicidal mentality. Still, it is a layman's knowledge and I don't pretend to anything deeper. The motivating factor in my choice of material—that is, choosing to write a true account of an actual murder case—was altogether literary. The decision was based on a theory I've harbored since I first began to write professionally, which is well over 20 years ago. It seemed to me that journalism, reportage, could be forced to yield a serious new art form: the "nonfiction novel," as I thought of it. Several admirable reporters—Rebecca West for one, and Joseph Mitchell and Lillian Ross—have shown the possibilities of narrative reportage; and Miss Ross, in her brilliant *Picture*, achieved at least a nonfiction novella. Still, on the whole, journalism is the most underestimated, the least explored of literary mediums.

George Plimpton's interview with Truman Capote was published in the *New York Times Book Review* on January 16, 1966, shortly after the appearance of *In Cold Blood*. Plimpton's own excursions into participatory journalism include *Paper Lion, Out of My League,* and *Mad Ducks and Bears.*

Why should that be so?

Because few first-class creative writers have ever bothered with journalism, except as a sideline, "hackwork," something to be done when the creative spirit is lacking, or as a means of making money quickly. Such writers say in effect: Why should we trouble with factual writing when we're able to invent our own stories, contrive our own characters and themes?—journalism is only literary photography, and unbecoming to the serious writer's artistic dignity.

Another deterrent—and not the smallest—is that the reporter, unlike the fantasist, has to deal with actual people who have real names. If they feel maligned, or just contrary, or greedy, they enrich lawyers (though rarely themselves) by instigating libel actions. This last is certainly a factor to consider, a most oppressive and repressive one. Because it's indeed difficult to portray, in any meaningful depth, another being, his appearance, speech, mentality, without to some degree, and often for quite trifling cause, offending him. The truth seems to be that no one likes to see himself described as he is, or cares to see exactly set down what he said and did. Well, even I can understand that—because I don't like it myself when I am the sitter and not the portraitist: the frailty of egos!—and the more accurate the strokes, the greater the resentment.

When I first formed my theories concerning the nonfiction novel, many people with whom I discussed the matter were unsympathetic. They felt that what I proposed, a narrative form that employed all the techniques of fictional art but was nevertheless immaculately factual, was little more than a literary solution for fatigued novelists suffering from "failure of imagination." Personally, I felt that this attitude represented a "failure of imagination" on their part.

Of course a properly done piece of narrative reporting requires imagination!—and a good deal of special technical equipment that is usually beyond the resources—and I don't doubt the interests—of most fictional writers: an ability to transcribe verbatim long conversations, and to do so without taking notes or using tape-recordings. Also, it is necessary to have a 20/20 eye for visual detail—in this sense, it is quite true that one must be a "literary photographer," though an exceedingly selective one. But, above all, the reporter must be able to empathize with personalities outside his usual imaginative range, mentalities unlike his own, kinds of people he would never have written about had he not been forced to by encountering them inside the journalistic situation. This last is what first attracted me to the notion of narrative reportage.

It seems to me that most contemporary novelists, especially the Americans and the French, are too subjective, mesmerized by private demons; they're enraptured by their navels, and confined by a view that ends with their own toes. If I were naming names, I'd name myself among others. At any rate, I did at one time feel an artistic need to escape my self-created world. I wanted to exchange it, creatively speaking, for the everyday objective world we all inhabit. Not that I'd never written nonfiction before—I kept journals, and had published a small truthful book of travel impressions: *Local Color*. But I had never attempted an ambitious piece of reportage until 1956, when I wrote *The Muses Are Heard*, an account of the first theatrical cultural exchange between the U.S.A. and the U.S.S.R.—that is, the "Porgy and Bess" tour of Russia. It was published in *The New Yorker*, the only magazine I know of that encourages the serious practitioners of this art form. Later, I contributed a few other reportorial finger-exercises to the same magazine. Finally, I felt equipped and ready to undertake a full scale narrative—in other words, a "nonfiction novel."

How does John Hersey's Hiroshima *or Oscar Lewis's* Children of Sanchez *compare with "the nonfiction novel?"*

The Oscar Lewis book is a documentary, a job of editing from tapes, and however skillful and moving, it is not creative writing. *Hiroshima* is creative—in the sense that Hersey isn't taking something off a tape-recorder and editing it—but it still hasn't got anything to do with what I'm talking about. *Hiroshima* is a strict classical journalistic piece. What is closer is what Lillian Ross did with *Picture*. Or my own book, *The Muses Are Heard*—which uses the techniques of the comic short novel.

It was natural that I should progress from that experiment, and get myself in much deeper water. I read in the paper the other day that I had been quoted as saying that reporting is now more interesting than fiction. Now that's *not* what I said, and it's important to me to get this straight. What I think is that reporting can be made *as* interesting as fiction, and done *as* artistically—underlining those two "as"es. I don't mean to say that one is a superior form to the other. I feel that creative reportage has been neglected and has great relevance to 20th-century writing. And while it can be an artistic outlet for the creative writer, it has never been particularly explored.

What is your opinion of the so-called New Journalism—as it is practiced particularly at The Herald Tribune?

If you mean James Breslin and Tom Wolfe, and that crowd, they have nothing to do with creative journalism—in the sense that I use the term—because neither of them, nor any of that school of reporting, have the proper fictional technical equipment. It's useless for a writer whose talent is essentially journalistic to attempt creative reportage, because it simply won't work. A writer like Rebecca West—always a good reporter—has never really used the form of creative reportage because the form, by necessity, demands that the writer be completely in control of fictional techniques—which means that, to be a good creative reporter, you have to be a very good fiction writer.

Would it be fair to say, then, since many reporters use nonfiction techniques—Meyer Levin in Compulsion, *Walter Lord in* A Night to Remember *and so forth—that the nonfiction novel can be defined by the degree of the fiction skills involved, and the extent of the author's absorption with his subject?*

Compulsion is a fictional novel suggested by fact, but no way bound to it. I never read the other book. The nonfiction novel should not be confused with the documentary novel—a popular and interesting but impure genre, which allows all the latitude of the fiction writer, but usually contains neither the persuasiveness of fact nor the poetic altitude fiction is capable of reaching. The author lets his imagination run riot over the facts! If I sound querulous or arrogant about this, it's not only that I have to protect my child, but that I truly don't believe anything like it exists in the history of journalism.

What is the first step in producing a "nonfiction novel?"

The difficulty was to choose a promising subject. If you intend to spend three or four or five years with a book, as I planned to do, then you want to be reasonably certain that the material will not soon "date." The content of much journalism so swiftly does, which is another of the medium's deterrents. A number of ideas occurred, but one after the other, and for one reason or another, each was eventually discarded, often after I'd done considerable preliminary work. Then one morning in November, 1959, while flicking through *The New York Times,* I encountered, on a deep-inside page, this headline: Wealthy Farmer, 3 of Family Slain.

The story was brief, just several paragraphs stating the facts: A Mr. Herbert W. Clutter, who had served on the Farm Credit Board during the Eisenhower Administration, his wife and two teen-aged children, had been brutally, entirely mysteriously, murdered on a lonely wheat and cattle ranch in a remote part of Kansas. There was nothing really exceptional about it; one reads items concerning multiple murders many times in the course of a year.

Then why did you decide it was the subject you had been looking for?

I didn't. Not immediately. But after reading the story it suddenly struck me that a crime, the study of one such, might provide the broad scope I needed to write the kind of book I wanted to write. Moreover, the human heart being what it is, murder was a theme not likely to darken and yellow with time.

I thought about it all that November day, and part of the next; and then I said to myself: Well, why not *this* crime? The Clutter case. Why not pack up and go to Kansas and see what happens? Of course it was a rather frightening thought!—to arrive alone in a small, strange town, a town in the grip of an unsolved mass murder. Still, the circumstances of the place being altogether unfamiliar, geographically and atmospherically, made it that much more tempting. Everything would seem freshly minted—the people, their accents and attitudes, the landscape, its contours, the weather. All this, is seemed to me, could only sharpen my eye and quicken my ear.

In the end, I did not go alone. I went with a lifelong friend, Harper Lee. She is a gifted woman, courageous, and with a warmth that instantly kindles most people, however suspicious or dour. She had recently completed a first novel *To Kill a Mockingbird*, and, feeling at loose ends, she said she would accompany me in the role of assistant researchist.

We traveled by train to St. Louis, changed trains and went to Manhattan, Kan., where we got off to consult Dr. James McClain, president of Mr. Clutter's alma mater, Kansas State University. Dr. McClain, a gracious man, seemed a little nonplussed by our interest in the case; but he gave us letters of introduction to several people in western Kansas. We rented a car and drove some 400 miles to Garden City. It was twilight when we arrived. I remember the car-radio was playing, and we heard: "Police authorities, continuing their investigation of the tragic Clutter slayings, have requested that anyone with pertinent information please contact the Sheriff's office. . . ."

If I had realized then what the future held, I never would have stopped in Garden City. I would have driven straight on. Like a bat out of hell.

What was Harper Lee's contribution to your work?

She kept me company when I was based out there. I suppose she was with me about two months altogether. She went on a number of interviews; she typed her own notes, and I had these and could refer to them. She was extremely helpful in the beginning, when we weren't making much headway with the town's people, by making friends with the wives of the people I wanted to meet. She became friendly with all the churchgoers. A Kansas paper said the other day that everyone out there was so wonderfully cooperative because I was a famous writer. The fact of the matter is that not one single person in the town had ever heard of me.

How long did it take for the town to thaw out enough so that you were accepted and you could get to your interviewing?

About a month. I think they finally just realized that we were there to stay—they'd have to make the best of it. Under the circumstances, they were suspicious. After all, there was an unsolved murder case, and the people in the town were tired of the thing, and frightened. But then after it all quieted down—after Perry and Dick were arrested —that was when we did most of the original interviews. Some of them went on for three years—though not on the same subject, of course. I suppose if I used just 20 per cent of all the material I put together over those years of interviewing, I'd still have a book two thousand pages long!

How much research did you do other than through interviews with the principals in the case?

Oh, a great deal. I did months of comparative research on murder, murderers, the criminal mentality, and I interviewed quite a number of murderers—solely to give me a perspective on these two boys. And then crime. I didn't know anything about crime or criminals when I began to do the book. I certainly do now! I'd say 80 per cent of the research I did I have never used. But it gave me such a grounding that I never had any hesitation in my consideration of the subject.

What was the most singular interview you conducted?

I suppose the most startled interviewee was Mr. Bell, the meat-packing executive from Omaha. He was the man who picked up Perry and Dick when they were hitchhiking across Nebraska. They planned to murder him and then make off with his car. Quite unaware of all this, Bell was saved, as you'll remember, just as Perry was going to smash in his head from the seat behind, because he slowed down to pick up another hitchhiker, a Negro. The boys told me this story, and they had this man's business card. I decided to interview him. I wrote him a letter, but got no answer. Then I wrote a letter to the personnel manager of the meat-packing company in Omaha, asking if they had a Mr. Bell in their employ. I told them I wanted to talk to him about a pair of hitchhikers he'd picked up four months previously. The manager wrote back and said that they *did* have a Mr. Bell on their staff, but it was surely the *wrong* Mr. Bell since it was against company policy for employees to take hitchhikers in their cars. So I telephoned Mr. Bell and when he got on the phone he was very brusque: he said I didn't know what I was talking about.

The only thing to do was to go to Omaha personally. I went up there and walked in on Mr. Bell and put two photographs down on his desk. I asked him if he recognized the two men. He said, why? So I told him that the two were the hitchhikers he said he had never given a ride to, that they had planned to kill him and then bury him in the prairie—and how close they'd come to it. Well, he turned every conceivable kind of color. You can imagine. He recognized them all right. He was quite cooperative about telling me about the trip, but he asked me not to use his real name. There are only three people in the book whose names I've changed—his, the convict Perry admired so much (Willie-Jay he's called in the book), and also I changed Perry Smith's sister's name.

How long after you went to Kansas did you sense the form of the book? Were there many false starts?

I worked for a year on the notes before I ever wrote one line. And when I wrote the first word, I had done the entire book in outline, down to the finest detail. Except for the last part, the final dispensation of the case—that was an evolving matter. It began, of course, with interviews—with all the different characters of the book. Let me give you two examples of how I worked from these interviews. In the first part of the book—the part that's called "The Last to See Them Alive" —there's a long narration, word for word, given by the school teacher who went with the sheriff to the Clutter house and found the four bodies. Well, I simply set that into the book as a straight complete interview—though it was, in fact, done several times: each time there'd be some little thing which I'd add or change. But I hardly interfered at all. A slight editing job. The school teacher tells the whole story himself—exactly what happened from the moment they got to the house, and what they found there.

On the other hand, in that same first part, there's a scene between the postmistress and her mother when the mother reports that the ambulances have gone to the Clutter house. That's a straight dramatic scene—with quotes, dialogue, action, everything. But it evolved out of interviews just like the one with the school teacher. Except in this case I took what they had told me and transposed it into straight narrative terms. Of course, elsewhere in the book, very often it's direct observation, events I saw myself—the trial, the executions.

You never used a tape-recorder?

Twelve years ago I began to train myself, for the purpose of this sort of book, to transcribe conversation without using a tape-recorder. I did it by having a friend read passages from a book, and then later I'd write them down to see how close I could come to the original. I had a natural facility for it, but after doing these exercises for a year and a half, for a couple of hours a day, I could get within 95 per cent of absolute accuracy, which is as close as you need. I felt it was essential. Even note-taking artificializes the atmosphere of an interview, or a scene-in-progress; it interferes with the communication between author and subject—the latter is usually self-conscious, or an untrusting wariness is induced. Certainly, a tape-recorder does so. Not long ago a French literary critic turned up with a tape-recorder. I don't like them, as I say, but I agreed to its use. In the middle of the interview it broke down. The French literary critic was desperately unhappy. He didn't know what to do. I said, "Well, let's just go on as if nothing had happened." He said, "It's not the same. I'm not accustomed to listen to what you're saying."

You've kept yourself out of the book entirely. Why was that— considering your own involvement in the case?

My feeling is that for the nonfiction-novel form to be entirely successful, the author should not appear in the work. Ideally. Once the narrator does appear, he has to appear throughout, all the way down the line, and the I-I-I intrudes when it really shouldn't. I think the single most difficult thing in my book, technically, was to write it without ever appearing myself, and yet, at the same time, create total credibility.

Being removed from the book, that is to say, keeping yourself out of it, do you find it difficult to present your own point of view? For example, your own view as to why Perry Smith committed the murders.

Of course it's by the selection of what you choose to tell. I believe Perry did what he did for the reasons he himself states—that his life was a constant accumulation of disillusionments and reverses and he suddenly found himself (in the Clutter house that night) in a psychological cul-de-sac. The Clutters were such a perfect set of symbols for every frustration in his life. As Perry himself said, "I didn't have anything against them, and they never did anything wrong to me—the way other people have all my life. Maybe they're just the ones who had to pay for it." Now in that particular section where Perry talks about the reason for the murders, I could have included other views. But Perry's happens to be the one I believe is the right one, and it's the one that Dr. Satten at the Menninger Clinic arrived at quite independently, never having done any interviews with Perry.

I could have added a lot of other opinions. But that would have confused the issue, and indeed the book. I had to make up my mind, and move towards that one view, always. You can say that the reportage is incomplete. But then it has to be. It's a question of selection, you wouldn't get anywhere if it wasn't for that. I've often thought of the book as being like something reduced to a seed. Instead of presenting the reader with a full plant, with all the foliage, a seed is planted in the soil of his mind. I've often thought of the book in that sense. I make my own comment by what I choose to tell and how I choose to tell it. It is true that an author is more in control of fictional characters because he can do anything he wants with them as long as they stay credible. But in the nonfiction novel one can also manipulate: if I put something in which I don't agree about I can always set it in a context of qualification without having to step into the story myself to set the reader straight.

When did you first see the murderers—Perry and Dick?

The first time I ever saw them was the day they were returned to Garden City. I had been waiting in the crowd in the square for nearly five hours, frozen to death. That was the first time. I tried to interview them the next day—both completely unsuccessful interviews. I saw Perry first, but he was so cornered and suspicious—and quite rightly so—and paranoid that he couldn't have been less communicative. It was always easier with Dick. He was like someone you meet on a train, immensely garrulous, who starts up a conversation and is only too obliged to tell you *everything*. Perry became easier after the third or fourth month, but it wasn't until the last five years of his life that he was totally and absolutely honest with me, and came to trust me. I came to have great rapport with him right up through his last day. For the first year and a half, though, he would come just so close, and then no closer. He'd retreat into the forest and leave me standing outside. I'd hear him laugh in the dark. Then gradually he would come back. In the end, he could not have been more complete and candid.

How did the two accept being used as subjects for a book?

They had no idea what I was going to do. Well, of course, at the end they did. Perry was always asking me: Why are you writing this book? What is it supposed to mean? I don't understand why you're doing it. Tell me in one sentence why you want to do it. So I would say that it didn't have anything to do with changing the readers' opinion about anything, nor did I have any moral reasons worthy of calling them such—it was just that I had a strictly aesthetic theory about creating a book which could result in a work of art.

"That's really the truth, Perry," I'd tell him, and Perry would say, "A work of art, a work of art," and then he'd laugh and say, "What an irony, what an irony." I'd ask what he meant, and he'd tell me that all he ever wanted to do in his life was to produce a work of art. "That's all I ever wanted in my whole life," he said. "And now, what has happened? An incredible situation where I kill four people, and *you're* going to produce a work of art." Well, I'd have to agree with him. It was a pretty ironic situation.

Did you ever show sections of the book to witnesses as you went along?

I have done it, but I don't believe in it. It's a mistake because it's almost impossible to write about anybody objectively and have that person really like it. People simply do not like to see themselves put down on paper. They're like somebody who goes to see his portrait in a gallery. He doesn't like it unless it's overwhelmingly flattering— I mean the ordinary person, not someone with genuine creative perception. Showing the thing in progress usually frightens the person and there's nothing to be gained by it. I showed various sections to five people in the book, and without exception each of them found something that he desperately wanted to change. Of the whole bunch, I changed my text for one of them because, although it was a silly thing, the person genuinely believed his entire life was going to be ruined if I *didn't* make the change.

Did Dick and Perry see sections of the book?

They saw some sections of it. Perry wanted terribly much to see the book. I had to let him see it because it just would have been too unkind not to. Each only saw the manuscript in little pieces. Everything mailed to the prison went through the censor. I wasn't about to have my manuscript floating around between those censors— not with those Xerox machines going clickety-clack. So when I went to the prison to visit I would bring parts—some little thing for Perry to read. Perry's greatest objection was the title. He didn't like it because he said the crime wasn't committed in cold blood. I told him the title had a double meaning. What was the other meaning? he wanted to know. Well, that wasn't something I was going to tell him. Dick's reaction to the book was to start switching and changing his story, saying what I had written wasn't exactly true. He wasn't trying to flatter himself; he tried to change it to serve his purposes legally, to support the various appeals he was sending through the courts. He wanted the book to read as if it was a legal brief for presentation in his behalf before the Supreme Court. But you see I had a perfect control-agent—I could always tell when Dick or Perry wasn't telling the truth. During the first few months or so of inter- viewing them, they weren't allowed to speak to each other. They were in separate cells. So I would keep crossing their stories, and what correlated, what checked out identically, was the truth.

How did the two compare in their recounting of the events?

Dick had an absolutely fantastic memory—one of the greatest memories I have ever come across. The reason I know it's great is that I lived the entire trip the boys went on from the time of the murders up to the moment of their arrest in Las Vegas—thousands of miles, what the boys called "the long ride." I went everywhere the boys had gone, all the hotel rooms, every single place in the book, Mexico, Acapulco, all of it. In the hotel in Miami Beach I stayed for three days until the manager realized why I was there and asked me to leave, which I was only too glad to do. Well, Dick could give me the names and addresses of any hotel or place along the route where they'd spent maybe just half a night. He told me when I got to Miami to take a taxi to such-and-such a place and get out on the boardwalk and it would be southwest of there, number 232, and opposite I'd find two umbrellas in the sand which advertised "Tan with Coppertone." That was how exact he was. He was the one who remembered the little card in the Mexico City hotel room—in the corner of the mirror—that reads "Your day ends at 2 p.m." He was extraordinary. Perry, on the other hand, was very bad at details of that sort, though he was good at remembering conversations and moods. He was concerned altogether in the overtones of things. He was much better at describing a general sort of mood or atmosphere than Dick who, though very sensitive, was impervious to that sort of thing.

What turned them back to the Clutter house after they'd almost decided to give up on the job?

Oh, Dick was always quite frank about that. I mean after it was all over. When they set out for the house that night, Dick was determined, before he ever went, that if the girl, Nancy, was there he was going to rape her. It wouldn't have been an act of the moment —he had been thinking about it for weeks. He told me that was one of the main reasons he was so determined to go back after they thought, you know for a moment, they wouldn't go. Because he'd been thinking about raping this girl for weeks and weeks. He had no idea what she looked like—after all. Floyd Wells, the man in prison who told them about the Clutters, hadn't seen the girl in 10 years: it had to do with the fact that she was 15 or 16. He liked young girls, much younger than Nancy Clutter actually.

What do you think would have happened if Perry had faltered and not begun the killings? Do you think Dick would have done it?

No. There is such a thing as the ability to kill. Perry's particular psychosis had produced this ability. Dick was merely ambitious—he could *plan* murder, but not commit it.

What was the boys' reaction to the killing?

They both finally decided that they had thoroughly enjoyed it. Once they started going, it became an immense emotional release. And they thought it was funny. With the criminal mind—and both boys had criminal minds, believe me—what seems most extreme to us is very often, if it's the most expedient thing to do, the *easiest* thing for a criminal to do. Perry and Dick both used to say (a memorable phrase) that it was much easier to kill somebody than it was to cash a bad check. Passing a bad check requires a great deal of artistry and style, whereas just going in and killing somebody requires only that you pull a trigger.

There are some instances of this that aren't in the book. At one point, in Mexico, Perry and Dick had a terrific falling-out, and Perry said he was going to kill Dick. He said that he'd already killed five people—he was lying, adding one more than he should have (that was the Negro he kept telling Dick he'd killed years before in Las Vegas) and that one more murder wouldn't matter. It was simple enough. Perry's cliché about it was that if you've killed one person you can kill anybody. He'd look at Dick, as they drove along together, and he'd say to himself, Well, I really ought to kill him, it's a question of expediency.

They had two other murders planned that aren't mentioned in the book. Neither of them came off. One "victim" was a man who ran a restaurant in Mexico City—a Swiss. They had become friendly with him eating in his restaurant and when they were out of money they evolved this whole plan about robbing and murdering him. They went to his apartment in Mexico City and waited for him all night long. He never showed up. The other "victim" was a man they never even knew—like the Clutters. He was a banker in a small Kansas town. Dick kept telling Perry that sure, they might have failed with the Clutter score, but this Kansas banker job was absolutely for certain. They were going to kidnap him and ask for ransom, though the plan was, as you might imagine, to murder him right away.

When they went back to Kansas completely broke, that was the main plot they had in mind. What saved the banker was the ride the two boys took with Mr. Bell, yet another "victim" who was spared, as you remember, when he slowed down the car to pick up the Negro hitchhiker. Mr. Bell offered Dick a job in his meatpacking company. Dick took him up on it and spent two days there on the pickle line—putting pickles in ham sandwiches, I think it was—before he and Perry went back on the road again.

Do you think Perry and Dick were surprised by what they were doing when they began the killings?

Perry never meant to kill the Clutters at all. He had a brain explosion. I don't think Dick was surprised, although later on he pretended he was. He knew, even if Perry didn't, that Perry would do it, and he was right. It showed an awfully shrewd instinct on Dick's part. Perry was bothered by it to a certain extent because he'd actually done it. He was always trying to find out in his own mind why he did it. He was amazed he'd done it. Dick, on the other hand, *wasn't* amazed, *didn't* want to talk about it, and simply wanted to forget the whole thing: he wanted to get on with life.

Was there any sexual relationship, or such tendencies, between them?

No. None at all. Dick was agressively heterosexual and had great success. Women liked him. As for Perry, his love for Willie-Jay in the State Prison was profound—and it was reciprocated, but never consummated physically, though there was the opportunity. The relationship between Perry and Dick was quite another matter. What is misleading, perhaps, is that in comparing himself with Dick, Perry used to say how totally "virile" Dick was. But he was referring, I think, to the practical and pragmatic sides of Dick—admiring them because as a dreamer he had none of that toughness himself at all.

Perry's sexual interests were practically nil. When Dick went to the whorehouses, Perry sat in the cafes, waiting. There was only one occasion—that was their first night in Mexico when the two of them went to a bordello run by an "old queen," according to Dick. Ten dollars was the price—which they weren't *about* to pay, and they said so. Well, the old queen looked at them and said perhaps he could arrange something for less; he disappeared and came out with this female midget about 3 feet 2 inches tall. Dick was disgusted, but Perry was madly excited. That was the only instance. Perry was such a little moralist after all.

How long do you think the two would have stayed together had they not been picked up in Las Vegas? Was the odd bond that kept them together beginning to fray? One senses in the rashness of their acts and plans a subconscious urge to be captured.

Dick planned to ditch Perry in Las Vegas, and I think he would have done so. No, I certainly don't think this particular pair wanted to be caught—though this is a common criminal phenomenon.

How do you yourself equate the sort of petty punk that Detective Alvin Dewey feels Dick is with the extraordinary violence in him—to "see hair all over the walls"?

Dick's was definitely a small scale criminal mind. These violent phrases were simply a form of bragging meant to impress Perry, who *was* impressed, for he liked to think of Dick as being "tough." Perry was too sensitive to be "tough." Sensitive. But himself able to kill.

Is it one of the artistic limitations of the nonfiction novel that the writer is placed at the whim of chance? Suppose, in the case of In Cold Blood, *clemency had been granted? Or the two boys had been less interesting? Wouldn't the artistry of the book have suffered? Isn't luck involved?*

It is true that I was in the peculiar situation of being involved in a slowly developing situation. I never knew until the events were well along whether a book was going to be possible. There was always the choice, after all, of whether to stop or go on. The book could have ended with the trial, with just a coda at the end explaining what had finally happened. If the principals had been uninteresting or completely uncooperative, I could have stopped and looked elsewhere, perhaps not very far. A nonfiction novel would have been written about any of the other prisoners in Death Row—York and Latham, or especially Lee Andrews. Andrews was the most *subtly* crazy person you can imagine—I mean there was just one thing wrong with him. He was the most rational, calm, bright young boy you'd ever want to meet. I mean *really* bright—which is what made him a truly awesome kind of person. Because his one flaw was, it didn't bother him *at all* to kill. Which is quite a trait. The people who crossed his path, well, to his way of thinking, the best thing to do with them was just to put them in their graves.

What other than murder might be a subject suitable for the non-fiction novel?

The other day someone suggested that the break-up of a marriage would be an interesting topic for a nonfiction novel. I disagreed. First of all, you'd have to find two people who would be willing—who'd sign a release. Second, their respective views on the subject-matter would be incoherent. And third, any couple who'd subject themselves to the scrutiny demanded would quite likely be a pair of kooks. But it's amazing how many events *would* work with the theory of the nonfiction novel in mind—the Watts riots, for example. They would provide a subject that satisfied the first essential of the nonfiction novel—that there is a timeless quality about the cause and events. That's important. If it's going to date, it can't be a work of art. The requisite would also be that you would have had to live through the riots, at least part of them, as a witness, so that a depth of perception could be acquired. That event, just three days. It would take years to do. You'd start with the family that instigated the riots without ever meaning to.

With the nonfiction novel I suppose the temptation to fictionalize events, or a line of dialogue, for example, must at times be overwhelming. With In Cold Blood *was there any invention of this sort to speak of—I was thinking specifically of the dog you described trotting along the road at the end of a section on Perry and Dick, and then later you introduce the next section on the two with Dick swerving to hit the dog. Was there actually a dog at that exact point in the narrative, or were you using this habit of Dick's as a fiction device to bridge the two sections?*

No. There was a dog, and it was precisely as described. One doesn't spend almost six years on a book, the point of which is factual accuracy, and then give way to minor distortions. People are so suspicious. They ask, "How can you reconstruct the conversation of a dead girl, Nancy Clutter, without fictionalizing?" If they read the book carefully, they can see readily enough how it's done. It's a silly question. Each time Nancy appears in the narrative, there are witnesses to what she is saying and doing—phone calls, conversations, being overheard. When she walks the horse up from the river in the twilight, the hired man is a witness and talked to her then. The last time we see her, in her bedroom, Perry and Dick themselves were the witnesses, and told me what she had said. What is reported of her, even in the narrative form, is as accurate as many hours of questioning, over and over again, can make it. All of it is reconstructed from the evidence of witnesses—which is implicit in the title of the first section of the book—"The Last to See Them Alive."

How conscious were you of film techniques in planning the book?

Consciously, not at all. Subconsciously, who knows?

After their conviction, you spent years corresponding and visiting with the prisoners. What was the relationship between the two of them?

When they were taken to Death Row, they were right next door to each other. But they didn't talk much. Perry was intensely secretive and wouldn't ever talk because he didn't want the other prisoners —York, Latham, and particularly Andrews, whom he despised—to hear anything that he had to say. He would write Dick notes on "kites" as he called them. He would reach out his hand and zip the "kite" into Dick's cell. Dick didn't much enjoy receiving these communications because they were always one form or another of recrimination—nothing to do with the Clutter crime, but just general dissatisfaction with things there in prison and . . . the people, very often Dick himself. Perry'd send Dick a note: "If I hear you tell another of those filthy jokes again I'll kill you when we go to the shower!" He was quite a little moralist, Perry, as I've said.

It was over a moral question that he and I had a tremendous falling-out once. It lasted for about two months. I used to send them things to read—both books and magazines. Dick only wanted girlie magazines—either those or magazines that had to do with cars and motors. I sent them both whatever they wanted. Well, Perry said to me one time: "How could a person like you go on contributing to the degeneracy of Dick's mind by sending him all this 'degenerate filthy' literature?" Weren't they all sick enough without this further contribution towards their total moral decay? He'd got very grand talking in terms that way. I tried to explain to him that I was neither his judge nor Dick's—and if that was what Dick wanted to read, that was *his* business. Perry felt that was entirely wrong—that people had to fulfill an obligation towards moral leadership. Very grand. Well, I agree with him up to a point, but in the case of Dick's reading matter it was absurd, of course, and so we got into such a really serious argument about it that afterwards, for two months, he wouldn't speak or even write to me.

How often did the two correspond with you?

Except for those occasional fallings-out, they'd write twice a week. I wrote them both twice a week all those years. One letter to the both of them didn't work. I had to write them both, and I had to be careful not to be repetitious, because they were very jealous of each other. Or rather, Perry was terribly jealous of Dick, and if Dick got one more letter than he did, that would create a great crisis. I wrote them about what I was doing, and where I was living, describing everything in the most careful detail. Perry was interested in my dog, and I would always write about him, and send along pictures. I often wrote them about their legal problems.

Do you think if the social positions of the two boys had been different that their personalities would have been markedly different?

Of course there wasn't anything peculiar about Dick's social position. He was a very ordinary boy who simply couldn't sustain any kind of normal relationship with anybody. If he had been given $10,000, perhaps he might have settled into some small business. But I don't think so. He had a very natural criminal instinct towards everything. He was oriented towards stealing from the beginning. On the other hand, I think Perry could have been an entirely different person. I really do. His life had been so incredibly abysmal that I don't see what chance he had as a little child except to steal and run wild.

Of course, you could say that his brother, with exactly the same background, went ahead and became the head of his class. What does it matter that he later killed himself. No, it's there—it's the fact that the brother *did* kill himself, in spite of his success, that shows how really awry the background of the Smiths' lives were. Terrifying. Perry had extraordinary qualities, but they just weren't channeled properly—to put it mildly. He was really a talented boy in a limited way—he had a genuine sensitivity—and, as I've said, when he talked about himself as an artist, he wasn't really joking at all.

You once said that emotionality made you lose writing control— that you had to exhaust emotion before you could get to work. Was there a problem with In Cold Blood, *considering your involvement with the case and its principals?*

Yes, it was a problem. Nevertheless, I felt in control throughout. However, I had great difficulty writing the last six or seven pages. This even took a physical form: hand paralysis. I finally used a typewriter—very awkward as I always write in longhand.

Your feeling about capital punishment is implicit in the title of the book. How do you feel the lot of Perry and Dick should have been resolved?

I feel that capital crimes should all be handled by Federal Courts, and that those convicted should be imprisoned in a special Federal prison where, conceivably, a life-sentence could mean, as it does not in state courts, just that.

Did you see the prisoners on their final day? Perry wrote you a 100-page letter that you received after the execution. Did he mention that he had written it?

Yes, I was with them the last hour before the execution. No, Perry did not mention the letter. He only kissed me on the cheek, and said, "Adios, amigo."

What was the letter about?

It was a rambling letter, often intensely personal, often setting forth his various philosophies. He had been reading Santayana. Somewhere he had read "The Last Puritan," and had been very impressed by it. What I really think impressed him about me was that I had once visited Santayana at the Convent of the Blue Nuns in Rome. He always wanted me to go into great detail about that visit, what Santayana had looked like, and the nuns, and all the physical details. Also, he had been reading Thoreau. Narratives didn't interest him at all. So in his letter he would write: "As Santayana says—" and then there'd be five pages of what Santayana *did* say. Or he'd write: "I agree with Thoreau about this. Do you?"— then he'd write that he didn't *care* what I thought, and he'd add five or ten pages of what he agreed with Thoreau about.

The case must have left you with an extraordinary collection of memorabilia.

My files would almost fill a whole small room, right up to the ceiling. All my research. Hundreds of letters. Newspaper clippings. Court records—the court records almost fill two trunks. There were so many Federal hearings on the case. One Federal hearing was twice as long as the original court trial. A huge assemblage of stuff. I have some of the personal belongings—all of Perry's because he left me everything he owned; it was miserably little, his books, written in and annotated; the letters he received while in prison . . . not very many . . . his paintings and drawings. Rather a heart-breaking assemblage that arrived about a month after the execution. I simply couldn't bear to look at it for a long time. I finally sorted everything. Then, also, after the execution, that 100-page letter from Perry got to me. The last line of the letter—it's Thoreau, I think, a paraphrase, goes, "And suddenly I realize life is the father and death is the mother." The last line. Extraordinary.

What will you do with this collection?

I think I may burn it all. You think I'm kidding? I'm not. The book is what is important. It exists in its own right. The rest of the material is extraneous, and it's personal, what's more. I don't really want people poking around in the material of six years of work and research. The book is the end result of all that, and it's exactly what I wanted to do from it.

Detective Dewey told me that he felt the case and your stays in Garden City had changed you—even your style of dress . . . that you were more "conservative" now, and had given up detachable collars. . . .

Of course the case changed me! How could anyone live through such an experience without it profoundly affecting him? I've always been almost overly aware of the precipice we all walk along, the ridge and the abyss on either side; the last six years have increased this awareness to an almost all-pervading point. As for the rest—Mr. Dewey, a man for whom I have the utmost affection and respect, is perhaps confusing comparative youth (I was 35 when we first met) with the normal aging process. Six years ago I had four more teeth and considerably more hair than is now the case, and furthermore I lost 20 pounds. I dress to accommodate the physical situation. By the way, I have never worn a detachable collar.

What are you going to work on now?

Well, having talked at such length about the nonfiction novel, I must admit I'm going to go on to write a *novel,* a straight novel, one I've had in mind for about 15 years. But I will attempt the nonfiction form again—when the time comes and the subject appears and I recognize the possibilities. I have one very good idea for another one, but I'm going to let it simmer on the back of my head for awhile. It's quite a step—to undertake the nonfiction novel. Because the amount of work is enormous. The relationship between the author and all the people he must deal with if he does the job properly—well, it's a full 24-hour-a-day job. Even when I wasn't working on the book, I was somehow involved with all the characters in it—with their personal lives, writing six or seven letters a day, taken up with their problems, a complete involvement. It's extraordinarily difficult and consuming, but for a writer who tries, doing it all the way down the line, the result can be a unique and exciting form of writing.

What has been the response of readers of In Cold Blood *to date?*

I've been staggered by the letters I've received—their quality of sensibility, their articulateness, the compassion of their authors. The letters are not fan letters. They're from people deeply concerned about what it is I've written about. About 70 per cent of the letters think of the book as a reflection on American life—this collision between the desperate, ruthless, wandering, savage part of American life, and the other, which is insular and safe, more or less. It has struck them because there is something so awfully inevitable about what is going to happen: the people in the book are completely beyond their own control. For example, Perry wasn't an evil person. If he'd had an chance in life, things would have been different. But every illusion he'd ever had, well, they all evaporated, so that on that night he was so full of self-hatred and self-pity that I think he would have killed *some*body—perhaps not that night, on the next, or the next. You can't go through life without ever getting anything you want, ever.

At the very end of the book you give Alvin Dewey a scene in the country cemetery, a chance meeting with Sue Kidwell, which seems to synthesize the whole experience for him. Is there such a moment in your own case?

I'm still very much haunted by the whole thing. I have finished the book, but in a sense I *haven't* finished it: it keeps churning around in my head. It particularizes itself now and then, but not in the sense that it brings about a total conclusion. It's like the echo of E. M. Forster's Malabar Caves, the echo that's meaningless and yet it's there: one keeps hearing it all the time.

Documentary Narrative as Art: William Manchester and Truman Capote

DONALD PIZER

Documentary narrative, as I understand the term, is that kind of prose work in which the author creates the impression that he has investigated the circumstances of an actual event and that he can prove the validity of his account of the event. Although documentary narrative has always been a major literary form (*Anabasis* is an early example), it has had its greatest vogue in recent years. The reasons for its current popularity are not yet entirely clear, but interest in the form seems to be related to the broad movement in contemporary art toward expression which attempts to communicate the "feel" of the actual: concrete painting, *cinema vérité*, and the living theatre. Whatever the causes for the popularity of documentary narrative, most major events— from sensational crimes to public disasters, including those of war— are soon followed by works which attempt to recreate these events. A few writers are absorbed enough in the form as form to use it to portray a "minor" occurrence. Lillian Ross's *Picture*, for example, is about the filming of *The Red Badge of Courage*. In works of this kind the form itself has an interest equal or superior to the subject. But in most instances—as in John Hersey's *Hiroshima* or Cornelius Ryan's *The*

Donald Pizer's essay appeared in the *Journal of Modern Literature*, September, 1971. He is a professor of English at NewComb College, Tulane University, and the author of several scholarly works, including *Realism and Naturalism in Nineteenth-Century American Literature* and *The Novels of Frank Norris*.

Longest Day—the choice of documentary narrative as a form seems to reflect the author's belief that the event itself is of such importance that it requires a form which intrinsically and immediately demonstrates the authenticity of the writer's account of that event.

I would like to discuss two modern examples of documentary narrative: William Manchester's *The Death of a President* and Truman Capote's *In Cold Blood*. The advantage of these examples, besides their familiarity, is that they are documentary narratives which deal with the similar subject of a murder in sufficiently dissimilar ways to permit a useful introductory discussion of the form. My choice of these works, however, results in the omission of two important kinds of documentary narrative. The first such omission, exemplified by Norman Mailer's *The Armies of the Night*, focuses on the writer himself as the major participant in the event. It brings documentary narrative close to autobiography, or vice versa. The second kind of work omitted is that in which the author depends entirely on first-person narrative, usually culled from tapes, as in Oscar Lewis' books. Both of these forms are documentary narrative, but they are special kinds and require separate discussion.

One way to begin a study of *The Death of a President* and *In Cold Blood* as documentary narratives is to consider briefly—before taking up each work in detail—the somewhat specialized meanings that "documentary," "narrative," and "art" have in connection with these and similar works. By "documentary" I mean that the writer tries to create an effect of circumstantiality, either by including verifiable documents and quotation or by appearing to do so. His emphasis on seemingly verifiable detail—the names of people and places, the full listing of the objects in a room or the contents of a suitcase, and much direct quotation—achieves the effect of documentation whether or not he includes or appends his sources. By "narrative" I mean that the writer pays exceptional attention to chronology. All narrative, of course, relies to some degree on the passage of time as a structural device. But in documentary narrative the writer is recurrently and explicitly exact about events in relation to time. His narrative technique thus contributes to the effect of documentary authenticity. By placing in immediate juxtaposition two of the seemingly most verifiable aspects of experience—objects and the movement of the clock—the writer seeks to persuade us that his account is accurate and authentic, since its principal components can be checked. Some documentary narratives include time-charts, a device which has the effect of making even more "solid"—that is, observable—the relationship between objects and time, a relationship which in essence is the event itself. By "art" I mean that the author imposes theme upon the event portrayed by means of his selection, arrangement, and emphasis of the details of his documentation and of his narrative. His theme may be merely an interpretation of what occurred during the particular event he is describing or it may be an interpretation of a large phase of experience which the event illustrates. But as in most literary works, verisimilitude is ultimately a means towards an end rather than an end in itself, although the author of documentary narrative may seek to suggest the contrary.

I

William Manchester's *The Death of a President: November 20-November 25, 1963* is documentary narrative at its most documentary. Both publisher and author note the extensive research involved in the project. "Operating out of headquarters in the National Archives," the dust jacket announces, "for two years [Manchester] worked twelve to fifteen hours a day, conducting a major historical investigation throughout Texas and elsewhere, accumulating forty-five volumes and portfolios of transcribed tapes, shorthand documents and exhibits. . . ." Manchester himself is almost absolute in his claims to authenticity. He tells us that he ignored as too limited the principal published work on the assassination, the twenty-six volume Warren Report. Rather, he relied on notes of participants, on his own interviews, and on his personal investigation. "Every scene described in the book was visited," he notes in his Foreword. "I crawled over the roof of the Texas School Book Depository and sat in Oswald's sixth-floor perch. I rode his Dallas bus, watch in hand." * His research has been so complete that "every statement, every fact, every quotation in my manuscript could be followed by a citation" (p. xi), and to substantiate this claim he appends a nineteen-page bibliography.

The book itself immediately calls attention to its documentary character by its chronological subtitle and by its end papers, one of which is a time-chart of the events of November 20-25, the other a map of the Kennedy funeral procession on November 25. Within the volume there are four additional, more detailed time-charts (Oswald's movements, the flight of Air Force One, etc.) and eight pages of maps and plans (the mortorcade route, a floor plan of Parkland Hospital's emergency area, a plan of Air Force One).

The text of *The Death of a President* is divided into four parts. The first, "Prologue: Lancer," is a brief account of the events of November 20 and of the background of Kennedy's Texas trip. The last, "Epilogue: Legend," summarizes events after November 25. Most of the work consists of "Book One: Charcoal" (the trip to Texas and

---

* William Manchester, *The Death of a President: November 20-November 25, 1963* (Harper & Row, 1967), p. xi. Subsequent references in the text are to this edition.

Kennedy's death) and "Book Two: Castle" (the return to Washington and events between November 22 and 25). Within these books, Manchester uses two basic narrative techniques, techniques which I call "simultaneous narrative" and "sequential narrative." The first is reserved for specific moments of great importance or great emotional impact: 12:21 P.M. on November 22 (nine minutes before the assassination), the assassination, certain moments during the return flight of Air Force One, dawn in Washington on November 23, and so on. In narrating the events of these moments, Manchester stops time in the sense that he describes (usually briefly) the activities or responses of many individuals at a precise moment. If the moment is one of action, he produces in effect a series of still photographs (or at most a montage of short newsreel clips) of those participating in the action, photographs which "freeze" the event within a variety of angles of vision and which therefore aid in clarifying the event as action. If the moment is one of emotional response, he produces a spectrum incorporating the possibilities within that response. Manchester's second and more frequently used narrative technique is that of overlapping but forward moving sequences of action. "At 4:40 P.M. Thursday, while the Kennedys were deplaning in Houston . . . , Lee Oswald had ended his day's work in Dallas . . ." (pp. 93-94). Manchester had already described the Kennedys' Houston activities after deplaning, but he refers back to a specific moment in that narrative to begin an account of Oswald's activities which will extend in time beyond that of his Kennedy narrative. Manchester is thus able to shift radically and frequently from one narrative segment to another because his constant reference to narrative moments that have already occurred creates a structure of interlocking narratives capable of supporting a great many disparate narratives. *The Death of a President* combines a forward moving chronological center and many narrative threads which are, in a sense, joined at that center. Unlike simultaneous narrative, sequential narrative is a common narrative device, though it is seldom used as fully or as elaborately as in documentary narrative of this kind.

The Death of a President is thus documentary narrative both in its overt display of documentary props (maps, time-charts, bibliographies) and in its complete dependence upon time as a narrative center. The book is documentary narrative in yet another way. Manchester uses some 350,000 words to recount the events of six days. This length derives principally from his commitment to reproduce as fully as possible the six days as verifiable detail. Since much of this detail is fundamentally trivial, even in the context of the assassination of a president, its effect, on the one hand, is to diffuse the impact and blur the significance of the assassination. On the other hand, Manchester's attention to detail supports the impression of authenticity in the work as a whole. The assumption of most readers is that a researcher who knows the location of each TV set in the White House during late November, 1963, must know the vital facts concerning the assassination itself.

The Death of a President has a number of major themes, some intended by Manchester, others emerging unintentionally out of his techniques as a documentary narrator. His most obvious theme is the combined one of "accuracy" and "honesty." He wishes to dispel the myths that have arisen about the Kennedy assassination and he wishes to deal fairly with the antagonists in the misunderstandings and disputes which followed the assassination. Manchester's techniques of exhaustive detail and of multiple point of view (the action viewed or responded to by many individuals) succeed in establishing this theme. That is, whatever the "true" circumstances of Kennedy's death or of the ill feeling which followed it, we feel that Manchester's account is reliable.

Manchester also seeks to capture the significance of the Kennedy assassination—not only how it occurred but why it occurred and what meaning its occurrence has. In this instance, however, Manchester's documentary narrative techniques hinder rather than advance his aim. Although he permits himself over six hundred pages to describe the events of six days, his reliance on time as a narrative center requires him to move comparatively swiftly from event to event. He foregoes any analysis in depth of the major figures in the assassination or of the social and political world of late 1963, since such analysis would weaken the priority of chronology. His attempt to introduce significance into his account is thus borne by his prose style, a style associated with popular news weeklies which seek to combine reportage and meaning for those who must read while they run. Manchester's prose abounds with titillating detail, with loaded metaphor, and with breezy one-sentence characterization. The effect of this method can be seen in the portrayal of Oswald. Rather than undertake a full discussion of Oswald, a task requiring both insight and considerable space, Manchester dismisses Oswald as relatively unimportant and finds a substitute villain in the more colorful and swiftly characterized eccentric right-wing world of Dallas. The meaning of the Kennedy assassination which emerges out of *The Death of a President* has a fairy-tale simplicity. Kennedy, the White Knight, is destroyed by the Evil Dragon of Hate, whereupon his Lady bears her grief nobly and his former retainers quarrel. There are subsidiary themes—for example, the criticism of the secret service and the Dallas police—but they, too, are neither moving nor profound. There is no way of knowing whether Manchester's triviality of mind is responsible for his technique of the swiftly told trivial detail, or whether this technique makes impossible any depth of insight or analysis. Whatever the cause, the effect of authenticity in the work is thus limited to events as external events.

Fairy tales are often charming, but their charm derives in part from a childlike view of experience.

There is a third, probably unconscious, theme in *The Death of a President*. Manchester comments at one point that "The events of November 22, 1963, were synchronic" (p. 277). On another occasion he notes that the ambulance carrying Kennedy's body to Bethesda Naval Hospital passed the White House at the precise moment that Johnson landed there via helicopter (p. 403). The first comment states a truism, the second is a minor illustration of the truism. Together the two remarks reflect Manchester's assumption that the chronological relationship between events is significant enough for this relationship to be in itself relevant to the cause and meaning of events. I call this assumption a theme because it arises out of and is inseparable from the impact of Manchester's technique. Although he set out to write a "plot" (a narrative with meaning), he has written a "story" (a narrative in which the relationship of events to time is assumed to have meaning). My terms are borrowed from E. M. Forster's well-known distinction. Forster comments that "the king died and then the queen died" is a story but that "the king died, and then the queen died of grief" is a plot. Manchester attempted to produce a documentary narrative with meaning. In his own words, he has incorporated into the book his "judgments" and "opinions." That is, he has reached certain conclusions about the events he is portraying, conclusions which should cause *The Death of a President* to resemble "the king died, and then the queen died of grief." But his technique, despite his conclusions, has been that of a story, "the king died and then the queen died." The impression of many readers that Manchester inadequately understands the events he is depicting stems not only from his unconvincing overt comments about these events but from his implicit theme that there is an inherent significance in the chronological relationship between events.

In all, *The Death of a President* illustrates many of the characteristics of a particular kind of documentary narrative. It communicates successfully both the external reality of certain sensational events and the emotional impact of these events on particular individuals—in this instance, the events of the moments immediately before, during, and after Kennedy's assassination. It fails, however, as a book, which is to say that it fails as successful art. This failure, as I have attempted to show, results principally from Manchester's inability to realize that his form is incapable of producing significant themes. Perhaps the most obvious and instructive example of Manchester's weakness in this regard is the lack of proportion in the work. Kennedy's assassination occurs approximately a quarter of the way through the book. Most of the last half of *The Death of a President* is an excruciating anti-climax during which the reader cries out for the foreshortening which an artist would bring to the narrative. But Manchester's form has committed him to lengthy accounts of arguments about White House office furniture, and so the possible relevant themes of the book—the causes, meaning, and effect of the assassination—are replaced by synchronic detail.

II

Although the subtitle of *In Cold Blood* is *A True Account of a Multiple Murder and Its Consequences,* Capote's documentary apparatus is much less evident than Manchester's. Capote's explicit claim to authenticity is confined to one sentence in his Acknowledgments: "All the material in this book not derived from my own observation is either taken from official records or is the result of interviews with the persons directly concerned, more often than not numerous interviews conducted over a considerable period of time." * The book lacks a bibliography, time-charts, and notes. Nevertheless, *In Cold Blood* leaves the impression of documentary authenticity. One way in which Capote gains this effect is by his extensive use of special kinds of "official records"—letters, diaries, written statements, and even an article in a learned journal—records which he identifies and quotes verbatim. His most important technique of documentary authenticity, however, is that of direct quotation from the "numerous interviews conducted over a considerable body of time." Perhaps half of *In Cold Blood* consists of such quotation in the form of monologue, dialogue, or snatches of conversation within authorial comment and summary narrative.

There is little doubt that Capote chose to rely on direct quotation of speech because he believed in the intrinsic merits of this technique. But it is worth noting that much of this quotation is in the form of conversation with an anonymous "journalist" or "acquaintance," a technique associated with the *New Yorker* "profile." *In Cold Blood* was apparently written specifically for initial publication in the *New Yorker,* and there is probably some connection between this intended outlet and Capote's recognition of the adaptability of a stylistic convention of *New Yorker* nonfiction. The advantages of this particular form of documentation, both in the *New Yorker* and in Capote's book, is that it not only creates an effect of authenticity but also permits theme to be introduced implicity rather than explicitly. Theme emerges out of what characters reveal about themselves in conversation and out of what other people say about them. The author appears to be an impartial chronicler of conversation; thus the themes present in his selection and arrangement of what has been said have a docu-

---

* Truman Capote, *In Cold Blood: A True Account of a Multiple Murder and Its Consequences* (Random House, 1965), p. 185. Subsequent references in the text are to this edition.

mentary impact—that is, they appear to be inseparable from the "truth" of reportage rather than to be "merely" authorial interpretation.

Capote is specific about time and dates, but *In Cold Blood* is in one sense a more relaxed chronological narrative than *The Death of a President*. "Time present" is approximately six months—from November 14, 1959, to early April, 1960—rather than six days. (Capote does extend the narrative to the execution of the murderers in April, 1965, but in greatly foreshortened form.) In another sense, however, Capote's narrative technique is considerably tighter, since it is more elaborately and consciously a means of thematic expression than is Manchester's.

Capote manipulates the chronolgy of narration in three ways. The first and most obvious is a modified form of what I called sequential narrative in *The Death of a President*. Of the four parts of *In Cold Blood*, the first three rely heavily on this form of narrative and the last uses it obliquely. Capote's sequential narrative differs from Manchester's in that each part of *In Cold Blood* is confined to two principal narrative threads, a technique which results in a powerful forward thrust in each part. In Part I, "The Last to See Them Alive," we follow Perry Smith and Dick Hickock on the one hand and the Clutter family on the other as each group moves through the day of November 14, 1959, toward the murder that night. The sequential narrative is broken down into short sections, each linked to the other not only by the forward moving time scheme but by our awareness that the two groups are drawing together geographically and that they will soon meet climactically. Capote's sequential narrative thus achieves narrative suspense as well as documentary authenticity, a combination present in Manchester only in those brief passages interconnecting Oswald's and Kennedy's actions on November 22. Parts II and III of *In Cold Blood* use dual sequential narrative in a slightly more diffuse form. Smith and Hickock remain one narrative thread, but the other is initially "all" Holcomb and Garden City, then the agents of the Kansas Bureau of Investigation, and finally Alvin Dewey, the KBI officer who personifies the perplexed outrage of both populace and police. Whereas Part I juxtaposed unsuspecting victims and approaching murderers for narrative climax, Parts II and III juxtapose fleeing criminals—and pursuing police. Part IV contains a less obvious dual sequential narrative. The technique is present, however, in the form of Smith and Hickock, who exist in time, and the "Corner" or gallows, their destiny, which is timeless. By continuously stressing the presence of the gallows, both as physical entity and as a presentiment in the minds of the prisoners, Capote's creates an effect similar to that in the first three parts—the inexorable coming together of two groups or units separated spacially but fated to converge. Capote's narrowing down of sequential narrative to two threads throughout *In Cold Blood* implies a theme quite different from that achieved by Manchester's juxtaposition of numerous synchronic events. Manchester's technique (though not his overt comments) suggests that coincidence governs human affairs whereas Capote's implies that a shaping destiny controls all life despite our unawareness of that destiny as it fulfills itself—a theme similar to that of Thomas Hardy in "The Convergence of the Twain."

Capote's second major narrative technique is also a more thematically forceful and relevant version of a technique used by Manchester. In his account of an event, Manchester occasionally recounts the background of that event. Because of his "quick-time" form, these excursions into the past are usually hurried and summary. Capote, however, often uses a present-time event primarily as a means of exploring the past. An obvious and even hackneyed example of this method occurs in Part II. The section opens in a Mexico City hotel room. Smith and Hickock have run out of money and are about to leave for California. While Dick sleeps, Perry Smith worries about the 2 P.M. check-out time and his two boxes of mementos that he must ship rather than take with him. As Perry looks through his boxes, several of the mementos are described in detail. Each represents an important phase of Perry's life, and each expands our awareness of his past and therefore our knowledge of his character. The section closes with some "present-time" having elapsed—it is now almost 2 P.M.—but the purpose of the section has been to create an impression of character rather than to narrate an event. It is also significant that the most important mementos are documents which are quoted verbatim: Tex John Smith's "A History of My Boy's Life," a letter by Perry's sister, Willie-Jay's "Impressions I Garnered from the Letter," and passages from Perry's diary. Thus the entire section is superficially documentary narrative at its most obvious: the event narrated occurs at an exact moment in time, and it relies heavily on verifiable documents. Yet Capote's purpose in the section, and in similar though less obvious passages in the book as a whole, is less to instill in the reader a belief in the verifiability of the event than to establish the authenticity of an intangible and unverifiable reality, the mind and heart of Perry Smith.

Capote's third major narrative technique is not present in *The Death of a President* or, indeed, in most documentary narratives. Works in this form usually maintain a consecutive narrative. That is, though an author may backtrack to pick up a narrative thread and though he may include certain material antedating the opening of his narrative (as Capote does in the Mexico City hotel room scene), he establishes in general a forward moving narrative without any important hiatuses. This respect for chronological order is, of course, related to the effect of authenticity, to the impression that events are being narrated as they indeed occurred. Capote, however, postpones narrating *the* major event of *In Cold Blood*, the murder of the Clutters, until he comes to the capture of Dick and Perry some months after the murder. There appears to be some justification for this narrative order in the fact that the Kansas police and the residents of Holcomb and Garden City know little about the murder until Dick and Perry are apprehended. But Capote had chosen early in the book, when describing the journey of Dick and Perry to Holcomb, to include experiences and thoughts of the two men which were known to him and to others only after their capture. Capote is completely omniscient throughout *In Cold Blood*, which means that he has wrenched the narrative of the murders out of chronological sequence for reasons other than respect for the limited awareness of a particular person or group.

Capote's most obvious reason for restructuring narrative order is to maintain suspense. Since we know from the beginning of the book that Dick and Perry commit the murders, we do not share the mystification of the residents of the area. But like the people of Holcomb and Garden City, we do not know the "what went on" and "why" of the night of November 14 in the Clutter house, and we wait expectantly for their disclosure. Capote's second and most important reason for manipulating the order of narrative is closely related to the thematic center of *In Cold Blood*—that is, to the character of Perry Smith. As we follow Perry and Dick in Parts II and III, Perry becomes more and more the focus of our attention. Gradually we are made aware of the complexity and depth of his character, in contrast to Dick, who is indeed the "small-time chiseler" that Alvin Dewey finally considers him. We learn of Perry's alcoholic mother and authoritarian father, of his miserable boyhood in homes and asylums, and of his thwarted artistic ambitions and his impossible child-like dreams. Perry has lived a loveless, frustrated life, and he has finally come to center his distrust and hatred on his family and particularly on his father, who "never gave me a chance." "I hate you," he tells his sister, speaking of those in his family who have had more opportunities than he or who he believes have obstructed his ambitions, "all of you—Dad and everybody" (p. 185). The effect of Capote's full dramatization of Perry's life is to make acceptable Dewey's response to a résumé of that life soon after Perry's capture. "He found it possible to look at the man beside him without anger—with, rather, a measure of sympathy—for Perry Smith's life had been no bed of roses but pitiful, an ugly and lonely progress toward one mirage and then another" (p. 246).

When Dick and Perry confess at the close of Part III, and when further disclosures about the murder are made early in Part IV, we are for the first time fully aware of the events of the night of November 14. We are, I think, initially surprised by the revelation of "what went on"—that Perry killed first Mr. Clutter and then the other three members of the family—for it was Dick who, before the murders, had spoken continuously of no witnesses and of the pleasures of killing. But we quickly realize that Capote's concentration on Perry throughout Parts II and III has anticipated the "what went on" by dramatizing the "why." In Part IV Perry's own self-analysis and the commentary of professional psychiatrists make explicit this "why." Perry killed Mr. Clutter (the initial murder, requiring the death of the rest of the family) for a number of reasons of increasing depth—because Dick's hesitancy and cowardice at the crucial moment was one more betrayal; because Mr. Clutter, a rich, imposing, and self-possessed man, was yet another figure of authority; and because Perry's hate of a "world" that had mistreated and misunderstood him could cause him to commit an "instinctive" murder, a murder which appears to be in cold blood because it is superficially emotionless. As Perry tells Donald Cullivan, " 'I was sore at Dick. The tough brass boy. But it wasn't Dick. Or the fear of being identified. I was willing to take that gamble. And it wasn't because of anything the Clutters did. They never hurt me. Like other people. Like people have all my life. Maybe it's just that the Clutters were the ones who had to pay for it' " (p. 290).

The principal themes of *In Cold Blood* can be described as a series of distinctions between what appears to be true and what is true. These distinctions or ironic relationships emerge out of Capote's narrative form; in other words, they are inseparable from Capote's technique of characterizing Perry Smith in depth before revealing his actions at the Clutter home. The most important thematic irony present in the book is that involved in its title. Although we assume initially that the Clutters are murdered in cold blood, we come to realize that Perry's actions on the night of November 14 stem from deep, uncontrollable emotions despite his surface dispassionateness while committing these acts. The title bears a second ironic meaning. Most of Part IV is devoted to the trial, imprisonment, and execution of Perry and Dick. In Capote's depiction of these events, the state of Kansas (representing "society") becomes the principal agent of death in cold blood because of its insistence upon an-eye-for-an-eye vengeance and because of its inadequate conception of criminal responsibility. Alvin Dewey, whom we have come to admire and trust, mirrors this ironic reversal. The relentless pursuer of the cold-blooded murderers of the Clutter family attends the execution of Dick and Perry. Dewey feels no compassion for Dick. "But Smith, though he was the true murderer, aroused another response, for Perry possessed a quality, the aura of an exiled animal, a creature walking wounded, that the detective could not disregard" (pp. 340-41). Dewey articulates an emotional realignment on our part which is the product of our understanding of Perry. We are now more moved by the fate of the murderer than that of the murdered, and we condemn the force that kills this wounded animal in cold blood. Capote's epigraph from Villon's *Ballade des pendus* is thus, by the close of *In Cold Blood*, an ironic commentary on the superficial meaning of the title of the book:

> Frères humains qui après nour vivez,
> N'ayez les cuers contre nous endurcis,
> Car, se pitié de nous povres avez,
> Dieu en aura plus tost de vous mercis.

In Cold Blood contains several other thematic ironies. The seemingly ruthless Dick who had chanted *"no witnesses"* and who runs down stray dogs is incapable of murder, whereas the hesitant Perry who attempts to make the Clutters comfortable and who prevents the rape of Nancy Clutter is the killer. The Clutter family itself, though in many ways an incarnation of the American Family, bears an ironic resemblance to the outcast Smiths. Both fathers are puritanical authoritarians, both mothers neurotic, both sons (Perry and Kenyon) introspective and moody. Only Nancy Clutter, the Becky Thatcher of her school play, is entirely appealing and only her death is permanently moving. (It is significant that while attending the execution of Perry and Dick, Dewey recalls a visit to the Garden City cemetery during which he was reminded of the dead Nancy by a chance encounter with her vibrantly alive friend, Sue Kidwell. The book closes with this intertwining of the two major sources of our compassionate involvement in the Clutter murders—the deaths of Nancy and Perry.) From the ironic portrayal of the Clutter family *In Cold Blood* widens in range to ironic representation of a large segment of American life. Holcomb and Garden City are almost exactly in the middle of the United States, and they are proud of their neighborliness and of a life free from the sins of the city. After the murders, however, they become centers of distrust and fear. And Perry Smith, the half-Indian son of a rodeo performer—the West personified—is a misshapen, slightly effeminate bed-wetter.

Capote also succeeds in involving the reader in an important theme which has significance independent of the particulars of the Clutter murder. Much of Part IV dramatizes the premise that conventional morality and criminal law are inadequate means of judging the acts of a Perry Smith. Perry's sister had written him: "You are a human being with a *free will*. Which puts you above the animal level" (p. 142); and the M'Naghten Rule states that a person who knows right from wrong at the time he commits a crime is responsible for that crime. Perry Smith, however, is not only a "wounded animal" but in the words of Dr. Joseph Satten, a psychiatrist interested in "motiveless murders," one of a class of individuals who "are predisposed to severe lapses of ego-control which makes possible the open expression of primitive violence, born out of previous, and now unconscious, traumatic experiences" (p. 299). Capote's portrayal of the character and fate of Perry Smith thus broadens into a dramatization of the gap between our contemporary knowledge of human nature and our archaic means of judging human acts. Unlike Manchester, who fails to convince us of any significance in the death of a president, Capote has led us to dwell on the social and ethical problems present in the death of a murderer.

***

Documentary narrative can vary in form and theme from William Manchester's total absorption in event as event to Truman Capote's exploration of event as meaning. Its adaptability suggests that it will continue to serve as a vehicle of experimental narrative by serious writers as well as a form of the higher journalism. Like all literary artists, the modern writer is confronted by the problems of the seemingly rival claims made upon him by his roles as observer and as maker. Documentary narrative, with its contrapuntal striking of the chords of "truth" and "art," appears to have found favor not only because it "solves" the problem but because it proclaims its solution loudly and clearly.

Part Four

DISSENT AND QUALIFICATION

Parajournalism, or Tom Wolfe and His Magic Writing Machine

DWIGHT MACDONALD

A new kind of journalism is being born, or spawned. It might be called "parajournalism," from the Greek *para*, "beside" or "against": something similar in form but different in function. As in parody, from the *parodia*, or counter-ode, the satyr play of Athenian drama that was performed after the tragedy by the same actors in grotesque costumes. Or paranoia ("against-beside thought") in which rational forms are used to express delusions. Parajournalism seems to be journalism—"the collection and dissemination of current news"—but the appearance is deceptive. It is a bastard form, having it both ways, exploiting the factual authority of journalism and the atmospheric license of fiction. Entertainment rather than information is the aim of its producers, and the hope of its consumers.

Parajournalism has an ancestry, from Daniel Defoe, one of the fathers of modern journalism, whose *Journal of the Plague Year* was a hoax so convincingly circumstantial that it was long taken for a historical record, to the gossip columnists, sob sisters, fashion writers,

The critic Dwight Macdonald's review of *The Kandy-Kolored Tangerine-Flake Streamline Baby*, one of the earliest critical examinations of Tom Wolfe's work, appeared in the *New York Review of Books*, August 26, 1965. Macdonald's analysis of Wolfe's *New Yorker* articles, referred to at the end of the review, appeared in the same publication on February 3, 1966.

and Hollywood reporters of this century. What is new is the pretension of our current parajournalists to be writing not hoaxes or publicity chitchat but the real thing; and the willingness of the public to accept this pretense. We convert everything into entertainment. *The New Yorker* recently qoted from a toy catalogue:

> WATER PISTOL & "BLEEDING" TARGETS! Bang! Bang! I got 'cha! Now the kids can know for sure who's [sic] turn it is to play "dead"! New self-adhesive "stick-on" water wounds TURN RED WHEN WATER HITS THEM! Don't worry, Mom! Won't stain clothing! "Automatic" pistol is a copy of a famous gun. SHOOTS 30 FT. Water Pistol & Wounds . . . 59c. 40 Extra Wounds . . . 29c.

And there was the ninety-minute TV, pop music and dance spectacular put on at Sargent Shriver's official request, with a disc jockey who calls himself Murray the K, in the hope of "getting through" to high school dropouts about what Mr. Shriver's Office of Economic Opportunity could do for them. Some Republican Senators objected on grounds of taste and dignity—the message was delivered by Murray the K jigging up and down in a funny hat as the big beat frugged on—but the program did stimulate a great many teenage inquiries. It "worked" in the same sense that parajournalism does.

The genre originated in *Esquire* but it now appears most flamboyantly in the *New York Herald Tribune*, which used to be a staidly respectable newspaper but has been driven by chronic deficits—and by a competitive squeeze between the respectable, and profitable, *Times*, and the less substantial but also profitable *News*—into some very unstaid antics. Dick Schaap is one of the *Trib's* parajournalists. "David Dubinsky began yelling, which means he was happy," he begins an account of a recent political meeting. Another is Jimmy Breslin, the tough-guy-with-heart-of-schmalz bard of the little man and the big celeb:

> Richard Burton, who had just driven in from Quogue . . . went straight for the ice-cubes when he came into his sixth-floor suite at the Regency Hotel. "Oh, I'd love a drink," he said. "Vodka." . . . "Humphrey Bogart," he laughed. "Bogey . . ." Burton has his tie pulled down and his eyes flashed as he told the stories. He tells a story maybe better than anybody I've ever heard. The stories are usually about somebody else. The big ones seem to have very little trouble thinking about something other than themselves. His wife kept hopping up and down getting drinks for everybody. She has long hair and striking eyes.

Right out of Fitzgerald, except he would have made a better job of describing Mr. Burton's wife.

But the king of the cats is, of course, Tom Wolfe, an *Esquire* alumnus who writes mostly for the *Trib's* Sunday magazine, *New York*, which is edited by a former *Esquire* editor, Clay Felker, with whom his writer-editor relationship is practically symbiotic. Wolfe is thirty-four, has a PhD from Yale in "American Studies," was a reporter first on the Springfield *Republican*, then on the Washington *Post*, and, after several years of writing mild, old-fashioned parajournalism for *Esquire*, raised, or lowered, the genre to a new level. This happened when, after covering a Hot Rod & Custom Car show at the New York Coliseum and writing a conventional, poking-mild-fun article about it (what he calls a "totem story"), he got *Esquire* to send him out to California where the Brancusis of hot-rod custom, or kustom, car design are concentrated. He returned full of inchoate excitements that he found himself unable to express freely in the usual condescending "totem" story because he was inhibited by "the big amoeba god of Anglo-European sophistication that gets you in the East." At the ultra-last deadline, Byron Dobell, Felker's successor at *Esquire*, asked him just to type out his notes and send them over for somebody else to write up. What happened was a stylistic break-through: "I just started recording it all [at 8 PM] and inside of a couple of hours, typing along like a madman, I could tell that something was beginning to happen." By 6:15 next morning he had a forty-nine page memo, typed straight along, no revisions, at five pages an hour, which he delivered to Dobell, who struck out the initial "Dear Byron" and ran it as was.*

The Kandy-Kolored Tangerine-Flake Streamline Baby is a collection of twenty-four articles written by Wolfe in the fifteen months after his stylistic break-through. It is amusing if one reads it the way it was written, hastily and loosely, skipping paragraphs, or pages, when the jazzed-up style and the mock-sociological pronouncements become oppressive. Since elaboration rather than development is Wolfe's forte, anything you miss will be repeated later, with bells on. He writes about topics like Las Vegas, Cassius Clay, Baby Jane Holzer, demolition car derbies, a pop record entrepreneur named Phil Spector, and a stock-car racing driver named Junior Johnson. A good read, as the English say. The fifth and last section, "Love and Hate, New York Style," is more than that. He is a good observer, with an eye for the city's style, and he would do very well as a writer of light pieces for, say, *The New Yorker*. "Putting Daddy On" and "The Woman Who Has Everything" are parajournalism at its best, making no pretense at factuality but sketching with humor and poignancy urban dilemmas one recognizes as real. "The Voices of Village Square" and "The Big

---

* [Editor's note: See Tom Wolfe, "Introduction to *The Kandy-Kolored Tangerine-Flake Streamline Baby*," page 29.]

League Complex" are shrewd and funny social comments—not the bogus-inflated kind he makes in his more ambitious pieces. Even better was "Therapy and Corned Beef While You Wait," which was in the advance galleys but doesn't appear in the book. Doubtless for space reasons, but why is it always the best parts they can't find room for?

A nice little book, one might say, might go to five thousand with luck. One would be wrong. *The Kandy-Kolored* (etc.) is in its fourth printing, a month after publication, has sold over ten thousand and is still going strong. The reviews helped. Except for Wallace Markfield in the *Tribune's* Sunday *Book Week,* and Conrad Knickerbocker's penetrating analysis in *Life,* they have been "selling" reviews. That Terry Southern should find it "a groove and a gas" and Seymour Krim "supercontemporary" is expectable, but less so other reactions: ". . . might well be required reading in courses like American studies" (*Time*); "He knows all the stuff that Arthur Schlesinger, Jr., knows, keeps picking up brand-new, ultra-contemporary stuff that nobody else knows, and arrives at zonky conclusions couched in scholarly terms. . . . Verdict: excellent book by a genius who will do anything to attract attention." (Kurt Vonnegut, Jr., *N.Y. Times Book Review*). *Newsweek* summed it up: "This is a book that will be a sharp pleasure to reread years from now when it will bring back, like a falcon in the sky of memory, a whole world that is currently jetting and jazzing its way somewhere or other." I don't think Wolfe will be read with pleasure, or at all, years from now, and perhaps not even next year, and for the same reason the reviewers, and the reading public, are so taken with his book now: because he has treated novel subjects—fairly novel, others have discovered our teen-age culture, including myself, seven years ago, in a *New Yorker* series—in a novel style. But I predict the subjects will prove of ephemeral interest and that the style will not wear well because its eccentricities, while novel, are monotonous; those italics, dots, exclamation points, odd words like "infarcted" and expressions like *Santa Barranza!* already look a little tired in his recent *Trib* pieces. As Mr. Knickerbocker writes, "There is no one as dead as last year's mannerist." A *memento mori* is another first book by a (really) young writer, Colin Wilson's *The Outsider,* which nine years ago went up like a rocket, and came down like one. The reasons for Colin Wilson's success were more interesting than his book, and so with Tom Wolfe' present vogue.

The distinctive qualities of parajournalism appear in the lead to "The Nanny Mafia":

All right, Charlotte, you gorgeous White Anglo-Saxon Protestant socialite, all you are doing is giving a birthday party for your little boy . . . So why are you sitting there by the telephone and your old malachite-top coffee-table gnashing on one thumbnail? Why are you staring out the Thermo-Plate glass toward the other towers on East 72nd Street with such vacant torture in your eyes?

"Damn it, I knew I'd forget something," says Charlotte. "I forgot the champagne."

The "knowing" details—Charlotte's malachite coffee table and her Thermo-Plate windows (and, later, her "Leslie II Prince Valiant coiffure") are fictional devices, reminding me of similar touches in the young Kipling's *Plain Tales from the Hills*. But Wolfe, who has publicly promised to write eight novels by 1968 and the sooner he gets at it and gives up journalism the better, is no Kipling but a mere reporter who is, ostensibly, giving us information—in this case that there is a mafia of superior, British-born nurses who tyrannize over socially insecure Park Avenue employers like Charlotte to such an extent that they don't dare give a children's party without providing champagne for the nurses. This may or may not be true—he rarely gives data that can be checked up on—but if it isn't, I don't think we would be quite as interested. Unlike Kipling's tales, it doesn't stand up as fiction. Marianne Moore defines poetry as putting real toads into imaginary gardens. Wolfe has reversed the process: his decor is real but his toads are dubious. Junior Johnson and Murray the K and Phil Spector and the kustom-kar designers are real, but somehow in his treatment come to seem as freely invented as Charlotte.

Stylistically, the above passage has the essential quality of *kitsch*, or a pseudo-cultural product manufactured for the market: the built-in reaction. The hastiest, most obtuse reader is left in no doubt as to how he is supposed to react to Charlotte with her malachite table and—later—"her alabaster legs and lamb-chop shanks . . . in hard, slippery, glistening skins of nylon and silk." As T. W. Adorno has noted of popular songs: "The composition hears for the listener." The specific *kitsch* device here is intimacy. Intimacy with the subject not in the old-fashioned sense of research, but an intimacy of style: the para-journalist cozies up, merges into the subject so completely that the viewpoint is wholly from inside, like family gossip. "All right, Charlotte, you . . ." There is no space between writer and topic, no "distancing" to allow the most rudimentary objective judgment, such as for factual accuracy. Inside and outside are one. It might be called topological journalism after those experiments with folding and cutting a piece of paper until it has only one side. There is also an intimacy with the reader, who is grabbed by the lapels—the buttonhole school of writing—often being addressed by Jimmy Breslin as "you."

It is hard to say just what Wolfe thinks of Charlotte, or of the real people he writes about. He melts into them so topologically that he seems to be celebrating them, and yet there is a peculiar and rather unpleasant ambivalence, as in his piece on Mrs. Leonard ("Baby Jane") Holzer, a rich young matron with lots of blonde hair whom he says he made "The Girl of the Year," that is, last year, there's another one now. I'm willing to grant his claim, but his piece seems to alternate between building up Baby Jane and tearing her down, damning with loud praise, assenting with not-so-civil leer. As for his readers, flattered though they may be to be taken so intimately into his confidence, made free of the creative kitchen so to speak, they are in the same ambiguous position. "Bangs manes bouffants beehives Beatle caps butter faces brushon lashes decal eyes puffy sweaters French thrust bras" one article begins, continuing for six more unpunctuated lines of similar arcana and if you don't dig them you're dead, baby. Every boost a knock.

But there is one value Tom Wolfe asserts clearly, constantly, obsessively: old he bad, new he good. Although he is pushing thirty-five, or perhaps because of it, he carries the American teenager's contempt for adults to burlesque extremes. His forty-seven-page ode to Junior Johnson, "The Last American Hero," ends: "up with the automobile into their America, and the hell with the arteriosclerotic old boys trying to hold onto the whole pot with their arms of cotton seersucker. Junior!" He contrasts his teen-age tycoon, Phil Spector, with "the arteriosclerotic, larded adults, infarcted vultures . . . one meets in the music business." Even Baby Jane—Baby! Junior!— loses her cool when she thinks of all those . . . adults: "Now she looks worried, as if the world could be such a simple and exhilarating place if there weren't so many old and arteriosclerotic people around to muck it up."

Those ten-thousand-plus purchasers of Wolfe's book are probably almost all adults, arteriosclerotic or not—I wonder what *his* blood pressure is—since there are so many of them still around mucking it up and also in a financial position to lay $5.50 on the line. So it's not a literal business of age—Junior and Baby Jane aren't exactly teenagers. Maybe more like how you *feel* sort of—"in" (new) or "out" (old)? I think the vogue of Tom Wolfe may be explained by two *kultur*-neuroses common among adult, educated Americans today: a masochistic deference to the Young, who are also, by definition, new and so in; and a guilt-feeling about class—maybe they don't deserve their status, maybe they aren't so cultivated—that makes them feel insecure when a verbal young—well, youngish—type like Wolfe assures them the "proles," the *young* proles that is, have created a cultural style which they either had been uncultivated enough to think vulgar or, worse, hadn't even noticed. Especially when his spiel is on the highest level—Wolfe is no Cholly Knickerbocker, he's even more impressive than Vance Packard—full of hard words like "ischium" and "panopticon" and heady concepts like "charisma" ("the [automobile] manufacturers may well be on their way to routinizing the charisma, as Max Weber used to say") and off-hand references to "high-status sports cars of the Apollonian sort" as against, you understand, "the Dionysian custom kind." Or: "The people who end up in Hollywood are mostly Dionysian sorts and they feel alien and resentful when they are confronted with the Anglo-European ethos. They're a little slow to note the differences between topside and sneakers, but they appreciate Cuban sunglasses." A passage like that can shake the confidence of the most arrogant Ivy League WASP. Or this:

> The educated classes in this country, as in every country, the people who grow up to [Wolfe writes in his Introduction] control visual and printed communication media, are all plugged into what is, when one gets down to it, an ancient, aristocratic aesthetic. Stock car racing, custom cars—and, for that matter, the jerk, the monkey, rock music—still seem beneath serious consideration, still the preserve of ratty people with ratty hair and dermatitis and corroded thoracic boxes and so forth. Yet all these rancid people [one assumes "ratty," "rancid," etc., are rhetorical irony but one can't be sure; with Wolfe for the defense you don't need a D.A.] are creating new styles all the time and changing the life of the whole country in ways that nobody even seems to record, much less analyze.

The publisher's handout puts it more frankly: "Tom Wolfe describes his beat as 'the status life of our time.' As he sees it, U.S. taste is being shaped by what were once its subcultures, largely teenage. . . He zeroes in on the new, exotic forms of status-seeking of a young, dynamic social class, 'vulgar' and 'common' to the Establishment, that has emerged since the war and that expresses the ordinary American's sense of form and beauty." No wonder the book is selling. In addition to appealing to our adult masochisms, it also promises a new sociology of taste. The post-war "culture boom" has greatly increased the number of Americans who are educated, in the formal sense they have gone through college, without increasing proportionately the number who know or care much about culture. There is, therefore, a large and growing public that feels it really should Take An Interest and is looking for guidance as to what is, currently, The Real Thing. The old *kitsch* was directed to the masses but the reader of Edna Ferber or even Will Durant would be put off, if only by its title, by *The Kandy-Kolored Tangerine-Flake Streamline Baby*, which is *kitsch* addressed to what might be called a class-mass audience, smaller and, educationally, on a higher level but otherwise not so different from the old one.

I don't think they will get their money's worth, for their *arbiter elegantiarum* is as uncertain as they are, his only firm value being old-bad, new-good. Not enough. It forces him to abstract "style" so aseptically from all other contexts that it becomes ambiguous even as a guide to taste. Writing of those kandy-kolored automotive aberations, he drops names desperately—Miró, Picasso, Cellini, the Easter Island statues, "If Brancusi is any good, then this thing belongs on a pedestal"—but his actual description of them and of their creators runs the other way. "Jane Holzer—and the Baby Jane syndrome—there's nothing freakish about it," he protests. "Baby Jane is the hyper-version of a whole new style of life in America. I think she is a very profound symbol. But hers is not the super-hyper-version. The super-hyper-version is Las Vegas." Rodomontade, whistling in the dark. He doesn't explain why Baby Jane is not freakish nor why she is a profound symbol of the new American style nor why Las Vegas is a super-hyper-profounder one, and his articles on her, and on Las Vegas ("the Versailles of America") lead me to opposite conclusions, which he often seems to share as a reporter if not as an ideologue. His most extreme effort is his praise of Bernarr Mac-Fadden's New York *Daily Graphic:* "Everybody was outraged and called it 'gutter journalism' and 'The Daily Pornographic.' But by god the whole thing had style . . . Even in the realm of the bogus, the *Graphic* went after bogosity with a kind of Left Bank sense of rebellious discovery. Those cosmographs, boy! Those confession yarns!" But the "cosmographs" were merely faked news photos, the confessions dreary fabrications, and that dear old *Graphic* in fact *was* gutter journalism in which no kind of rebellion, Left or Right Bank, was involved. Wolfe's term for its subtle quality is "the *aesthetique du schlock*"—*Schlock* being Yiddish for *ersatz* or phony—and it applies to his other discoveries in "the new American style." O, they're tenting tonight on the old camping ground.

There are two kinds of appropriate subjects for parajournalism. The kind Tom Wolfe exploits in the present book is the world of the "celebs": prize-fighters, gamblers, movie and stage "personalities," racing drivers, pop singers and their disc jockeys like Murray the K ("The Fifth Beatle"), impresarios like Phil Spector ("The First Tycoon of Teen") entrepreneurs like Robert Harrison (whose *Confidential* magazine, the classic *old* one (1952-1958) you understand, Wolfe salutes as "the most scandalous scandal magazine in the history of the world," adding: "*Confidential* was beautiful. This may be a hard idea to put across . . . but the fact is the man is an aesthete, the original *aesthete du schlock*," who as a teenage employee of the *Graphic* received the stigmata direct from Bernarr MacFadden) and pop-art-cum-society figures like Andy Warhol, Huntington Hartford (an antipop popper), and Mrs. Leonard Holzer.* The other kind of suitable game for the parajournalist—though not Tom Wolfe's pigeon —is the Little Man (or Woman) who gets into trouble with the law; or who is interestingly poor or old or ill or, best, all three; or who has some other Little problem like delinquent children or a close relative who has been murdered for which they can count on Jimmy Breslin's heavy-breathing sympathy and prose.

Both celebs and uncelebs offer the same advantage: inaccuracy will have no serious consequences. The little people are unknown to the reader and, if they think they have been misrepresented, are in no position to do anything about it, nor, even if such a daring idea occurred to them, to object to the invasion of their privacy. The celebs are eager to have their privacy invaded, welcoming the attentions of the press for reasons of profession or of vanity. While the reader knows a great deal, too much, about them, this is not real knowledge because they are, in their public aspect, not real. They are not persons but *personae* ("artificial characters in a play or novel"—or in para-journalistic reportage) which have been manufactured for public consumption with their enthusiastic cooperation. Notions of truth or accuracy are irrelevant in such a context of collusive fabrication on both sides; all that matters to anybody—subject, writer, reader—is that it be a good story. To complain of Wolfe's Pindaric ode to Junior Johnson that his hero couldn't be all that heroic is like objecting to Tarzan as unbelievable.

But of late Tom Wolfe has attempted more solid, resistant sub-jects. As his colleague, Mr. Breslin, might put it, he's been fighting above his weight. There was that front-page review of Norman Mailer's *An American Dream* in the Sunday Tribune's *Book Week* (which Richard Kluger edits in a more substantial and, to me, interesting way than Clay Felker's set-'em-up-in-the-other-alley technique with *New York*). As the French say, the most beautiful parajournalist cannot give any more than he has, and the only way Wolfe could explicate his low estimation of the novel was to jeer at the author's private life and personality—or rather his *persona*, this being the aspect of people Wolfe is at home with—followed by some satirical excursions on tangential matters like the ludicrous discrepancy between Mailer and

---

* Wolfe unaccountably missed Christina Paolozzi, a young Italian noblewoman who achieved celebdom by no more complicated strategy than stripping to the waist and allowing *Harper's Bazaar* to photograph her, from the front. But Gay Talese, an *Esquire* alumnus who now parajournalizes mostly in the *Times*—in a more dignified way, of course—includes her in his recent collection, *The Overreachers*, along with Joshua Logan, Floyd Patterson, Peter O'Toole, Frank Costello, *e tutti quanti*.

Dostoevsky and the even more laughable crepancy between Mailer and James M. Cain. *C'est amusant mais ce n'est pas la critique.* Not that I disagree with his low estimate of *An American Dream.* Mr. Kluger asked me to review it and I declined for lack of time. If I had accepted, I should also have slated it but I don't think I would have thought of going into Mailer's personality and private life if only because there is so much in the printed text to criticise. But Tom Wolfe doesn't seem to be much of a reader.

A week or two later, he took on a subject of much greater mass and resistance, *The New Yorker,* with which he grappled in the April 11th and 18th issues of Clay Felker's *New York.* The perfect target for two young(ish) men on the make with a new magazine competing for the same kind of readers and advertisers. Part One was headed "Tiny Mummies! The True Story of The Ruler of 43rd Street's Land of the Walking Dead!" It sketched in bold strokes, letting the facts fall where they may, an action painting of a bureaucratic, arteriosclerotic, infarcted organism that was dead but didn't know enough to lie down and of William Shawn, its editor, "the museum curator, the mummifier, the preserver-in-amber, the smiling embalmer" who took over after Harold Ross died in 1952.* The second part debunks the magazine itself: "For forty years it has maintained a strikingly low level of literary achievement"—compared, that is, to *Esquire* and *The Saturday Evening Post.* There is no space here to consider the truth of these propositions or the methods by which Wolfe attempts to demonstrate them beyond noting that, as a staff writer with an office at *The New Yorker* for the last thirteen years, I find his facts to be often not such, especially when some atmospheric touch depends on them; his snide caricature of Shawn to be a *persona* (convenient for his purpose) rather than the real person I know; his evaluation of the magazine to be hung on a statistical gimmick it would be courteous to call flimsy; his research such as it is wouldn't get by the editor of a high-school yearbook; and his ignorance of *The New Yorker's* present and past—he thinks Ross was trying to imitate *Punch* —remarkable even for a Doctor of American Studies turned parajournalist.

Somehow Tom Wolfe has managed to miss a target broad enough to have profited by some sensible criticism. He has also revealed the ugly side of parajournalism when it tries to be serious: to deal with a forty-year run of a weekly magazine and to fabricate a *persona* without the collaboration of the person involved. What with his own

---

* "Infarcted" sums up Wolfe's stance: *"Pathol.* a circumscribed portion of tissue which has been suddenly deprived of its blood supply by embolism or thrombosis and which, as a result, is undergoing death (necrosis), to be replaced by scar tissue." Necrosis! Scar tissue! Santa Barranza! Eeeeeeeeeee!

reading block and Shawn's refusal to be interviewed—his privilege, I should think, perhaps even his constitutional right, cf., Justice Brandeis on "the right to privacy"—Wolfe was reduced to speculations on the nature of the magazine and its editor. These are sometimes plausible, sometimes not, but they always fit into a pattern that has been determined in advance of the evidence, like Victorian melodrama or the political tracts we used to get from Germany and Russia in the Thirties.* It is not surprising that Wolfe got away with it, making an instant reputation as a rebel and bad man which didn't do any harm to his book later. The first resource of a parajournalist is that his audience knows even less than he does—and it was a bold, slashing attack on a sacred cow, an Institution, The Establishment. That fellow Wolfe, he really gave it to *The New Yorker!* David and Goliath. It's hard for the class-mass audience to see that, today, Goliath is sometimes the good guy. He's so much less entertaining than David.

---

* These are generalizations and parajournalism, which thrives on generalization, cannot be understood unless it is examined in specific detail. For such an examination of Tom Wolfe's *New Yorker* Caper see my analysis of his technique, from boldly asserted unfacts to rhetorically insinuated untruths, in a forthcoming issue of this paper.

The New Confusion

WILLIAM L. RIVERS

Anyone who hopes to understand what is happening in the world today must begin by trying to understand what is happening among those we rely upon to report and interpret the human enterprise—the journalists. That won't be easy. Not even the journalists are certain. It is clear that something called the New Journalism is taking hold— a slippery hold in some cases—all over the country. But what is it? Many newspaper editors seem to think of the New Journalism as the practice of injecting opinion into the news columns—and view it with the horror of a slaver who discovers that the blacks in the hold are out of their chains and advancing on the ship's bridge. Many reporters argue that it is not opinion writing in the editorial-page sense, but they sneer at the editors' quaint passion for "objectivity," arguing that tell-it-like-it-is-with-me is the only route to the real truth.

If there were nothing more to the New Journalism, we could simply choose sides and argue it out. But the problem is much larger and fuzzier. Some consider the underground press the New Journalism. The revival of muckraking—overground and underground—is sometimes called the New Journalism. To complicate everything completely, though, two genuine New Journalists, Tom Wolfe and Gay Talese,

William L. Rivers teaches in the Department of Communication at Stanford University and writes regularly for *The Progressive,* in which "The New Confusion" appeared in December, 1971. Among his books are *The Opinionmakers* and *The Adversaries: Politics and the Press.*

both ex-newspapermen who now write magazine articles and books, are concerned not with opinion, personalized news, or muckraking, but with developing new and artful techniques of gathering and reporting facts. If we must also take account of Norman Mailer's nonfiction—and if *that* isn't New Journalism, what is?—what we have is the New Confusion.

If this continues, the dangerous practices will soon become so tangled with the valuable techniques that the valuable will be lost. Everette Dennis of Kansas State University begins to unravel the confusion in his introduction to a collection of student-written articles titled *The Magic Writing Machine*. He identifies the journals founded by newsmen who despaired of the conventional press and started their own papers as *alternative journalism*. The best examples are Bruce Brugmann's *San Francisco Bay Guardian*, Ronnie Dugger's *Texas Observer*, and the late Gene Cervi's *Cervi's Journal* (published in Denver), all of which focus, often fiercely, on matters that conventional papers cover scantily or not at all. The many little journals produced by proponents of a counter-culture Dennis calls *underground journalism*. He identifies the reporting that uses the tools of the scientific method and survey research as *precision journalism*. Phil Meyer of the Knight Newspapers is one of the few practitioners of this form, which tries to push journalism toward science while all the others are pushing it toward art.

These need attention, and I propose to cover them in future articles for *The Progressive*. Here, the focus is on what Dennis calls *advocacy journalism*, which I consider dangerous, and *new nonfiction*, which can be valuable.

It is hardly possible to take account of the danger of advocacy in the news without reviewing the old debate, objectivity versus interpretation. Although advocacy and interpretation are quite different, recalling that debate provides a needed historical context.

Until the coming of Franklin Roosevelt's New Deal, the average reporter wrote a formula. He sought to fashion a clear and concise straight news story, starting with the who, what, when, and where of an event and proceeding toward the end by placing factual details in descending order of interest and importance (a device primarily designed to enable editors to cut stories from the bottom up). His job was to try to hold a mirror up to an event and show its surface. Explaining why it had occurred and brooding over what should be done about it were the missions of the editorial writers and the columnists. A few reporters, primarily foreign correspondents and Washington correspondents, had been given license to interpret the news and explain and clarify complex events. But almost everyone else was limited to straight news reporting.

With the advent of the New Deal, the old forms suddenly seemed inadequate. Washington correspondents of the time say they can fix on the exact moment when "the old journalism" failed utterly: the day in 1933 when the United States went off the gold standard. They appealed to the White House for help in reporting that baffling change, and a Federal Government economist was sent over to clarify the new facts of economic life. They tried to explain what *he* explained, without much success.

The increasing complexity of public affairs made it difficult to confine reporting to the strait jacket of unelaborated fact. Relaying exactly what a Government official said, or what Congress did, was often misleading: Even facts didn't speak the truth. Moreover, reporters discovered that they were, in effect, running errands for the Establishment and enshrining the status quo; the sources of news releases, press conferences, and official statements were usually men with position and power. Somewhat hesitantly, reporters like Paul Anderson and Marquis Childs of the *St. Louis Post-Dispatch* and, a bit later, James Reston of *The New York Times* began to build the interpretative reporting structure that made its way back to city rooms everywhere.

The trend was fiercely debated. Ten or twelve years ago, it split the top level of the great *Louisville Courier-Journal*. Editor Barry Bingham argued: "The need for interpretative reporting becomes more insistent week by week." At the same time, Executive Editor James Pope attacked the interpreters, maintaining that "by definition, interpretation is subjective and means to 'translate, elucidate, construe . . . in the light of individual belief or interest. . . .' Interpretation is the bright dream of the saintly seers who expound and construe in the midst of the news." To Pope and others, interpretative reporters were simply abandoning objective journalism. But the *Courier-Journal* has become an excellent interpretative newspaper.

Lester Markel, the able and acid retired Sunday editor of *The New York Times*, who was the most insistent advocate of interpretation, argued several years ago in *The Saturday Review* that no form of reporting could really be defined as "objective":

> The reporter, the most objective reporter, collects fifty facts. Out of the fifty he selects twelve to include in his story (there is such a thing as space limitation). Thus he discards thirty-eight. This is Judgment Number One.
>
> Then the reporter or editor decides which of the facts shall be the first paragraph of the story, thus emphasizing one fact above the other eleven. This is Judgment Number Two.
>
> Then the editor decides whether the story shall be placed on Page One or Page Twelve; on Page One it will command many

times the attention it would on Page Twelve. This is Judgment Number Three.

This so-called factual presentation is thus subjected to three judgments, all of them most humanly and most ungodly made.

Such arguments and the findings of behavioral scientists seem to have persuaded nearly everyone that humans cannot be objective in the machine-like sense. Most of the proponents of objectivity now argue that it is a goal worth striving for even if it is not quite attainable.

Choosing sides in this debate is difficult because both kinds of reporting should have a place in newspapers and on news programs. The proponents of interpretation are right in arguing that mere facts can mislead, that facts must be placed in a context that gives them meaning. The reporter who explains facts and clarifies the meaning of events serves us well. Those who favor interpretation are also right in holding that a reporter can interpret the news—or analyze it, if you prefer—without becoming an advocate. The ultimate test is whether the writing is slanted in such a way that we can determine the reporter's personal views. The best example of journalistic balance is provided by Richard Strout, who writes admirable interpretative news for *The Christian Science Monitor* that does not even hint at his own leanings, and who writes equally admirable opinion pieces, suitably labeled by the *Monitor's* "Opinion and Commentary" heading —often on the same topics.

The root of the matter is made clear by James Carey of the University of Illinois, one of the most thoughtful professors of communication, who points out, "There must be greater stylistic freedom among modern journalists and a more fluid definition of news if only because the pace of social change continually presses the journalist into situations for which the conventional styles and conventional news definitions disable both perception and communication."

Proponents of objective reporting, on the other hand, are right in arguing that few reporters are capable of interpreting complex events, either because they do not know how to explain, clarify, and analyze without advocating, or because they know too little about the subjects they are reporting to do more than present the surface of an event. Even seasoned reporters can differ sharply, as the March issue of *The Progressive* made clear by quoting these sentences from two of the best Washington correspondents:

> To be blunt about it, almost nobody believes President Nixon's budget except the high officials who put it together—and it's probable that even some of them have their doubts.
> —HOBART ROWEN, "Credibility Is Lacking in Nixon Budget," *The Washington Post*, January 31, 1971

In general, then, insofar as decisions and judgments made at this stage are important, this budget appears to receive fairly high marks for credibility.

—EDWIN L. DALE, JR., "The Budget Gap—Nixon Receives an A for Credibility," *The New York Times*, January 31, 1971

How facts can be variously interpreted was also demonstrated when the Stanford News Bureau released information on gifts to the university for the 1970-71 fiscal year.

The university-published *Campus Report* headed its story:

HIGHEST NUMBER OF DONORS IN STANFORD HISTORY

The *San Francisco Chronicle* headline said:

STANFORD AGAIN RAISES $29 MILLION IN GIFTS

The *Palo Alto Times* story was headed:

DONATIONS TO STANFORD LOWEST IN FOUR YEARS

The student-published *Stanford Daily* announced:

ALUMNI DONATIONS DECLINE; BIG DROP FROM FOUNDATIONS

These headlines accurately reflected the stories they surmounted —which were also accurate. Stanford did have more donors than ever, as the *Campus Report* story said. It did raise more than $29 million for the fourth consecutive year, as the *Chronicle* said. Donations were the lowest in the past four years, as the *Palo Alto Times* reported. The total was lower than in 1969-70 and it included less foundation money, as the *Stanford Daily* said. As proponents of objective reporting contend, a positive or negative stance can make all the difference.

Those who argue for objective reporting are also right in contending that many events do not lend themselves easily to interpretation —some are not *worth* interpreting—especially at the hot moment of their occurrence. It is nonsense to try to analyze a fast-breaking event as it happens, far better to allow time for fact-gathering and reflection. This means that there is still need for who-what-when-where news, which should be followed later by reflective interpretation clearly labeled as such.

Advocacy journalism is a long step beyond interpretation. Reading it is much like going back a hundred years or so, when a U.S. Senator found his speech described by a friendly reporter as "full of marrow and grit, and enunciated with a courage which did one's heart good to hear. No mealy-mouthed phrases . . . but strong and stirring old English, that had the ring of the true metal." Another reporter described the same man: "a soft, catlike step; a keen, snaky eye; a look and address now bold and audacious, and then cringing and deprecatory, his whole air and mien suggesting a subdued combination of Judas Iscariot with Uriah Heep."

A rationale for the modern version of this kind of reporting comes from Ray Mungo, one of the young founders of the Liberation News Service, who argues in his book, *Famous Long Ago:*

> *Facts* are less important than *truth* and the two are far from equivalent, you see, for cold facts are nearly always boring and may even distort the truth, but Truth is the highest achievement of human expression. . . . Now let's pick up a 1967 copy of the Boston *Avatar,* and under the headline "Report from Vietnam, by Alexander Sorenson" read a painfully graphic account of Sorenson's encounter with medieval torture in a Vietnam village. Later because we know Brian Keating, who wrote the piece, we discover that Alexander Sorenson doesn't exist and the incident described in *Avatar,* which moved thousands, never in fact happened. But because it has happened in man's history, and because we know we are responsible for its happening today, and because the story is unvarnished and plain and human, we know it is *true,* truer than any facts you may have picked up in the *New Republic.*

Mungo's approach is so dangerous that it is fortunate that little advocacy journalism goes this far. Most of it is in the form of reports on real events in which the writer makes his personal leanings quite clear. Strong beliefs—especially the conviction that the status quo must be challenged—are surely the chief reason a wave of advocacy journalism has reached the newsrooms, but there is another: impatience with the blandness of both objective reporting and interpretation. A recent personal experience illustrates the point. Stanford University has suspended Associate Professor Bruce Franklin, a self-proclaimed Maoist, because he participated in actions that led to violence on the campus. (He may be dismissed as a result of a hearing that is going on at this writing.) I wrote an article on the Franklin case for the May-June, 1971, issue of *Change: The Magazine of Higher Education.* Unlike news stories and interpretative stories in newspapers and in news broadcasting, many magazine articles can reflect the views of the writer, but I tried to keep my views out of the article in the hope that a balanced interpretation would make the issues clear. But even I can see that the article is dull reading. I could have written a richer and livelier piece had I not been so careful to present everything impartially, but blandness is often the price of "on the other hand" journalism.

It is a price worth paying to achieve objectivity, but the flavor and richness of advocacy are fascinating lures. A talented reporter working on a piece that allows him to vent his views—say, a critical review, or an article for a journal of opinion—often writes joyously, especially if his usual work is constricted by the rules of objective reporting or interpretation.

Many readers seem to be similarly lured. Although concern with the state of the world may be the chief reason for the growing popularity of journals of opinion like *The Progressive, The New Republic,* and *National Review,* many readers are drawn to journalism that carries the bite of opinion.

Whatever the reasons for its appeal, advocacy journalism is dangerous when it creeps into the news columns of newspapers and into news broadcasts. If we are to understand events, reporters must first use the tools of objective reporting and interpretation to answer simple questions: What did President Nixon (or Spiro Agnew, or Senator Muskie) actually say last night? What precisely took place in the trial of Angela Davis? What are the issues in the dispute about the actions of Daniel Ellsberg, or J. Edgar Hoover? With these matters established, it is time to comment upon them and take sides—in editorials and opinion pieces.

I do not agree with Nicholas von Hoffman, *The Washington Post* columnist, who lamented in a recent column that Tim Wicker, *The New York Times* columnist and associate editor, speaks from political platforms and commits himself to partisan causes. Wicker, whose commitment is properly expressed in his columns, may find it difficult, as von Hoffman writes, to "avoid becoming the voice of a political faction," difficult to be "his own man, writing his own opinions even when they hurt The Movement." But columnists who are not so publicly and personally engaged have their leanings, offer their opinions, and are lured by spokesmen for causes. Wicker's commitment is actually different in degree, not in kind. But von Hoffman's plea that the journalist stand as a man apart—"a grouchy, suspicious, nasty, introspective monk, a horrid, raggedy thing no faction would care to capture"—is an excellent perscription for the reporter as compared with the columnist.

If the young reporters insist upon advocacy in the news—as a good many do—journalism stands to lose a hard-won prize: a professional stance that keeps most publishers and broadcast executives in the counting room where they belong and out of the news departments.

Most of the techniques of the new nonfiction are probably as valuable as advocacy journalism is dangerous. In some hands, they add a flavor and a humanity to journalistic writing that push it into the realm of art. Moreover, the new nonfiction is the only part of the New Journalism that actually *is* new. One can find all the other aspects here or there in practices that are centuries old.

How the new nonfiction began is not at all certain. A form of it appears in Truman Capote's *In Cold Blood,* but not long after that book was published I participated in a television panel discussion with Meyer Levin, the author of *Compulsion,* who had trouble staying calm enough to plug his own new book of that time because he was aflame about Capote's claim that he had invented a new art form. Levin claimed that *he* had perfected it long before.

My own view is that Lillian Ross deserves the credit for inventing the form because of her series in *The New Yorker* in 1952 on the filming of *The Red Badge of Courage*, which was later published as the book, *Picture*. She used the central technique of what is now the new nonfiction: recreating scenery and atmosphere scene after scene.

Of course, journalists had been writing scenes for years. Anecdotes, which are usually little scenes, have appeared here and there in newspaper and magazine articles for decades. But Miss Ross built scene upon scene so artfully that one critic called *Picture* "the first piece of factual reporting to be written in the form of a novel."

The importance of scene-building was stressed by Tom Wolfe in an article in the September, 1970, issue of *The Bulletin* of the American Society of Newspaper Editors:

> The first time I realized there was something new going on in journalism was one day in 1962 when I picked up a copy of *Esquire* and read an article by Gay Talese entitled "Joe Louis at Fifty."
>
> "Joe Louis at Fifty" wasn't like a magazine article at all. It was like a short story. It began with a scene, an intimate confrontation between Louis and his third wife:
>
> " 'Hi, sweetheart,' " Joe Louis called to his wife, spotting her waiting for him at the Los Angeles Airport.
>
> "She smiled, walked toward him, and was about to stretch up on her toes and kiss him—but suddenly stopped.
>
> " 'Joe,' she snapped, 'where's your tie?'
>
> " 'Aw, sweetie,' Joe Louis said, shrugging, 'I stayed out all night in New York and didn't have time.'
>
> " 'All night!' she cut in. 'When you're here with me all you do is sleep, sleep, sleep.'
>
> " 'Sweetie,' Joe Louis said with a tired grin, 'I'm an ole man.'
>
> " 'Yes,' she agreed, 'but when you go to New York you try to be young again.' "
>
> The story went on like that, scene after scene, building up a picture of an ex-sports hero now fifty years old. . . .
>
> I couldn't believe this stuff. How did this guy Talese ever get in on all this intimate byplay in the latterday life of Joe Louis? *He piped it.* That was it. *He faked the quotes, goddamn it*—which was precisely the cry of self-defense that many literati would sound over the next five years as New Journalism began to shake up the literary status structure.
>
> Talese hadn't piped it, of course. He was *there* all the time, and that was the simple secret of that.

The new nonfiction has other facets. Like the novelist, Talese presents the thoughts of his subjects, a technique that he calls "interior monologue." In *The Kingdom and the Power*, his book on *The New York Times*, Talese wrote of Clifton Daniel, who was then managing editor:

> There were times when Daniel felt that Catledge was sufficiently satisfied with the way things were going, or was sufficiently un-interested, to allow Daniel free rein. During such periods Daniel felt a pleasant identity with the photographs of the men on the wall—Van Anda and Birchall, James and Catledge. He felt confi-dence in himself as an executive, satisfaction in the reporters or critics whom he had hired, reassurance in the style in which *The Times* was covering the world. While Daniel often gave the im-pression of vain-gloriousness and was unquestionably proud of his title, he also saw himself as an instrument of the institution, a good soldier, a loyal subject, and there was not a man in the build-ing who was less likely to betray a corporate secret than Clifton Daniel.

Wolfe, who is the most ardent spokesman for the new nonfiction, is a scene-builder, of course. Perhaps his chief distinction is that he colors every scene with rich detail and memorable metaphors. In *Radical Chic and Mau-Mauing the Flak Catchers*, Wolfe describes an OEO bureaucrat:

> This man comes out, and he has that sloppy Irish look like Ed McMahon on TV, only with a longer nose. But he doesn't have to open his mouth. All you have to do is look at him and you get the picture. The man's a lifer. He's stone civil service. He has it all down from the wheatcolor Hush Puppies to the wash'n'dry semi-tab-collar shortsleeve white shirt.

There is so much more to the work of the new nonfiction writers that it sometimes seems that the only device of the novelist they avoid is fictionizing—and some of their critics accuse them of *that*. The critics were on solid ground not long ago when *New York* magazine published a long, absorbing article by Gail Sheehy about a prostitute named Redpants. Then *The Wall Street Journal* revealed that the only trouble with the article was that Redpants doesn't exist. She was a composite of several prostitutes.

It is equally difficult to recommend the kind of new nonfiction pioneered by Norman Mailer, which blends advocacy and personal reporting techniques. Like *Esquire*, which is a triumph one month and a disaster the next, Mailer's ups and downs are total. But the main objection is that Mailer has misled too many young imitators. They see him focus upon himself in that strange third-person style: "The phone rang one morning, and Norman Mailer, acting upon his own principle of war games and random play, picked it up. That was not characteristic of Mailer." They fail to see that Mailer recounts how events affected him *and* his view of events, which is often penetrating reportage. Most of his young imitators are merely self-indulgent. One who cured himself, a thoughtful young graduate assistant in journalism at the University of Illinois named Daniel J. Balz, observed in the September/October issue of *Columbia Journalism Review:* *

> Norman Mailer's *Armies of the Night,* as most now recognize, pushed us even farther because hundreds of us had gone to the Pentagon, either as participants or reporters, and had failed to come to grips with it in any way comparable to Mailer. Of course we blamed that on form, not on ourselves. We didn't relate Mailer's earlier political pieces, his reports on the 1960 and 1964 conventions, to the Pentagon book. We simply related the book to what we had written—form against form—and believed Mailerian thoughts rested in all of us, waiting to be sprung.

All in all, the techniques of the new nonfiction are worth promoting. The visual quality of the reporting brings people and political institutions alive in a way that makes conventional journalism seem bloodless. The new nonfiction requires saturation research—many interviews and intense observation—and thus shows us the superficiality of the newspaper norm, the single-interview story. But the best reason for promoting the new nonfiction is that mastering it is so demanding that reporters will have no energy left for advocacy.

---

* [Editor's note: See Daniel J. Balz, "Bad Writing and New Journalism," page 288.]

Notes on
the New Journalism

MICHAEL J. ARLEN

It's probably easier than it should be to dismiss the articles which appeared recently in *New York* magazine on the subject of "The New Journalism." In the first place, the articles, which were by Tom Wolfe (himself a founding member of *New York* and author of *The Kandy-Kolored Tangerine-Flake Streamline Baby*), had most of the defects of the form he was extolling—the pop sociology, the easy cultural generalities—with few of the compensating attractions—the dramatic scene-setting, the impressionistic color (such as had made, for instance, his own piece on the stock-car racer Junior Johnson so vivid and fascinating to read). "The voice of the narrator, in fact, was one of the great problems in non-fiction writing," Dr. Wolfe now intoned. Also: "The modern notion of art is an essentially religious or magical one . . ." etc. Also: "Queen Victoria's childhood diaries are, in fact, quite readable." Also: "Literary people were oblivious to this side of the New Journalism, because it is one of the unconscious assumptions of modern criticism that the raw material is simply 'there.'" And so forth. In the second place, although it must have been fun to work at the *Herald Tribune* in its last few years of existence—when and where, according to Wolfe, the birth of New Journalism mostly occurred—he manages to describe this great

Michael J. Arlen's article appeared in the *Atlantic*, May, 1972. He writes for the *New Yorker* and is the author of *Living-Room War, Exiles,* and *An American Verdict.*

moment in Western cultural life with a school-boy reverence which somehow doesn't leave anyone else much breathing room, a combination of Stalky & Co. and The Day That Curie Discovered Radium. In Tom Wolfe's world, in fact (as he might say), there is perpetual struggle between a large and snooty army of crumbs, known as the Literary People, who are the bad guys, and Tom's own band of good guys: rough-and-tumble fellows like Jimmy Breslin, dashing reporters such as Dick Schaap, the savvy nonintellectuals, the aces, the journalistic guerrilla fighters, the good old boys who "never guessed for a minute that the work they would do over the next ten years, as journalists, would wipe out the novel as literature's main event."

It's easy enough to fault this sort of treatment of a complicated subject. A bit too simpleminded. Too ingroupish. Me and My Pals Forge History Together. All the same, it seems to me that beneath, or despite, the blather, Tom Wolfe is right about a lot of it. And very wrong too. And journalism is perhaps in the kind of muddle it's in today not, lord knows, because Tom Wolfe sat down at his bench one day and invented a new art form, but because people in general, editors as well as writers as well as readers, have had trouble figuring out how to deal with this terrain that he and many, many other journalists have steadily been pushing their way into over a period of a good many years.

To begin with, of course, one can say that the New Journalism *isn't* new. That's a favorite put-down: the New Journalist prances down the street, grabbing innocent bystanders by the lapels, and breathlessly (or worse, earnestly) declaiming about his "new fictional techniques," or his "neo-Jamesian point of view," or his "seeing the world in novelistic terms" and all the rest of it, while the Old Literary Person gazes out his window and mutters: "New Journalism, indeed! What about Addison and Steele, eh? What about Defoe? What about Mencken? Joe Mitchell? Hemingway? Mark Twain?" That's right in a sense, but not, I think, in the most meaningful sense. It's right, at any rate, that there's been a vein of personal journalism in English and American writing for a very long time. For example, Defoe in his *Journal of the Plague Year* developed for *his* subject the same sort of new techniques that the New Journalists discovered yesterday —namely, he wrote it in the manner of a personal autobiographical narrative, and made up the narrative (although not the details, which he got from records and interviews) since he was about five years old when the incident took place. For example, Joseph Mitchell published a remarkable series of pieces in *The New Yorker* in the early 1940s on New York fish-market life—full of impressionistic detail, and centering on a man whom he had also invented: Mr. Flood. In a prefatory note to the first piece, Mitchell wrote: "Mr. Flood is not one man; combined in him are aspects of several men who work or hang out in Fulton Fish Market, or who did in the past. I wanted these stories to be truthful rather than factual, but they are solidly based on facts."

Here, by the way, is the opening passage from "Old Mr. Flood":

> "*A tough Scotch-Irishman I know, Mr. Hugh G. Flood, a retired house-wrecking contractor, aged ninety-three, often tells people that he is dead set and determined to live until the afternoon of July 27, 1965, when he will be a hundred and fifteen years old. 'I don't ask much here below,' he says. 'I just want to hit a hundred and fifteen. That'll hold me.' Mr. Flood is small and wizened. His eyes are watchful and icy blue, and his face is . . .*"

Here is the opening to *The Earl of Louisiana*, by A. J. Liebling:

> "*Southern political personalities, like sweet corn, travel badly. They lose flavor with every hundred yards away from the patch. By the time they reach New York, they are like Golden Bantam that has been trucked up from Texas—stale and unprofitable. The consumer forgets that the corn tastes different where it grows. That, I suppose, is why for twenty-five years I underrated Huey Pierce Long . . .*"

Here is the opening to *Homage to Catalonia*, by George Orwell, published in 1938:

> "*In the Lenin Barracks in Barcelona, the day before I joined the militia, I saw on Italian militiaman standing in front of the officers' table. He was a tough-looking youth of twenty-five or six, with reddish-yellow hair and powerful shoulders. His peaked leather cap was pulled fiercely over one eye. He was standing in profile to me, his chin on his breast, gazing with a puzzled frown at a map which one of the officers had opened on the table. Something in his face deeply moved me. It was the face of a man who would commit murder and throw away his life for a friend . . .*"

And here is the opening of Tom Wolfe's piece on Phil Spector, the rock music figure:

> "*All these raindrops are high or something. They don't roll down the window, they come straight back, toward the tail, wobbling, like all those Mr. Cool snowheads walking on mattresses. The plane is taxiing out toward the runway to take off, and this stupid infarcted water wobbles, sideways, across the window. Phil Spector, 23 years old, the rock and roll magnate, producer of Philles Records, America's first teen-age tycoon, watches . . . this watery pathology . . . it is sick, fatal . . .*"

According to Tom Wolfe and the various unofficial histories of New Journalism, something marvelous, exciting, dramatic—a light of revelation—happened to Old Journalism in the hands of the young hotshots at *Esquire* and the *Herald Tribune*. Since then, the novel has never been the same. A new art form was created. And so forth.

I wonder if what happened wasn't more like this: that, despite the periodic appearance of an Addison, or Defoe, or Twain, standard newspaper journalism remained a considerably constricted branch of writing, both in England and America, well into the nineteen twenties. It's true that the English had this agreeable, essayist, public-school-prose tradition of personal observation, which filtered down into their newspapers. *"As I chanced to take leave of my café on Tuesday, or Wednesday, of last week, and finding myself sauntering toward the interesting square in Sarajevo,"* the English correspondent would write, *"I happened to observe an unusual, if not a striking, occurrence . . ."* Even so, in spite of the "I," and the saunterings, and the meanderings, and the Chancellor-Schmidlap-informed-me-in-private business, English journalism was for the most part as inhibited, and official, and focused as was the society which paid for it and read it.

In America there was much of the same thing—some of it better, a lot of it worse. The American daily press didn't go in as strongly for the sauntering *I*, except for the snobbier Eastern papers, which presumably were keen to imitate the English style. The American press rested its weight upon the simple declarative sentence. The no-nonsense approach. Who-What-Where-When. Clean English, it was later called when people started teaching it at college. Lean prose. Actually, it was two things at once. It was the prose of a Europe-oriented nation trying to put aside somebody else's fancy ways and speak in its own voice. But it was also the prose of the first true technological people—Who? What? Where? When? Just give us the facts, ma'am—the prose of an enormously diverse nation that was caught up with the task (as with the building of the railroads) of bridging, of diminishing this diversity.

In those days, when something happened, an event—a hotel fire, for example—newspapers generally gave you certain facts, embedded in an official view. No matter that the reporter himself, personally, was a hotshot, a drinker, a roarer, an admirer of Yeats, a swashbuckler of the city room; in most instances he gave you the official view of the fire. Where it was. How many people got burned. How much property got damaged. What Fire Commissioner Snooks said of the performance of his men. And so forth.

Then, after the First World War, especially after the literary resurgence in the nineteen twenties—the *writers'* world of Paris,

Hemingway, Fitzgerald, etc.—into the relatively straitlaced, rectilinear, dutiful world of conventional journalism appeared an assortment of young men who wanted to do it differently. Alva Johnson. John McNulty. St. Clair McKelway. Vincent Sheean, Mitchell, Liebling. And god knows who else. A lot of them worked for the old *Herald Tribune.* Later, many of them connected in one way or another with *The New Yorker.* What they did to journalism I think was this: first, they made it somehow *respectable* to write journalism. A reporter was no longer a crude fellow in a fedora. He was a widely informed traveler (like Sheean), or had an elegant prose style (like McKelway), or a gusto for listening and finding out things (like Mitchell or Liebling). Second, when they looked at this same hotel fire, and how it had been covered by their predecessors and colleagues, they noted that, at the Fire Commissioner's briefing, for the most part no one started his camera, or pencil, until the Fire Commissioner came into the room, and walked to the lectern, and opened his Bible, and began to speak. One imagines that these young men saw things otherwise. Movies were already by then a part of the culture, although admittedly a lowly part of the culture. Motion was a part of the new vocabulary. And total deference to the Fire Commissioner, or to the General, or to the Admiral, had already begun its twentieth-century erosion. The *new* thing, it seems to me, that the writer-journalists of the 1930s and 40s brought to the craft was a sense, an interest, in what went on before (and after) the Fire Commissioner came into the room. What did he do when he got on the elevator downstairs? Did he drop a quarter on the floor? What were his *movements?* For the first time in conventional reporting people began to move. They had a journalistic existence on either side of the event. Not only that, but the focus itself shifted away from the Fire Commissioner or the man who owned the hotel, and perhaps in the direction of the man who pumped the water, or the night clerk at the hotel across the way. Thus: reduced deference to official figures. (For example: James Agee's *Let Us Now Praise Famous Men.*) Personal touches. Dialogue—in fact, real speech faithfully recorded. When you read a McKelway piece on Walter Winchell, for example, you found a public hero taken to task, you found out what Winchell did when he wasn't in the public view, and you heard him speak—not quotes for the press, but what he said when he was ordering a ham on rye. "I'll have a ham on rye." Few reporters had done that before. Newspapers hadn't had the space. And besides (editors said), who wants to know what Bismarck had for breakfast, or what his ordinary comments sound like.

Then time passes. The scene shifts—everybody shifts. The nineteen fifties. The nineteen sixties. Tom Wolfe writes that he came out of college, or graduate school, burdened like the rest of his generation with the obligation to write a novel—only to discover suddenly that the time of the novel was past. I don't know whom Tom Wolfe was talking to in graduate school, or what he was reading, but back in the early nineteen fifties you didn't have to read every magazine on the newsstand to realize that a fairly profound change was already taking place in the nation's reading habits. Whether it was *Collier's, The Saturday Evening Post,* or *The New Yorker,* most magazines, which had been preponderantly devoted to fiction, were now increasingly devoted to nonfiction. It was also true, even then, that the novel itself was changing—changing, to be sure, as it had been since Henry James first gazed upward and noticed that the roof was off the cathedral. It was becoming easier, possibly, and more profitable, to become a novelist-disguised-as-screenwriter; but harder, perhaps, to become, and stay, a novelist of imagination and interior truth, which is what people increasingly seemed to be wanting of them. Mostly, in fact, one hears about the Death of the Novel from journalists, or from novelists-turned-journalists. And although there is only one *Painted Bird,* or *Separate Peace,* or *Play It As It Lays* produced in every twenty thousand books, people, the audience, still seem to be looking for *that* one; and the impress of each of those few books, I suspect, is still stronger and more lasting than nearly all the rest.

This brings us to the present state of the craft: the New Journalism. There is no getting around the point, I think, that a number of writers in the last dozen years have been exerting a steady (and often a self-dramatizing) push at the already-pushed boundaries of conventional journalism. I think of Gay Talese in many of his *Esquire* pieces, and especially in his last book, *Honor Thy Father.* I think of Terry Southern's magazine pieces, also for the most part in *Esquire.* Norman Mailer writing in *Harper's* about the peace march to the Pentagon, and the presidential campaign of 1968, and then in *Life* on the moon shot. Tom Wolfe and Breslin and Gail Sheehy and a whole lot of people who write for *New York.* Dan Wakefield in *The Atlantic.* John McPhee and Truman Capote in *The New Yorker.* A whole lot of people—sometimes they all seem to be the same person—who write in *The Village Voice.* Also: Nicholas von Hoffman, David Halberstam, Marshall Frady, Barry Farrell; and obviously a great many others. My guess is that anyone who denies that the best work of these writers has considerably expanded the possibilities of journalism—of looking at the world we're living in—is hanging on to something a bit too tightly in his own past. And on the other hand, that anyone who feels a need to assert that the work, especially the whole work, of these men composes a new art form, and a total blessing, is by and large talking through his hat.

Consider the mythic hotel fire we were talking about. Today, when a New Journalist tells it, there is likely to be *no* deference to an official version—if anything, perhaps a semiautomatic disdain of one. There is virtually no interest in the traditional touchstone facts, the *numbers*—the number of people dead, or saved, or staying at the hotel, the worth of the jewelry, or the cost of damage to the building. Instead, there are attempts to catch the heat of the flames, the *feel* of the fire. We get snatches of dialogue—dialogue overheard. A stranger passes by, says something to another stranger, both disappear. Rapid motion. Attempts to translate the paraphernalia of photography—the zoom lens, film-cutting. Disconnection. And nearly always the presence of the journalist, the writer—*his* voice. Our event, in fact—the fire—has seemingly changed in the course of time from (once) existing solely as an official rectilinear fact, to (later) a more skeptically official, looser, more written, human account, to (now) its present incarnation in New Journalism as a virtually antiofficial, impressionist, nonfactual, totally personal account of a happening—which often now is only permitted to exist for us within the journalist's personality.

The chief merits and demerits of New Journalism seem then as basic as these: the merit is—who really wants to read about this fire as it is likely to be presented in the *New York Times* or in a standard newspaper report? For those who *do* want to, the standard newspaper will give you the traditional facts: the number of people in the hotel, the number of people killed, who owns the hotel, etc. The standard newspaper conisders these facts important, because (apparently) the standard newspaper for the last seventy-five years or more has considered these facts important. Here is the beginning of a front-page story in the *New York Times* on the controversial and emotional subject of housing in Forest Hills: "*A compromise plan to end the fight over the Forest Hills low-income housing project has been worked out by top aides of Mayor Lindsay, including former Deputy Mayor Richard R. Aurelio, and has been discussed privately with leaders of blacks and Jews and with high-ranking officials. The plan would call for a scaling-down of the Forest Hills project by about a third and the revival of the project for the Lindenwood section of Queens that was recently killed by the Board of Estimate. The Lindenwood project, however, would be smaller than the earlier one. . .*" If this is the voice of conventional journalism speaking to us about our world, it is likely to find an increasingly restless, disconnected audience. The voice speaks too thin a language. The world it tells us about so assiduously seems but a small part of the world that is actually outside the window—seems a dead world, peopled largely by official figures, and by procedural facts, and written about in a fashion which is doubtless intended to be clear, and clean, and easy to understand, but which instead is usually flat, and in-human, and nearly impossible to connect to.

If then the merit of New Journalism is that it affords us the possibility of a wider view of the world, a glimpse of the variousness and disorder of life, its demerits, I think, are that these possibilities are so seldom realized, or at such cost to the reality-mechanism of the reader. For instance, in the matter of our hotel fire; there is no need, it seems to me, for a journalist today to relate all the traditional facts (especially since most of them, in this sort of story, are basically concerned with Property); but if he is to tell it as a *real* story, an account of an event that actually happened, I think there is a very deep requirement on the part of the reader (usually not expressed, or not expressed at the time) that the objects in the account be real objects. If the fire took place at the Hotel Edgewater, probably one ought to know that much, and certainly not be told that it was the Hotel Bridgewater. "But what does it matter?" says the New Journalist. "That's not the important thing, is it?" In many ways it isn't, but in serious ways it is. It's a commonplace by now that contemporary life doesn't provide us with many stable navigational fixes on reality; and that we need them, and have trouble, privately and publicly, when we are too long without. Families. Schools. The Government. Movies. Television. None of these contribute much anymore to informing us of the actual objects in the actual room we move about in. Journalism *should* materially help us with this, but all too rarely does—is either too conventionally timid, or, with the New Journalist, too often (I think) gives up the task of telling us of the actual arrangement of the objects, or at any rate of trying to find out, get close to it, in favor of the journalist's *own* imposed ordering of these objects.

By no means all New Journalism is careless. Talese, for example, seems to be remarkably meticulous as to detail. Mailer's account of the march on the Pentagon seems to have been extremely faithful to what happened. There are other examples, although not, I suspect, all that many. *A careful writer.* That was Joe Liebling's way of praising a fellow journalist, his highest praise. There are probably few careful writers around anymore. And few careful editors. Few careful generals. Few careful stockbrokers. Few careful *readers.* This doesn't seem to be a very careful period we are living in. Relationships seem to break apart . . . carelessly. Wars are waged . . . carelessly. Harmful drugs are put on the market . . . carelessly. A soldier kills ("wastes") two hundred unarmed civilians . . . carelessly; and his countrymen, when told of this, first don't want to hear, then turn away . . . carelessly. The point is not that it is a better or worse era than Liebling's, nor that there is any sure way of measuring it—but it is different.

And swirling all about us—still swirling, although the motion has somewhat abated—has been the great sexual lather of the 1960s. It was in the sixties, wasn't it, that we first had the miniskirt? Wife-swapping. Sex clubs. Swinging. The Pill. The sexuality of Kennedy politics. The new dances. Grove Press best sellers. *I Am Curious Yellow*—and showing at a chic theater. The sexual emancipation of women. Kaffeeklatsches about the clitoral orgasm. All those strident sexy costumes—the cutout clothes, the glaring colors, the *threads* that lawyers started to wear on weekends, the big wide ties, the side-burns. Esalen. Touch therapy. Everybody (it seemed) committed to being sexy, or at any rate aware of it, or at any rate trying to deal with it. Since then, some of the stridency has quieted down a bit. Sex in writing, for instance, seems to be less insistent and obligatory. We've just had *Love Story,* haven't we? Fashion magazines have started muttering about a Return to Elegance, whatever that may mean. But it was back in the sixties that New Journalism made its big push—a debut which Tom Wolfe seems to think derived from some magic confluence of the stars, or at least from some solemn discovery of the Death of the Novel. I wouldn't say that it wasn't *at all* the way he says it was—but my guess is that a lot of what's happened in New Journalism has as much to do with the New Carelessness of the times, and the sexual stridency of writers (and of nearly everyone else), as it has to do with attempts to evolve freer journalistic techniques.

At any rate, the new journalistic techniques have produced a mightily uneven body of work. Some of it is as good as, for instance, Wolfe's own *Electric Kool-Aid Acid Test*—but much of it—for example a recent piece in *Rolling Stone* by Hunter Thompson on the New Hampshire primaries—is slipshod and self-serving. Partly this is because of the times we live in, and how both writers and readers respond to the times. Partly, too, it's because—with one, or two, or two-and-a-half exceptions—there are virtually no prose editors anymore. Already in reporting, one notes that what used to be called a reporter is now called an "investigative reporter"; the reporter is presumably the fellow who informs us that the President is now standing in the doorway of the plane. And in editing, the person who deals with the bloody manuscript is now somebody called the "copy" or "text" editor, and works in a small office behind the broom closet; while the Editor, of course, is the man having lunch with Clifford Irving. Editors today lunch, and make deals, and assign subjects—"concepts"—and discourse airily on the "new freedom" which they now provide writers; which in fact means that the Editor can remain at lunch, and not be much bothered on his return by a responsibility to his writer's story, or to his writer's subject, because he usually has none, claims none. And writers, for their part, are just as keen to escape the strictures of traditional editing—as indeed are so many others in our society to escape the traditional strictures of *their* lives, marriages, families, jobs; and possibly for the same sort of reasons.

Writers. Writer-journalists. It is clearly a splendid thing, a sexy thing, to be a writer-journalist these days. Admirals, aviators, bishops—everyone has his day. Today it is the journalist (and some others). He declaims about the end-of-the-novel while he hitchhikes on the novel. He has small patience for the dreary conventions of the Old Journalism, although he rides upon its credibility, on the fact that most people will buy and read his work on the assumption (built up by his predecessors) that when he writes: "Startled, the Pope awoke to find the Hotel Bridgewater in flames," it was indeed the Bridgewater, not the Edgewater, and that it was, in fact, the Pope. Even so, this is not the worst of crimes. When people complain too much about inaccuracy, or inattention to detail, it seems to me they are usually talking about something else, perhaps a larger, muddled conflict of life-views.

Where I find the real failure in New Journalism, or in much of it anyway, is in the New Journalist's determination and insistence that we shall see life largely on *his* terms. Granted one knows, by now, the pitfalls of conventional "objectivity." One is aware of the inaccuracies and timidities which so often have resulted from on-the-one-hand . . . on-the-other-hand reporting. Still, there is something troubling and askew in the arrogance—and perhaps especially in the personal unease —that so often seems to compel the New Journalist to present us our reality embedded in his own ego. A classic example of this, I thought, was Mailer's *Of a Fire on the Moon,* with its generalities about engineers and scientists—generalities which seemed less concerned with what scientists or engineers might be, even if one could generalize about them, than in the ego-ability of the writer to generalize about them. Lesser talents and egos than Mailer are less noticeable, although it seems to me that much, if not most, routine New Journalism—I am thinking of the dozens of pieces about movie stars and politicians that appear in magazines each year—consists in exercises by writers (admittedly often charming, or funny, or dramatically written exercises) in gripping and controlling and confining a subject within the journalist's own temperament. Presumably, this is the "novelistic technique." But in fact Madame Bovary is a creature of Flaubert's—regardless of whether Flaubert once spent a summer in Innsbruck with a lady who looked vaguely like her, and who expressed dissatisfaction with her husband. Whereas Phil Spector, for example, in the Tom Wolfe piece, or Bill Bonanno in *Honor Thy Father,* or George Meany in a *Harper's* piece by John Corry all are real people, *nobody's* creatures, certainly not a journalist's creatures—real people whose real lives exist on either side of the journalist's column of print. The New Journalist is in the end,

I think, less a journalist than an impresario. Tom Wolfe presents . . .
Phil Spector! Jack Newfield presents . . . Nelson Rockefeller! Norman
Mailer presents . . . the Moon Shot! And the complaint is not
that the New Journalist doesn't present the totality of someone's life,
because nobody can do that—but that, with his ego, he rules such thick
lines down the edges of his own column of print. Nothing appears to
exist outside the lines—except that, of course, it does. As readers, as
audience, despite our modern bravado, I don't think we show much
more willingness, let alone eagerness, than we ever did to come to terms
with this disorder—the actuality, the nonstorybook element in life.
And it seems to me that, on the whole, the New Journalist (despite *his*
bravado) hasn't risked much in this direction either; and if you think
none of it matters, my guess is you're wrong.

So What's New?

LESTER MARKEL

To some like the dawn of a historic day in literature, to others like the onset of a plague of editorial locusts, the "New Journalism" has moved into the limelight, for all to survey, to ponder, to wonder. It is panelled on television, it is debated in newspaper seminars, it achieves first page attention twice in the course of a year in the once-always-*August*-and-now-je-*June Bulletin* of the ASNE.

The "New Journalism," its high priests contend, supplies a fresh and essential approach to reporting, making possible the Revelation of The Truth. The "New Journalism," its critics insist, is a bad Baedeker, a false map to editorial turnpikes; rather than providing direction to the Verities, it leads to credibility detours.

The argument proceeds heftily and deserves full scrutiny. Before assessing the pros and cons, however, this should be made 72-point clear: despite the fascination of many newspaper editors with the subject and despite the obvious yen of *The Bulletin* helmsmen to explore the theme to its ultimate adjective, the doctrine has little relevance to the daily newspaper. Nevertheless, it has created confusion in the editorial sancta, lured young reporters into strange byways and induced in copyreaders a dangerous tolerance for these meanderings.

Lester Markel's article was published in the January, 1972, issue of *The Bulletin* of the American Society of Newspaper Editors. He was formerly Sunday Editor of the *New York Times*.

Therefore, this present screed: an effort to define the "New Journalism," to new-journalize the "New Journalists," and, to demonstrate why the concept cannot and should not take the place of the misnamed "Old Journalism"—a label applied contemptuously by the New-J's, even though most of them do not or choose not to understand it.

In his search for enlightenment, this road-company Diogenes has aimed his flickering lantern at both the product and the producers of the New-J. He has examined numerous dissertations on the subject and questioned some of the high priests of the order. He has read Truman Capote, who started it all with his *In Cold Blood*, which he anointed a "nonfiction novel." He has talked with Clay Felker, editor of *New York* magazine, patron saint and one of the keepers of the New-J aviary; with Tom Wolfe, the articulate unofficial Secretary and Scribe of the sect; and with Gay Talese, whose ardent devotion to the New-J is attested by *The Kingdom and the Power,* in which he told All (and More) about the "not-so-good-not-so-gray" *New York Times,* and *Honor Thy Father,* in which he performed the same kind of hysterectomy on the Mafia.

First, then, the search for a definition.

Tom Wolfe (in an article in the ASNE *Bulletin* of September 1970) remarks that the "New Journalism" requires "all three talents, reporting, analysis and, above all, the dramatic techniques of fiction. . . . The basic units of reporting are no longer who-what-when-where-how-and why but whole scenes and stretches of dialogue. The 'New Journalism' involves a depth of reporting and an attention to the most minute facts and details most newspapermen have never dreamed of. To pull it off you casually have to stay with the people you are writing about for long stretches . . . days, weeks, even months."

Gay Talese (in "Author's Note" to *Fame and Obscurity*) offers this: "The 'New Journalism,' though often reading like fiction, is not fiction. It . . . seeks a larger truth than is possible through the mere compilation of verifiable facts, the use of direct quotations, and adherence to the rigid organizational style of the older form. The 'New Journalism' allows, demands in fact, a more imaginative approach to reporting. . . . I attempt to absorb the whole scene . . . and then I try to write it all from the point of view of the persons I am writing about, even revealing whenever possible what these individuals are *thinking.*" *

As an added starter there is Gloria Steinem, that formidable combination of Joan of Arc and Carry Nation, who (also in the ASNE *Bulletin*—of February 1971) scorns the "who-when-where-what-why

---

* [Editor's note: See Gay Talese, "Author's Note to *Fame and Obscurity,*" page 35.]

story"—a formula which "in inverted pyramid form is not one for writers; it's one for telegraph operators." She defines the New-J as the "old journalism of the days before the telegraph when news stories were done in essay form, or short story form, or some literary form. . . . You can only make sense of a situation by giving the human viewpoint, which is opinion." (Opinion?) *

In their writings, as cited above, the New-J's appear to have little doubt about the definition and validity of the concept. They seem to agree that they are trying to apply the "techniques of fiction" to non-fiction—"reporting in depth," "psychological insights," "meaningful dialogue," "truth not merely facts." This involves, they explain, a deep and long process of inquiry, the kind of insight (imagination?) that "factual reporting" cannot achieve.

Yet conversations with some leading New-J's reveal differences over interpretation, procedure and even nomenclature. Some of them, the elite, do an intensive job of investigating; one might label them, prosaically, the "Diggers." Others who assume the title do only casual and often careless investigation; one might dub them the "Skimmers." The "Diggers" vehemently disavow the "Skimmers" as false preachers of the faith and polluters of the New-J stream.

But these divisions into castes are minor compared to the divergences over definition and philosophy. For example: Mr. Talese speaks constantly of the "New" in comparison with the "Old" journalism; Mr. Felker deplores the use of both terms. Again: Mr. Talese talks of the "techniques of fiction"; Mr. Wolfe concedes that maybe the word "fiction" should not be used and that more accurately the process should be described as one that employs "all the techniques known to prose." (He is wary, as understandably he should be, that the word "fiction" implies to the innocent bystander something that is "fictitious.")

Some practices of the New-J's bother me no end—the portrayal of a composite rather than a single character (only thus, they hold, can the profile be rounded and complete); the collapsing of a sequence of happenings over a considerable period into a single episode of a single day (only thus, they contend, can the typical event be portrayed); the reporting of talk that might or should have taken place, even if it didn't (only thus, they believe, can the subconscious be brought to the surface for the reader to behold); a casual regard for "facts." ("It is often possible," says David Freeman, "for facts to get in the way of real truth.")

Out of my readings and my conversations these conclusions emerge: first, that the "New Journalism" is really not new; second, that

---

* [Editor's note: See "Gloria Steinem: An Interview," page 76.]

only in the broadest sense, is it journalism; and, third, that many of the New-J's fail to recognize that the "New" is not a substitute for the "Old" journalism and that journalism generally has been in process of change even if they have failed to notice it.

As for the newness of the concept, surely reporting in detail and in depth reaches far back in literature. As Mr. Wolfe points out, as one instance, Boswell's accounts of Dr. Johnson's doings would certainly qualify as "New Journalism"; and there are countless other examples. Moreover, the elite among the New-J's talk about the techniques not as a "discovery" but as a "rediscovery"; Clay Felker rejects the phrase as inaccurate and conducive to malpractices.

Consider then the word "journalism." It is derived from the French *journal* (daily), which in turn stems from the Latin *diurnal*, the adjective for *dies* (day). In the strict sense, it does not contemplate reporting and writing "for long stretches—days, weeks, even months"; it is concerned with the happenings of the day, with the news. Nevertheless, I accept as colleagues those who practice reporting in depth for weeklies and monthlies as well as dailies. But I feel that the New-J's should more properly be called "factual fictionists" or possibly "deep-see reporters" rather than journalists.

Now, about the "Old Journalism" so-called. The New-J's never deign to define it; they tag it as the "who-what-when-where-how-and-why school" and let it go at that. So one asks: is it not the job of the news-gatherer and the news-purveyor to answer these questions with as much insight as he can? Are the facts to be ignored? How do the New-J's, I inquire, propose to cover, for the same or the next day's newspaper, stories such as the admission of China to the United Nations, or Phase II of the Big Freeze, or an Attica outbreak or the shooting of a Kennedy? Of the 12 to 14 articles on the first page of the average newspaper, at least 10 cannot be covered in minute detail or with the dialogue and the colorful sidelights which the New-J's prescribe. There is simply not the time to do this kind of job, desirable as it may be, unless the newspaper is willing to yield the news field entirely to that other medium—television.

Furthermore, the New-J's depend in large degree on intimate glimpses and interviews—"whole scenes and stretches of dialogue" to achieve Mr. Wolfe's "basic units of reporting." There seems to be involved here a process that approaches the psychoanalytical technique. But the greater, the much greater, part of the news concerns events, rather than personalities, and obviously you cannot put a happening on the couch.

I am concerned too on the score of objectivity—an ideal which, even though it is rarely realized, should be kept constantly in the foreground. Often, I discover, the New-J's become caught up emotionally with their subjects in the course of their long association with them—and neutrality becomes difficult; judgment must be unfogged by sentiment. Moreover, a conclusion based on the weighing of facts is surely more easily and more soundly reached than one based on probing into the subject's "thinking" or one in which "imagination" is given full rein.

Thus, there are many pitfalls for even the most expert of the New-J's. In the hands of the lesser and more amateur practitioners, the dangers are legion—the tendency to produce actual instead of factual fiction; to skimp on the amount of research required for a well-rounded piece, to indulge in flights of fancy phrases; to throw all pretense of objectivity to the winds and let prejudice take over; in short, to perform as sociologists or psychoanalysts rather than reporters. This kind of thing is happening and will happen much more frequently and disastrously if editors open the doors too widely to the New-J's. And there is the danger that the credibility gap, perilously wide now, will be further extended.

Editors should keep in mind what the New-J's seem or choose to forget: that the "Old Journalism" is in process of important change and that various fresh approaches have been introduced into daily newspaper work. Increasing accent is being put on interpretation—the effort to make the news clear and relevant for the reader; to provide for him the setting, the sequence and significance of events and, whenever possible, an approximation of the truth (some indication as to which is the more believable of contradictory statements). Reporting in depth is taking place in increasing degree; pieces that even the most fervent New-J's might applaud are being published, profiles with insights, roundup or trend stories.

I concede that such pieces do not appear as often as they should, but a start has been surely made. And if the newspaper is to have an important future, publishers and editors should combine forces to make it more comprehensive, more understandable, more relevant and, above all, more credible.

In the light of these various findings and observations, I urge the editors of daily newspapers to keep their sense of proportion about the New-J's and I implore the pilots of The ASNE *Bulletin* not to accord them first page interviews, even if they are mini-dress, maxi-I.Q. ladies. And, most ardently, editors should repulse those among the New-J's who would apparently substitute for who, what, when, where, how and why—for all these eternal and absolute basics—a large IF.

Editor's Notes
on the New Journalism

HAROLD HAYES

The New Journalism has now become so established that it is apparently recognizable whenever and wherever its practitioners seek to perform it. Gay Talese's new book, *Honor Thy Father,* is complimented by *Newsweek* as "one of the New Journalism's finest achievements." "The New Journalism," sternly warns *The Wall Street Journal,* "Is Sometimes Less Than Meets The Eye." In the past year, at least three journalism historians have called on these offices to shed light on this brand-new school of journalism. Even the New Journalists themselves—a gymnasium full of ill-assorted egos, ranging from the brilliant to the banal—genuflect graciously when described in such terms. Yet the New Journalism is without a working definition. Some call it a form of reporting in which the writer stands at the center of the event; *The Wall Street Journal* says it is a technique of compressing facts in order to distill reality; and the Columbia Graduate School of Journalism defines it as a form of "subjective reality—the attempt to report events with the techniques of fiction." That it is *new* is the one point upon which all parties agree. It must be hell these days for the poor news reporter in Topeka, sitting there punching out his one-sentence, monosyllabic leads, wondering how many light-years he must travel in order to get with it.

Harold Hayes' comments on the New Journalism appeared in the "Editor's Notes" column of *Esquire* in January, 1972.

The problem with such definitions is not that they are too broad; rather that they are not definitions at all. "New" must carry the full freight of description, and here the connection is meaningless. Those who refer to the New Journalism see as its leading practitioners Gay Talese, Tom Wolfe and Norman Mailer. Yet except for their admiration for one another, Talese and Wolfe have very little in common. The work of neither man is related to that of Norman Mailer, each of the three having arrived at his station by following different routes. The journalism of Talese is comparable to the earlier work of Lillian Ross, to Joe Mitchell before Ross, to Alva Johnston before Mitchell, and so on back. Tom Wolfe's first manuscript in his modern voice (*The Kandy-Kolored Tangerine-Flake Streamline Baby*) suffered only minor deletions when submitted to this magazine, but significantly these deletions were made because they bore too marked a similarity to the voice of Holden Caulfield in *Catcher in the Rye*. Even Mailer, whose splendid variations in technique seem born of the occasion, owes more to past influences than present. If there is a school to emerge from the work of these men, then it is only a school of coincidence, and certainly it it not "new." In 1930 Edmund Wilson stood squarely in the center of events, more than likely compressed a few facts, and most assuredly used the technique of fiction in writing *Frank Kenney's Coal Diggers;* so did James Agee in reporting on Southern poverty in *Let Us Now Praise Famous Men* (1941); and so did George Orwell on many notable occasions, especially in *Homage to Catalonia*, his most personal account of the Spanish Civil War. To my knowledge, *The American Mercury, Vanity Fair, Harper's* (the pre-Sixties *Harper's* under Jack Fischer, who was the first, I believe, to publish the nonfiction of James Baldwin), and *The New Yorker* could produce encyclopedias on variations of the form currently defined and designated as New Journalism. The wealth to be found from mining magazine journalism somewhat prior to the day before yesterday is embarrassing—or should be to historians of the New Journalism and others who persist with the term.

It is easy enough to think of older examples out of the recent past of this magazine but they would be irrelevant to the issue since *Esquire* of the late Fifties and Sixties is considered a birthplace of the school. The publisher of this magazine—its editor in the Thirties and Forties—has suffered more movements than any editor I know. When asked his opinion on the subject, he recalled with some pleasure a *Nouveau Journalisme* lead sentence from *Paris Match* in the Thirties: "J'ai su que la main qui tenait l'allumette pour ma cigarette était celle d'un *gangster!*—"I knew that the hand which held a match to my cigarette was that of a gangster!" Santa Baranza! Send the Mau Mau flak catchers to put out the fire on the moon! Who can wait to see what happens next!

About six years ago, our Backstage editor, the late Alice Glaser, asked that old New Journalist, Dwight Macdonald, how he would describe his role as a writer. Mcdonald sent over an unfinished eight-page manuscript in which he characterized himself as a "literary journalist," one who sees no need to restrict himself to conventional journalistic forms in writing about matters of journalistic interest. Here the matter should rest, for "literary journalism" is a definition which allows any writer with ambitions beyond the restrictions of newspaper journalism to write as well as he is able. It is certainly no distinction for a writer of substance to be lauded as a modern innovator simply because he writes in a manner unfamiliar to non-New Journalists—more precisely, Old Journalists. Old Journalists are concerned solely with the conveying of information as briskly and effectively as possible within a stylitsic framework which is familiar to most readers. But literary journalism allows, indeed encourages, conceptual writing and there is nothing new about conceptual writing except when there occurs the ever-new miracle of a single writer's originality—that of a Mailer, a Talese, a Wolfe—responding to his own singular concepts, and no matter the point in time at which this wondrous intersection occurs.

The 'New Journalism' We Need

GERALD GRANT

Several months after Benjamin Bradlee left *Newsweek* to become managing editor of the Washington *Post,* a series of staff shakeups began. After the first wave one of the editors invited a dozen young city staff reporters to lunch. As he sipped his Dubonnet on the rocks we nervously wondered about our fate. Most of what he said now escapes me. But I have a vivid recollection of his curiosity about the social circles we traveled in. Whom did we see? What parties did we go to? Whom did we know? His point was that a good deal of what went on in Washington could be learned at dinner parties—or at least that those who were able to establish a social relationship with sources after working hours were most likely to be privileged to the inside story on the job. Some of the best journalists in Washington had grown in reputation as their sources had grown in responsibility; in some cases they had been lucky enough to be classmates.

At the time his message struck me as mildly offensive. Not that it was pointless; his own prominent social connections had not hurt his career. As I look back, however, his inquiry no longer strikes me as saying so much about upward mobility of journalists as about patterns of thought in journalism. His comments underscored the idea that

Gerald Grant, a former Nieman Fellow and *Washington Post* reporter, is an associate professor of sociology and education at Syracuse University. His article appeared in the *Columbia Journalism Review,* Spring, 1970.

talent in journalism is often a skill for finding out what somebody *else* thinks or knows about something. It may be an oversimplification, yet it is true that lively concern for whom a journalist knows reflects weak appreciation for how he thinks.

What separates most journalists from the few great ones is that the latter are not content with knowing what their sources think. They exhibit an independent intelligence that seeks to wrest meaning from the torrent of events rather than acting as mere transmission belts. They ask better questions because they have a better concept of what the "story" is.

There are some journalists who think, as Richard Hofstadter has said, in terms of configuration and style, thus delineating patterns as well as describing events. One recalls the work of Philip Meyer of the Knight Newspapers, who has effectively used social science skills to analyze current issues; of the perceptive reporting of Joseph Lelyveld and Anthony Lukas of the *New York Times;* of the probing exemplified by the work of Laurence Stern's and Richard Harwood's Insight Teams on the *Washington Post.* There has been a gratifying tendency on a number of papers such as *Newsday* and the *Los Angeles Times* to give reporters the time and freedom to do serious, thoughtful journalism. But as Daniel P. Moynihan said in his brilliant eulogy for Paul Niven, "[Journalism is] that most underdeveloped, least realized of professions. Not a profession at all, really. Rather a craft seeking to become such out of the need to impose form on an activity so vastly expanded in volume and significance as desperately to need the stabilizing influence of procedure and precedent and regularity."

Max Ways, in a *Fortune* article last October entitled "What's Wrong with News: It Isn't New Enough," attributes journalism's shortcomings to its failure to adopt new forms and new defintions of "the story." As a result of applying old yardsticks to events, he says, journalism continues to focus on what can be easily measured and told, to the neglect of more complex and important events unfolding in the society. But were the yardsticks ever any good? My guess is that journalism in 1870 failed in much the same ways it does today. The underlying explanation, then as now, is the kind of mental habits and attitudes most journalists bring to bear on events.

Journalists work by a code that makes many of them moral eunuchs. The professional, in print at least, generally pretends to be without opinions or convictions. His objectivity differs from that of the scientist who demands freedom to develop a fresh hypothesis but then remains objective in the sense that he will look in an unprejudiced way at the results of his experimentation.

Reportorial objectivity has been under vigorous attack by the "New Journalists." Citing Norman Mailer and others, they rightly sense that newsroom objectivity may result in untruth. It masks feelings and stifles imagination. More importantly, it can produce a trained incapacity for thought in the young journalist. Unconsciously he comes to believe that what he thinks doesn't matter. He regards himself as a conduit. The reporter calls an expert for a quote as an unfortunate shortcut to thinking the problem through himself. He asks not what do I think, but what do they think? That can be a habit difficult to break. He seldom has a sense of personal responsibility for what he writes.

This is why Michael Arlen, writing in *Living Room War,* is right when he characterizes much current journalism as propaganda. Not that experts shouldn't be interviewed, or that reporters must be philosopher-kings; but they should be something more than tape recorders. Most journalists are caught in a nether world. They are neither men of action, forced to confront a problem by struggling with it in an operational sense, nor men of true imagination or contemplation.

Yet uncritical enthusiasm for the New Journalism of passion and advocacy may cost more in the loss of the valuable skepticism of the traditional newspaperman than can be gained through the new involvement. The trouble with advocacy may be that it leads writers who haven't thought or felt much to portray cardboard emotions. Most readers would rather hear the experts. The challenge is to make sense out of the experts and of events. We don't need a whole new breed of novelists in action; we need more cogent journalism that tells us about problems rather than sketching conflict, that gives us the arguments rather than two sets of opposing conclusions. We do not need more passion but more intellect, more understanding.

While there are heartening signs of change, it remains depressingly true that the rewards in journalism tend not to go to the writer who painstakingly thinks a problem through and expresses the subtleties, but to the author of jazzy personality pieces, scoops, and exposés. Exposés are nominated for prizes (often rightly so, of course) while a complicated piece of analysis wins the epithet "thumbsucker." These attitudes are related to the city-room environment where keen—often counterproductive—competition encourages reporters to jealously guard their scoops and current projects even from their co-workers. There is no incentive for the kind of intellectual sharing and discussion of first drafts that is common in an academic community or in any profession where the contributions and criticisms of one's colleagues are considered essential.

Work tends to be defined as scurrying about and asking questions. It is the rare reporter who has the fortitude to sit at his desk and read a book on a subject he intends to write about. Not infrequently one reads a long newspaper series—in which hundreds of man hours of reporting and travel time have been invested—and it is glaringly obvious that some of the most basic books written in that field have not been glanced at by the writers. I once asked Nicholas von Hoffman of the *Washington Post* how he avoided the usual pitfalls of newspaper writing. His exaggerated reply: "I never read newspapers."

Interestingly, von Hoffman was in his thirties when he turned to journalism, having been a community-action organizer with Saul Alinsky. Perhaps that thought-provoking apprenticeship also protected him from learning the bad intellectual habits that are bred into many young reporters. There may be something of a pattern in his experience, although it could just as well be explained by genetic endowment. The careers of a number of exceptional journalists reveal some catalytic intellectual experience outside the newsroom: Walter Lippmann's association with Santayana and his diplomatic experience; David Broder's opportunity to break out of the usual journalistic formulas on the *Congressional Quarterly;* Nick Kotz's background of Phi Beta Kappa and study at the London School of Economics before his present assignment with the *Des Moines Register* and *Tribune;* Willie Morris' residence at Oxford before tackling the *Texas Observer*, and now the editorship of *Harper's;* Anthony Lewis' immersing himself in the Harvard Law School as a Nieman Fellow before doing his exceptional reporting on the U.S. Supreme Court; Alan Barth's sojourn with the Schlesingers while he was a Nieman; Joseph Lelyveld's Fulbright year in Southeast Asia before joining the *Times*.

Journalists pride themselves on being generalist-specialists. Ridicule of academic specialties ranks high as newsroom sport. Yet the methods by which journalists are trained tend to be extremely narrow, even though most are probably college graduates. On most large papers today reporters specialize early in fields in which few have any general background: transportation, politics, education, or perhaps even elementary education. But the academic, whose specialty or current research may be narrowly focused, usually has had a broad intellectual base that emphasizes the interrelationships of knowledge and common methods of inquiry. The journalist learns his lore on the job. He is steeped in the concrete and specific phenomena pertaining to his beat, learning in the syncretic, associative way. Thus, he often lacks a broad conceptual framework of his subject, or a method of analysis. Hence he is usually very good in predicting what will happen tomorrow, but seldom about the shape of things five years from now. Similarly, he often remains unaware of historical parallels of current events, or of cross-cultural comparisons.

The aims of journalism differ crucially from those of scholarship. The academic investigating police behavior, for instance, wants to tell it all once, thoroughly, exhaustively. His intellectual aim is to formulate a theory or model that will explain the seemingly variable surface events, and perhaps predict the shape of things to come. The newspaper has a vested interest in the concrete and specific, in telling the same story again and again in a way that makes it sound new and different. Thirteen petty robberies must be written in a way to make them sound as different and interesting as possible.

Both approaches have their strength, however. If the journalist often obscures the general truth in mountains of fact, the scholar frequently remains blinded to the specific truth of a particular situation because of his faith in his abstractions, and occasionally, his ideology. Noam Chomsky has shown in *American Power and the New Mandarins* how frequently the latter is true. He convincingly pairs Neil Sheehan's description in the *New York Times* of fetid slums in Saigon with some scholarly accounts of the supposed benefits of American-sponsored "urbanization" in Vietnam. He writes:

> Many have remarked on the striking difference between the way the press and the visiting scholar describe what they see in Vietnam. It should occasion no surprise. Each is pursuing his own craft. The reporter's job is to describe what he sees before his eyes; many have done so with courage and even brilliance. The scholarly adviser and colonial administrator, on the other hand, is concerned to justify what he has done and what he hopes to do, and—if an expert as well—to construct an appropriate ideological cover, to show that we are just and righteous in what we do, and to put nagging doubts to rest.

Paradoxically, the limited generalization characteristic of most journalism is often a great strength. It doesn't care what the general theory is, but what is true in this particular instance. Ignorance of what is supposed to be true may have the productive result of puncturing myth or forcing scholars to re-evaluate old evidence.

Much more could be said of the sins of academe—of its petty jealousies, blindness, and irrelevancies. My aim, however, has been to probe the roots of what Norman Isaacs of the *Louisville Courier-Journal* once called the "mental prearrangement" that passes for thought among many journalists. More weight could be given to exceptions to some of the norms cited. But the point is precisely that there are such norms, though they are increasingly being violated.

The more general question that obtrudes is how can the norms be changed? To begin with, journalism schools could profitably follow the developments of law, education, and business schools whose faculties are no longer top-heavy with former practitioners, although they have an important place. Faculty are needed from the academic disciplines who are interested in applying their knowledge to the problems of mass media and who will teach students more thoughtful modes of analysis in a realistic setting. Such new faculty could also play a vital role in strengthening journalism schools' much-neglected role of critically assessing the performance of the press.

Newspapers should also recruit from law schools and graduate schools of sociology and political science. A great many more skilled young academics in the social sciences could be attracted to new careers in the mass media if given responsibility to tackle significant issues. Newspapers need not become miniature graduate schools, but neither should they produce the kind of shabby analysis that they do of city budgets and school reading scores. Personnel practices must change. Salaries must rise. Sabbaticals should become standard. Research assistants will be needed. Change might be so drastic as to free the average reporter from drudgery and scut work in the way that the average elementary school teacher has been liberated in New York City. The costs of carrying out these suggestions might prove a considerable financial drain on many smaller papers—at least until their benefits could be established. For that reason, such programs ought to be worthy of foundation support.

But these are long-term changes. What about now? Newpapers have only begun to take advantage of outside expertise. Academic skepticism of "newspaper writing" can be overcome with the right kind of assurances from sensitive editors that copy will be responsibly handled (not to mention massage of professorial egos with promises of the right kind of display). This puts a premium on editors who are aware of the outside expert's area of competence and interest and who can frame issues in an intellectually stimulating way. Outsiders should also be involved in seminar-like lunches, planning sessions and critiques of coverage. This use of experts as "consultants" has become fairly common among magazines but is employed less frequently by newspapers.

A bolder necessary step is to go beyond hiring the free-lance talents of academics to hiring the academics themselves. But the twist here is to employ them for their skill as teachers, as catalysts who would develop new concepts and methods of reporting. Distinguished teachers and thinkers could be brought to newspapers for short periods to head special projects and reporting teams. Some might come on sabbatical; others for only a semester or a few months or weeks. They might come from think tanks, foundations, publishing houses, and universities as well as from the ranks of freelances and other diverse social critics. Why not ask Ralph Nader, Saul Alinsky, or James Baldwin as well as sociologist Nathan Glazer, psychologist Robert Coles, economist Robert Lekachman? There are scores of candidates, though perhaps not all as well known, in every large city.

Under such a system, a small team of reporters might be assigned to work for a month preparing a series on the police, or an assessment of educational programs in the slums, or a survey of changing racial attitudes. They might work with a political scientist, a sociologist, a social psychologist. They would read and jointly discuss several books and perhaps a half-dozen relevant articles, attempting to define issues, identify historical trends, decide where reportorial energies should be directed.

Instead of rushing out to interview sources, reporters might spend time digging into census documents, examining attitudinal research, and drawing some conclusions of their own. There would be some debate about what the story is—with one result that the series would not be, like so many others, merely an elaboration of the obvious. Interviews would not be sought until there was some evaluation of what had been written, what the questions were, and the kinds of sources that could best answer them. In the case of the racial attitude series, reporters would have a chance to learn about constructing a survey, how data is fed into a computer, and some elementary notions about principles of statistical inference.

David Riesman, commenting on a draft of this article, noted that more reflective social scientists are under attack today by some of their radical activist colleagues. Although generally enthusiastic about the suggestions here, he added, "I could imagine the ironies of academicians in the newsroom being more journalistic than the journalists."

One should not overlook the benefits that would accrue to academics as a result of immersion in the newsroom. They would come away with a more realistic sense of the possible, of how complicated things really are in the concrete. It might broaden the outlook of many scholars about what their fields of inquiry ought to include. It could prove an interesting testing ground for many kinds of hypotheses and have benefits in research terms, including research about the mass media. New and better academic publications might be another by-product. The hostility of many journalists toward academics—perhaps a result of their unconscious resentment at their dependence on the experts—might be reduced. There might be a similar gain in understanding on the part of the academics, who are frequently jealous of the journalists' power (and angry at what they regard as its misuse), and who sometimes resent journalists who "cream off" the fruits of their research.

The whole notion of a newspaper as an educational institution—internally as well as externally—is central to this concept. The possibilities of encouraging greater cross-fertilization within the newsroom are limitless. Outsiders would be astonished at how little information or expertise is exchanged or developed among newspaper staffs, which have an exceptional range of talent and great opportunities for such development. A consulting firm like Arthur D. Little would close tomorrow if internal staff growth processes were as moribund as those on even our largest newspapers. Newspapermen, though they would vigorously deny it, jealously guard their imagined status and small prerogatives within the newsroom, and nothing in the way the place operates is likely to encourage them to do otherwise. One way is to bring in a catalyst from whom all learn as they teach each other. The multiplier effects of such a process could be surprising. Journalism could expand your mind.

In and Out of
Universal City

BENJAMIN DEMOTT

Bad moment for bringing out a new novel. Especially bad for a little book, familiar pattern—love, renunciation . . . Current Critical Trend Unfavorable. New Involved Journalism is all the rage. Involved Journalism is a personification of a vision, says Nat Hentoff (following Norman Mailer) in the *Evergreen Review*. "Who needs fiction?" says Professor Kazin in the *Atlantic Monthly*. "Who needs fiction in order to learn what is constantly reported by . . . the magazines, newspapers, college textbooks, and television set?"

—The line is hard to dispute. You want to say: "Involvement is a cage. Freedom is precious. Stories liberate." But merely saying so—it sounds whiny. What's the point? And as for demonstrating, actually trying to show where and how storymaking (and reading) can straighten people out, keep a man in one piece: could you even begin to do that without soaring into hubris—or tailing off into another tale?

The time is early May, close to the end of term. A foundation aide up from New York talks awhile in my office and then offers

Benjamin DeMott is a professor of English at Amherst College and the author of *The Body's Cage* and *A Married Man*, both novels. His essays are collected in *You Don't Say, Surviving the 70's,* and *Supergrow: Essays and Reports on Imagination in America,* in which this article is reprinted. It originally appeared in the *Antioch Review,* Spring, 1969, with the title "In and Out of Universal City: Reflections on the New Journalism and the Old Fiction."

a gig. Fly out to Hollywood, observe some TV film-making, write answers to a few questions about the production dynamic, supplies of unused talent and imagination, etc., and add any thoughts bearing on the immediate business (the immediate business is Educational Television, Methods of Improving). The trip can be scheduled in reading period, guidance on "the coast" assured (an independent producer attached to Universal City promises to cooperate). As for—oh, yes—money: we're staying in tight on this, but "a skinny hundred a day and expenses," will that do? . . .

The flight west (at the end of the month) is cozy, and I settle in on a Sunday night at a motel I've stayed at before—a block or two off Hollywood Boulevard, on the corner of Yucca and Something Else. (I'm not totally green. Behind me a year or two is a stretch as a writer-consultant in ETV, and a turn, before cameras, as an interviewer —in Hollywood, at that.) In the morning I go to work. I drive out to Universal City, meet my people, observe shooting on sound stages and the back lot, attend a script conference, a casting conference, a rap session and a gabfest, and begin "interviewing" producers, writers, coordinators, directors. Succeeding days are the same, and the notes pile up. ("Carol, darling, take your own time to sit down. Don't feel obligated to do it on the cue." . . . "Okay, it's *between* a rewrite and a polish." . . . "Are you going to eat that during the shot?" . . . "We need an inch under Ben." "Give Ben an inch and he'll take a mile." . . . "Roll'em and go." . . .)

On toward dinnertime in the evening I walk over with the producer and his helpers to the projection room to watch the day's prints. (The footage is for *Run for Your Life,* a serial dramatic show about a young man with a year to live.) Afterward, sliding out of most invitations, I drive back to my motel, swim in the pool, mix a drink, eat alone, late, at this or that Pow Beefhouse along La Cienaga, and return home to work for an hour, pulling notes into paragraphs. Several days of this and I say my thankyous, pack up, and fly home. My "report" takes a weekend to finish (the foundation man likes it)—whereupon exams come in and the gig's up. . . . A trip, another carbon MS in a manila folder, a vanished check—day in the life of a culture reporter/professor . . . The story in theory ends here.

Suppose for a moment, though, that we wanted to go on with it—in the New Style, in Involvedese—with an eye to clarifying differences between new journalism and old novels. Could it be done? Is there a formula to follow? Guidelines for tyro Involveders? Hints? Rules? The answer is Yes of course, rules aplenty. In some particulars, indeed, the forms and conventions of Involvedese are as tight as those of an aubade. (The conventions include a set tone—conscientious embitterment; a set conflict—Good Guy vs. Bad Guy within the reporter; a set pattern of character development—the reporter is first a clown, then a heel, then a seer, and a set climax or reversal or peripeteia —exposure of the Involved Audience's vanity and hypocrisy.)—But why so many words, as the wave said to the fisherman. Let's run the junket through the involving machine and look at the scenario that comes forth.

The first sight, naturally, is my public Universal City self, angled to reveal a naïf, a Country Joe clownishly enjoying the local magic, sloping about in a mist of stock responses. . . .

Item: A projection-room audition. After the dailies, the producer watches clips of starlets—casting is incomplete for a segment due to start filming in the morning. A face pleases him. Backwind: he looks again. The girl speaks only a single line in the clip. Striking wide eyes. "Get her," is the word to the casting people. They set out on a telephone search. My heart races. I'm hot for the sweepstakes: will A Star be born? They give up after half an hour, and in a different but still charged mood, I think: Sad, sad . . . Poor child. So near yet so far. Who'll ever know?

Item: A moment on the sound stage. Star and ingenue playing to each other. (PAUL [almost a whisper]: "I'm sorry, Kate. I'm sorry." KATE: "Oh, Paul . . . I've never blamed you—") Beautiful. I love it. I sigh with the ingenue, turn away with her, share the inexplicability of things that keeps them from life together, a future. . . . The director snaps his fingers, signaling the end of the take, and delightedly I catch a glance—shy? approving?—that passes between Star and girl. They like each other, then? They're together, really together? I'm in rapture.

Item: Script conference. A new young director calls on the producer to complain about the logic of the script he's to direct the following week. A recent Harvard grad, producer of the undergraduate version of Kopit's first play. Attractive, personable . . . I don't follow the talk closely enough—miss my chance to find out how sharp the lad is, whether he's another slumming Harvardian or someone earnestly trying to redeem his assignment. Plain enough why I wander off: "in my heart" I already know the score. He's a Harvard, isn't he? That means he's okay. Harvard in Hollywood sticks up for integrity, and rightly so. People respect people who stand up for themselves. You're damn straight. Up quality! Up taste! Reinhart!

—Well and good: we've got a tease and a theme—reporter as nit. It needs underlining and development. More confession, more personification of the vision. How about a backward glance, like so—

I've always been a boob out in Hollywood. I gored on stereo-types the last time too. In my educational telly days, I plumped for a D. W. Griffith bio-special that presented the man as a noble artist-voyager afloat on a sea of muck. (Camera tight on bronze Hollywood Boulevard sidewalk star bearing Griffith's name, as the voiceover laments—during pullback to twoshot—the chewing gum that pedes-trians grind into his memory.) Nor is that the half of it. I'm forever sucking up to local values out there. It's true. Was I not ecstatic—on this trip—when asked for my views at a script conference? Did I not become embarrassed about my drab professorial rented compact car? At home it's easy to be properly sniffish about posh car con-spicuousness, but out there—The Truth is, I'm *extremely vulnerable to corruption.* Going in and out of the gate I avoided the guard's eyes; I was downright furtive.

And the night I accepted an invitation to dine with a Biggie—more sin. We climb out of the chauffeured car in Bel Air; I follow the cigar through the voluptuous house, single-file line of march, children, maids, dogs, hanging on, hoping to delay our passage. (Same bit every night, the man says, patting this one, shaking that one off.) And we slip out a side Dutch door through a lush garden to a pool house—domesticity left behind, sweet young bird waiting on pool ter-race to make drinks. "We" three eat by ourselves, chuckling, happy, *yé-yé,* we here, they there. . . . Did I speak up for the family? for good solid middle-class values? I did not. I read my way deep into this alien pattern: two worlds, eh? servants and children in one, yes, grown-ups separate, hmmmmm. Mmmmmmmm?

—Pause here, frowning—a moment of perplexed search for self-understanding. Or for self-justification or for a rationalization. Per-haps my finkery was actually good manners. (Would it not have been rude to confront hospitality with a solemn endorsement of family togetherness?) Perhaps the sucking up was determined in my youth—spells cast over me in the Fantasy Theater off Sunrise Highway in hometownville. Saturday afternoon, endfolded, glass bell over me, hurrying away from the flicks. Safe in the schoolyard, screened from sight, I fight the air and smash chins (if the flick's been Gable or Gar-field), or, if it's Sophisticated Comedy, I light my Sensation with Bill Powell's insouciance and speak out in Cary Grant's voice. Having once adored the glamour, having once given up my whole self to it, having once become a mere echo, could I have expected to break out of myself in the real Hollywood? . . .

—Okay: we've made it to the middle. Our line thus far—for the Involvedese Scenario—is that in the daytime Uni-City was Fun City for me. A place where my mind cut off altogether and I shuttled about from one act of identification to another—fool, fraud, boozer, comic, happy sunshine sycophant.

But at night—here's a key moment: we're turning toward The Deeper Guilt—at night and the following weekend I stopped shuttling. Another character rose up in me and held the floor: the foundation fink, the "culture critic." I try to be fair to him at first. I say, In a way the culture critic was doing the best he could. We have to have people like that. It's a condition of The Culture. The Culture Critic had specific questions to answer about morale, taste-levels, and the like. He was just doing his job. Ah but *no*, dammit. (This is an emotional outburst.) I *loved* the job. I was shameless. My behavior as Culture Critic was downright treacherous. Did I so much as hesitate, for instance, before invoking alienation theory behind my hosts' backs? No, I did not, witness this paragraph of my report:

> . . . no community interest or shared sense of responsibility for the finished segment of a series show unifies production staff and performers, directors, men on the set. . . . The executive producer . . . and his immediate associates are usually visible to others chiefly in entrepreneurial roles: they are artificially drawn off into a separation—as "coordinators" of ungraspable multiplicities. . . . Stereotypes of art versus business harden. Tensions, frictions, suspicions deplete trust. Feelings of powerlessness burgeon. . . . The performer retreats into a reductive sense of himself, experiences no sense of control over the production as a whole, and at length dwindles into self-pity. . . .

Furthermore I savaged the product itself, never hinting how I dug The Stars:

> *Run for Your Life* is fairly described as a fantasy. The *shtick* is the imminent death of the hero, which places him beyond ordinary moral chastisement (whatever the behavior, decency would feel compelled to forgive it). The hero has a positive obligation to sin. He was created as a sophisticated, attractive, appetitive hero— and if such a figure were to form a permanent relation with a girl, he would be guilty of self-indulgence, or even of cruelty itself. The character of his situation therefore establishes or suggests a world in which promiscuity is probity—and that world is scarcely unwelcoming to mass fantasy and desire. If the imminence of death were constantly stressed, true enough, the fantasy would be contained or qualified. But here again the executive producer is alert—too alert—to the substance of the program's appeal. He remarks that he avoids scripts which make much of the death theme and turn the viewer's face too blankly toward reality.

Even at the moment of final survey, I held to my lying condescension, and spoke in pained distaste:

> There are elements of garish pseudo-sophistication in various segments of *Run for Your Life,* and the dialogue abounds in three-dot waffle. (Sample provided.) But the precedents for this warmed-over Sagan—if not for promiscuity and bloody socking matches— in the radio soaps of the thirties and in sentimental ladies' fiction of the late nineteenth century are past counting. Neither show nor hero is an inexplicable phenomenon, a freak of culture. Both are continuous with America, part of a seamless cultural whole. What is unappetizing about them is also unappetizing about Ford Galaxies, Holiday Inns, Hollywood Boulevard between Highland and Vine, the teary-sincere orator in LBJ, the smile of the airline stewardess, *Valley of the Dolls,* many commencement speeches, and perhaps half the articles in this month's issues of the "quality" magazines. Style, discipline, clarity of thought, fullness of understanding are lacking—and the heart is nevertheless somehow vaguely felt to be in the right place.

Am I not a wretched soul to have set myself up so high? Am I not a hypocrite to have left my own clowning goof-off response so far behind!

—Time for the kicker, the close. We need a moment wherein "I" the Involved Reporter get it in the ear, am *caught out* in my fundamental insincerity and guilt. No problem: life supplies the *shtick.* Within months of my trip to "the coast" my two opposing selves—Detached Critic and Secret Showbiz Buff—clanked against each other noisily in public, did they not? Knowing only the part of my nature that I cheesily dressed out for them, the producers of *Run for Your Life* trustingly wrote me into one of their scripts. Ben Gazzara, Star, takes down a book "By Benjamin DeMott" from the shelf of a new girl friend's apartment, and comments in a way suggesting that anyone who reads my work must be highly educated and a person of Natural Taste. At the time I was asked to release my name for this use, I was touched. Showbiz, ah, Showbiz! But time passes. They catch up with you. At the end of a class last spring, a spiky straight-A student wheels up to incorruptible me and says, You were on TV last night, a real lousy show, how come? Feeling the tide of his disillusionment (Say it isn't so, Prof), I hung there suspended, as I hang here in the final paragraph of this swell piece of Involved Reportage. I hang suspended and then pretend puzzlement, not having the courage to face him.

But though I acknowledge no complicity, turn away, I am—at least for an instant—nailed. And you know it, Reader, don't you? You wanted it. You want to whip me. Chew me. You're rejoicing because I got what I deserved, right? So you see? *You're another.*

No compassion. We're all [obscenity] together and it was ever thus. Whereupon we

GO TO BLACK

As should be said at once, an essay that fleshed out the model above with appropriate details, intensities, and dirty words wouldn't by any means be useless. It could put a reader in touch with several bits of conventional wisdom about contemporary life—as for example that even on holiday people see their inner world as conflict-ridden; and that a man's fantasies rouse contradictory responses—joy, shame—inside him; and that the objectifying culture which seeks to neutralize "the personal" imposes strains and falsehoods; and that, responding to this pressure, people discipline themselves, separate their parts and arrange them in hierarchies, in order to create a viable professional self.

But despite these reminders, these occasional gestures at something beyond the Involved Reporter, the actual function of such writing isn't, as the small scenario should show, to bring a world into general view. On the contrary, the function is to explore a literary mode of self-suspicion. The explorations are often witty, sometimes intense. There is a certain play within the tone of embitterment. It flexible enough to accommodate ruefulness and embarrassment (see Andrew Kopkind on serving *Time* in the *New York Review of Books*), as well as earnest, caring, self-childing (see Murray Kempton defining, in *The Spectator*, his feelings of guilt after the murder of Bobby Kennedy). A disciplined reporter occasionally makes his guilt felt in a piece without explicitly focusing on it—see Tom Wolfe's piece on a father-son, adman-hippie confrontation in the Village (*The Kandy-Kolored Tangerine-Flake Streamline Baby*), or Rex Reed's account of a family Sunday at the Paul Newmans', unaccredited sightseers and tourists milling outside while Reed is well treated within (*New York Sunday Times*, September 1, 1968).

But too often the impression, no matter what the precise tonal register or level of discipline, is that form has preceded substance. Selection of details both from outward events and inward response lights up discontinuity, opportunism, insincerity; personal rumination curves repeatedly, deterministically, toward the occasion when the reporter "finds himself out." Conscious from the start of an obligation ever to inch his way toward a more solidly cynical idea of a person, the writer speaks always with a self-deprecatory tic.

The tic has a history, naturally, and a sociology as well. Reductive versions of humankind have been standard items in Western thought for longer than a century. Psychiatry has enlarged the market, as Seymour Krim—his essay "Making It" (1968) is a landmark in the development of Involvedese—once pointed out:

> In the climate we all make it in, the age of suspicion, putdown, sneer, needle, it's almost inevitable that a swinging person is going to probe himself for the hidden motivations in the way he acts, makes his little scenes. Introspection is the private playground of every brain around, there's no escaping it, and especially in New York where psychiatry has gotten such an incredible play is there a used condom of doubt that drags down every full-hearted gesture into the subway mire of the psyche's triple-dealing [sic]. Face it, man—nothing is safe in our world from the meanest interpretation, nothing is pure or uncomplex, nothing but *nothing* escapes from the enlarged vocabulary of analysis that our quick and unhappy minds grind out for sheer dissonant sport.

And the appetite for cynical views of the person is now fed everywhere in the media. Think of the endless series of Feiffer cartoons (Instant John Osborne, Instant Underground Man) showing sad-faced middle-class types abusing their moral character, and then being congratulated by their audience:

> Your Honor [says a Feiffer character in panel one] . . . Ladies and Gentlemen of the jury [panel 2] . . . I have great potential but no follow through [3]. . . . I have contempt for the values of success but I secretly hunger to be successful [4]. . . . I don't know what love is, which is why I avoid all serious relationships [5]. . . . I make a great show of interest in other people but I'm *really* only interested in myself [6]. . . . I've never deliberately hurt anyone in my life but I always feel guilty [7]. . . . I throw myself on the mercy of the court [8]. . . .

In the next-to-last panel the jury speaks:

> The jury finds the defendant a fine, insightful person who is not afraid to be brutally honest with himself.

And in the last panel the man departs, slick, buoyant, smug in briefcase and cigarette holder. "Justice triumphs," is his conclusion. The message is: Self-love is a disease beyond remedy. You cannot confess without strengthening your sense of invulnerability. "He who despises himself esteems himself as a self-despiser." The evil in me is beyond my capacity to name and know. From the trap of guilt there's no possibility of escape.

Or think of the insistence with which the same ground theme sounds in the work of the literary masters of Involvedese—witness the central passages of Norman Mailer's *Armies of the Night,* wherein the writer details his guilt at not spending another night in jail:

. . . a failure of nerve always presented the same kind of moral nausea. Probably he [Mailer] was feeling now like people who had gone to the Pentagon, but had chosen not to get arrested, just as such people, at their moment of decision, must have felt as sickened as all people who should have marched from Linclon Memorial to the Pentagon, but didn't. The same set of emotions could be anticipated for all people who had been afraid to leave New York. One ejected oneself from guilt by climbing the ladder—the first step back, no matter where, offered nothing but immersion into nausea. No wonder people hated to disturb their balance of guilt. To become less guilty, then weaken long enough to return to guilt was worse than to remain cemented in your guilt.

"That passage," says Mr. Hentoff, not only "draws you in," it "brings you the news about the rest of your life." And again the news is that "for the rest of our life" we must wear another man's dirty shirts.*

News of this kind resembles dogma more than things as they are, and some who are in close touch with their own full human complication are likely to resist it. Sustaining an uncomplacent, non-beamish resistance is impossible, however, without protection from cynicism about the person—and what protection can be found? I can mumble commonplaces and truisms at guilt-mongers. I can talk to myself about the connectedness of human parts, about the interdependency of self-love and self-criticism, about the intimate relation between human fantasy and social hope. I can remind myself that the common (and absurd) daydream of escape from conditioned existence into Absolute Integrity or Beauty or Guiltlessness is at the same time a force charging me to invent new models of life, and reinvigorating old standards of assessment. I can lay it down that men's dignifying severities of self-scrutiny have roots in indulgence, that responsibilities begin in irresponsibility, and that the compulsion to believe the worst of ourselves—the style of conscientious embitterment, dutiful self-hatred—is in fact a vanity, a fleec-lined hair shirt, bearing no relation to genuine humility or genuine pride, and invariably deflecting both understanding and the will to modify or re-create the conditions.

But, expressed thus, these truths are the merest chat, worthless until the meaning is known from inside. And the case is—coming at last to the point—that there are few surer ways into that meaning than through imaginative writing. To say this, to say that fiction alone draws us out from the cage of self into caring, knowledgeable concern for the life that is not our own, isn't to claim that novelists and storytellers are untouched by high-fashioned self-hatred. Neither is it to

---

* [Editor's note: See Nat Hentoff, "Behold the New Journalism—It's Coming After You!", page 49.]

say that journalism by literary men never draws a person out in the fashion described. (There are hints of conscience-nagging in George Plimpton's *Paper Lion;* the writer one or twice damns himself for an interloper, etc. But because his subject permits lightheartedness, and because he himself has virtually a lover's feeling for the charm of his own fantasy, he can bear to let his reader see beyond him.)

It is to say, though, that creating a story, whether as writer or reader, is an act capable of liberating people from the boring predictabilities of self-regard. That creation is a means of living into the interdependency of "best self" and "worst self," and of pushing beyond artificial borders, beyond official moral simplifications of human motivation, beyond this year's lit-establishment tone and style of self-assessment, into a clearer, denser, fresher world. Reading or writing, I indulge my desire or need to be someone else, to be a different person in a better world—and am reminded that this desire is at once an indulgence and a moral distinction—and am lifted (briefly, that is true, only briefly) by this "literary" experience to a kind of behavior both as judge and as fantasist that possesses unfaked dignity. I oscillate between permissible identifications with other human beings and an attainable detachment. I sense contrarieties pressing inside the next man. I'm elevated by the act of judging deeds that aren't mine, but that are yet known to me from within.

And it *is* the judgment—that act of judging—that's most exhilarating. Reading and writing fiction is far from a murky love-in or flower kiddies' ball. It is an act requiring sympathy, since "understanding" is the goal—but not an extravagant sympathy of the kind that chokes the sense of justice. Reading *Anna Karenina* I'm not simply bewildered or amused that Oblonsky can at the same time be wretched about his faithlessness to Dolly and tickled by some wisp of recollection of the "bewitching" governess. I don't simply take this response or conduct in a forgiving spirit, or regard it as a determined event, inescapable. I come at its inevitability from within. I feel the regrettable yet, for him, oddly pleasing limitlessness of what we cannot control. I understand that the conscience that pains Oblonsky also delights him by reminding him of his personal attractiveness. I am unremittingly aware of the reciprocities of what is called "virtue" and what is called "vice," conscious of the hollowness of appeals to Integrity as a separable entity in itself, alert to the complex process by which new vanities and new moral aspirations wake to life simultaneously within human beings. And *yet none of this knowledge paralyzes me.* I assess the relative significance of the character's conscience in my inward experience as I read; I understand that Oblonsky is a small man, less than a man can be, and in the act of understanding I rise for a while above the naïf or gull within me, above my smallness, and out of chichi self-contempt.

A voice says: It sounds mysterious. Reading and writing fiction equal judging yourself from outside, judging another from within. . . . Can you tell it simpler, please?

It's not, finally, a simple matter, I suppose. And for that reason people who talk about fiction in terms of volume of news, competition with Huntley-Brinkley, or with Mailer at a convention, or Capote at an execution, seem to me (I confess) dim. A story is an orchestration or score of sympathy and judgment, penetration and objectification: now the one predominates, now the other, but both are always at hand, stimulating each other, letting us out of ourselves, calling us back to judge our trip. I need such scores for several reasons. Partly because through them it's possible to touch a life of feeling or an idea of personhood superior to the one in current journalistic fashion, yet not so far beyond me as that still proposed by the religious establishments. Partly because the possession of a means of motion forth from the self spins me out of simplicities of self-laceration and doom-mongering. Partly because, through the novel—again: either by writing or reading it—I touch my borders, such as they are, become an expanded constructive sympathy, an expanded self. No more rewinding myself perpetually onto the spindle of a passive shame: I spring with the word toward its target and take the force of the impact from within.

—Fine, oh, fine, says a harsher voice: I get it. Writing fiction is an ego rub. It builds self-satisfaction. It lets you like yourself.—You think that's proper? In a time like this we should go about savoring our beauties and excellences?

Well, it hurts to say so, true. And no use pointing out, defensively, that there are complacencies in stylized guilt (the news of my whole life) as well as in shrugging self-acceptance. For, once that point is made, you're back again in abstract argument, speaking up solemnly for some famous elusive "balanced attitude toward life," etc. Who can know what balance is? The best I know is that I like truth of the sort implicit in Thoreau's lovely springy sentence: "When I am condemned and condemn myself utterly, I think straightway, 'But I rely on love for some things.'" I like, that is to say, a truth of resiliency, a truth about how we spring out, spring back, aren't by any means "indomitable," yet seldom are put down by sorrow or guilt, can cross over, can know from within. Such truth doesn't belong to the new journalism; the mode is too uniformly blackish and self-accusatory. But in the bright book of life, the novel, you can sometimes touch it— which is why, even in a bad moment, people will get on with the work.

—Well and good, says one last voice, kinder and more relaxed. But you've not said how it really went out there, have you? Out in Hollywood? You remember you started—

How it *really* went? In the end that's another subject, not at all close to the one in view here (is fiction finished?). It is the subject of values shaken, the challenge of fantasy—not fit stuff (to repeat) either for Involvedese or for the lingo of the Culture Critic. The subject does come up, though, in something of mine available for a price downtown—a book that has, for a stretch, a Hollywood setting. The work is called A Novel, and I can speak of it at any time without feeling pushy, guilty, or the like. For the idea of speaking of it is only to rouse a pleasant memory. Thinking back on "the work," talking about it, I remember writing it—the experience rushes into mind, the freedom, sense of perfectability. . . . How happy I was!—happiness being nothing more nor less than a road by which it does seem possible truly to get there from here.

On Epidemic First Personism

HERBERT GOLD

When it first occurred to me that perhaps the current fad for first person parajournalism, where the reporter—me, say—looks into his own heart for information about politics, war, or suffering, and tells what he finds there in long loping sentences all stuffed with literary allusion and neighborhood bar slang—I'm a scholar and good fellow, too—may have gone too far, I decided to spend a few days away from my wife and five lovely children in order to explore my angst-ridden contemporary soul for one of the deepest and truest articles I have ever written. Syntax, structure, and information would be no obstacle to my quest for self-analysis. Outré! Right on! I must seek to discover whether delicious solipsism, the deepest religion of my kind, can ever supplant horrid egotism, the disease of others. But first, let me tell you about my childhood in Cleveland . . .

About a hundred years ago Dostoevsky assaulted his fellow novelist Turgenev with this accusation: When T. describes a shipwreck, with children drowning, what he describes is the tears running down his own cheeks. See! Turgenev is sad. See! Turgenev is moved. See sensitive Turgenev.

It wasn't entirely just. And yet, if it was unfair to Turgenev, it remains true to a recurrent weakness among writers. The lust to make

Herbert Gold's reservations about first-person journalism appeared in the *Atlantic*, August, 1971.

an evocation which comes alive for readers, providing an almost religious communion of souls, sometimes degenerates into mere me-me-me-singing. In the fantastic heart of writers there is always the temptation to justify, to brag and confess, to make their own immortal souls the prime issue for everyone else. And now, as writers become celebrities, they are being rewarded for this childish frailty. Confessional operetta, the one-man show starring a howling, complaining, bragging, spangled, bangled, and adjective-crazed prose ingenue, is the literary fashion of the time. First personism has become an epidemic contagion.

The reporter headed for trouble spots doesn't wear his William Holden trench coat anymore, but knows what is expected of him: "How I Got Drunk in the Middle East."

The crusading lady writer, spellbound by deep questions of essence and being, begins with a theme and a title: "Thoughts on the Role of Women in Our Society While I Squeeze My Hated Husband's Blackheads."

The English philosopher C. E. M. Joad defined decadence as "dropping the object." That is, an overelaborate architecture tells us that the object for which the building was built is forgotten. The decadent construction stands pretending to be one thing—a church, a bank, a restaurant—but is, in fact, a monument to euphemism, cleverness, or historical nostalgia. In the same way, an involuted, self-displaying rhetoric is careless of argument. It may use the vocabulary and gesture of original thinking, and evoke the standards of the past (or of the future), and hurtle with an energy of conviction, but the real purpose is not to discover but to display. We might ask of some contemporary styles: Is the speediness a haste to learn the truth, or is it merely another speedy ego trip? Are all the good stunts necessary to outwit stubborn ignorance and habit, or are they intended merely to show us the author's latest postures?

The first-person arias of the Wolfettes and Mailerlings center the whole world in the self of the writer. They don't do their job of telling and sharing experience. Instead, they sacrifice knowledge for a parading of personality—the wistfully arrogant group personality of the quintessential *New Yorker* writer, the bluffy Southern heartiness of the traveler for the recent *Harper's*, the anxious deprecation of *New York* magazine's new conservative chicness, the bleary sexual confession of the *Village Voice*, the run-on truth-speed-paranoia mumble of many of the underground journalists, the rollicking buffoonery of *Rolling Stone's* and *Esquire's* fine young chaps. Many of these writers are talented, and I name few names because, to paraphrase Vladimir Nabokov, anonymous dispraise hurts a little less. I've taken a turn or two myself in the past.

Perhaps these writers should be writing fiction. To make oneself larger is an impulse legitimately gratified through the magnifying vision of the fictive imagination. But it's a spoiled self-display to take a matter of life and death for others—rats in slums, poison in food, war, and miseries—and use it to show the tears on your own cheeks. Many articles now tell us all about the problem of the writer's jet reservations, the Holiday Inn in which he stays, his loneliness at night, his menu and his wine card—all material better described in his expense account—and only then get to the entertainer or revivalist or politician he is interviewing. The delight in self, the lack of delight in subject matter, implies a serious ultimate judgment which ought to be faced by the first-person journalist: What matters? Does the world matter? Does anything matter but me? Is there anything out there? Is my business to stroke myself, and let the voyeuristic reader watch while telling him he is learning something, practicing sympathy or intelligence? Beyond the game of prose, is there something which is not a game?

Back in the mid-fifties the critic Norman Podhoretz wrote a magazine article in which he predicted that the new American art form would be . . . magazine articles.* People want to *know*, he said, and fiction is tuckered out. The novelists will be too impatient to suffer the long incubation of fiction. They want the immediate joy of publication now, renown now, and the gratifying contact with the great and the ignoble which touring journalists can have.

Well, Podhoretz's prediction turned out to be prophetic. Magazine readers and editors wearied of the objective homogeneity of traditional cottonspeak article prose, and also of the breathless backward-reels-the-mind pseudo-excitement of traditional anonymous jazziness. The individual voices of talented writers provided a fresh perspective on the real world: Norman Mailer, Tom Wolfe, James Baldwin, Gore Vidal, Paul Goodman, Joan Didion. First they were writers, then they were celebrities, and then the prose is in danger. The prose is in danger right away with their epigone.

Not that anyone wants to return to the term paper as the model for objective seriousness, or Pete Martin visiting the stars as a model for intimacy. The women's lib journalists—Sally Kempton and Vivian Gornick, for example—sometimes build to touching climaxes of misery as they equate the troubles of the world with their own dramatic troubles with men. With some subjects—rock music, say, or the Film Star Interview, a form which has become almost as classic and familiar as the sonnet—it's proper that the article be an exploration into the deepest heart of America or Hollywood by a talented, lonely, and

---

* [Editor's note: See Norman Podhoretz, "The Article as Art," page 125.]

scared pop-writer. Surely it's not important to treat Grand Funk Railroad or Raquel Welch as more than an occasion for a lonely meditation on Me and the Media, Me and Your Friendly Neighborhood Sex Goddess.

But enough already. There really is a real world out there. "As I was saying to my wife only last night as I strove to write this piece" is probably a phrase that leaps unforgettably to the scissors in the final version. The writer sets himself up as judge and jury, and the reader is entitled to know what his standards are, but he might just as well leave out the personal advertisements. Jack Newfield's running romance with the Kennedys let us in on every twist and turn of his aching heart, but what we really wanted to know about each of the Kennedy brothers was what they meant to the rest of us, not how Jack Newfield's nose was continually clogged with difficult feelings. A little objectivity is not a dangerous thing. We need to hear the subject more than we need to hear the heroic writer's conversations with his intimates. Tacitus, Tolstoy, Coleridge—to take three raconteurs at random—discussed the real world and also used the word "I." But they discussed the real world of history, morality, or art. The "I" was located firmly. First-person journalism is not a new phenomenon. It's only the celebrity-mongering, the offering of the self for sale by flashy wordsmithing selfs, that seems very modern. (Hemingway's decline was the last generation's sad example.) The trouble comes when there's not enough world and too much self.

It used to be thought that popular magazines flattered their readers by giving them pablum. Now, in a time avid for stimulation and personality, there's pepper in the pablum. It used to be that journalists buried themselves like cynical monks, telling who-what-where-when-how, and leaving out the why. Now, trying to give the meaning of it all, the playful parajournalists lie down like puppies, howling operatically, their four paws in the air, scratching their own bellies. For many years Norman Mailer tried to avoid the use of the word "I" by referring to himself as "One," as in the (sample) phrase, *One predicts the apocalypse as one suffers cancer-producing Muzak.* Now, in his moonshot, he has taken to the astrological plural, calling himself "Aquarius." In either case, the "I" is central to the thought, and the Mailerlings get a confused message. What is good in Mailer is the participation in a real world. What the epigone reads is that he sure gets away with talking about himself a lot.

At its best, the first person singular can reflect the context of events, give a passionate depth sounding, resonate with social need, answer for a moment the avidity for touch and intimacy which is one of the diseases of mass society, and thus truly justify what *this writer* says, feels, suffers. And sometimes, for example, Norman Mailer (on the police at the Pentagon), Tom Wolfe (on the East Side girl with everything), Gloria Steinem (interviewing Pat Nixon for *New York* magazine), George P. Elliott (on pornography in *Harper's*), Tom Williams in *Esquire* (on the touching and dreadful innocence of hard hats), Wilfrid Sheed in almost any of his film and book reviews make the interaction of touring self and throbbing subject an occasion for both light and heat.

The personal reportage of Joan Didion brilliantly evokes the starved privacy of Americans, no matter what her ostensible subject. Have Medium, Will Travel. Writers often surprise themselves with what they celebrate—homosexuality, the Manson case, women's lib, Bobby Seale, or the opening of a tennis ranch—and as they meet each other, crisscrossing the country on the magic wings of the expense account, they must sometimes fret about what they will either discover or sweep noisily under the rug, depending on their talent and sense of responsibility.

Stendhal said that the ideal style would be that of the Napoleonic code, direct, unambiguous, impersonal, cool. Well, writers aren't laying down the law; they don't have Napoleon's authority; and therefore, if they hope to make a strong case, they need to arouse passion by giving a strong whiff of personality, of soul, as Stendhal himself understood in his novels. But the ideal of a crystalline transparency and objectivity is one which needs to be recalled in a time of self-important muttering, grousing, and self-display. The mystery of personality is a proper fuel in making art; it may be the essential one. But the magazine article is not a TV talkshow interview *of* the self *by* the self, in which a writer emits sounds about his own greening with the illusion that he in his own body and soul makes up most of what is significant about America (or Amerika). That's dropping the object. That's confusing one's own wet cheeks with the heaving seas, the perplexed children, and the shipwreck.

"Say, fella," said Enrico Banducci, proprietor of Enrico's Coffee House where all us high-living first-person journalists hang out in San Francisco, "say, Herb, how'd you do on that article criticizing first-person journalism?"

"I think I did good this time, Reek," I said (all us intimate first-person journalists like to call him Reek). "I think I really hit the ole ball this time, Bandooch," I said (all of us first-person journalists like to rotate our vocabularies when we're referring to our contact with stories out there in real life).

"That's just dandy," answered my colorful bar-owning pal. "Then can I tell Susie you'll pay up your tab?"

Bad Writing and
New Journalism

DANIEL J. BALZ

In the preface to his book *The Courage of Turtles*, Edward Hoagland makes an offhand but telling comment about one of the problems of current journalism. "First-person journalism is fashionable now," he writes, "though the excess of its practitioners are going to kill off its fashionability soon." It is a perception that could be applied to the entire range of writing called the New Journalism.

Much of the critical discussion about the New Journalism has centered on what it is doing to the art of reporting. Those problems were discussed by Gerald Grant in these pages.* The feeling among many reporters is that New Journalism has allowed emotions to substitute for facts, instead of to amplify them, and that this has produced sloppy reporters and in some cases, shallow stories—something New Journalism is supposed to prevent. Grant wisely asked that the New Journalism take the form of more thorough research, more study of the literature in a specific field, more discussion among reporters about the stories they are covering, more reliance on academic experts, and

Daniel J. Balz was a graduate student in journalism at the University of Illinois when his article appeared in the September/October, 1971, issue of the *Columbia Journalism Review*. He is presently an economics reporter with the *National Journal*.

---

* [Editor's note: See Gerald Grant, "The 'New Journalism' We Need," page 263.]

most importantly, more reliance on one's own brain—in short, a New Journalism based not so much on subjective feelings and senses but on more arduous research and independent thinking.

But that is only one facet of the New Journalism: reporting. The other is writing. If we are to expend greater effort in gathering material for a story, at least as much effort should be given to writing it. Grant wrote: "We don't need a whole new breed of novelists in action. . . . We do not need more passion but more intellect, more understanding." Although I agree with his overview I don't think it would hurt if reporters asking to play by the rules of New Journalism had more of a novelist's sense for writing.

The freedoms of current journalism, just as they have given rise to sloppy reporting, also have fostered sloppy writing. Not that there hasn't been poor writing in newspapers before ("The difference between literature and journalism is that journalism is unreadable and literature is not read," Oscar Wilde once observed), but if we are to continue to argue for more freedom in newspaper writing, we should demonstrate more awareness of how and when to use it.

I am of that generation of writers unduly influenced by the delights of Tom Wolfe, and I am also of that generation labeled as activists, or "advocacy journalists," by older members of the media. We have been subjected to a number of pressures, including peer-group pressure, that have led us away from journalistic forms popular a decade ago toward something we believed, with the encouragement of our elders, was better.

I do not mean to rediscover here the roots of the New Journalism, for that has been covered before. But as in other areas of society we were attempting to find a better way to tell the story, and so we grasped quickly for what was new. Unfortunately, we still seem to be grasping for something we don't really understand.

In a Columbia University discussion between Wolfe, Gay Talese, and Harold Hayes of *Esquire*, printed in the January, 1970, issue of *Writer's Digest*, Hayes said that as good as Wolfe was, he had probably ruined a generation of writers.* I am not so sure that Wolfe has ruined us so much as he fooled us. We all read in the introduction to *The Kandy-Kolored Tangerine-Flake Streamline Baby* how, after many false starts, he sat down one night and hammered out his piece on customized cars in one great burst, and how *Esquire* knocked off the DEAR BYRON from the beginning and took it unchanged.** And we read his marvelous articles, with all those exclamation points and dashes

---

* [Editor's note: See "The New Journalism: A Panel Discussion with Harold Hayes, Gay Talese, Tom Wolfe, and Professor L. W. Robinson," page 66.]
** [Editor's note: See Tom Wolfe, "Introduction to *The Kandy-Kolored Tangerine-Flake Streamline Baby*," page 29.]

and gassy colors and hip talk, and we were lulled into believing that journalism was easy if editors would loosen the reins a bit.

We didn't penetrate his aqua Malacca malaise enough to realize it wasn't the colors or the punctuation or the hip talk that made Tom Wolfe good. It was instead the abilities of a Ph.D. in American Studies to see things in our society which no one else recognized as being significant. Nor did we consider his apprenticeship on papers like the *Washington Post* or the *Herald Tribune*.

Dan Wakefield used to say in a class he conducted at the University of Illinois that some of the best writing we would do would be in letters to friends because we would not feel the inhibitions of form. And we were a little disappointed when things we wrote still sounded rough and shallow, for we had failed to listen when he had said that if we all sat down and said, "I'm going to write this piece like it's a letter to my friend," that we would be no better off than before.

Norman Mailer's *Armies of the Night*, as most now recognize, pushed us even farther because hundreds of us had gone to the Pentagon, either as participants or reporters, and had failed to come to grips with it in any way comparable to Mailer. Of course we blamed that on form, not on ourelves. We didn't relate Mailer's earlier political pieces, his reports on the 1960 and 1964 conventions, to the Pentagon book. We simply related the book to what we had written—form against form—and believed Mailerian thoughts rested in all of us, waiting to be sprung.

Such influences have caused experimentation with style, form, and subject matter, and that is hopeful. Newspapers today are livelier for it. But after several years of this journalistic thaw there is still an indication that we are no more comfortable with these new forms than we were when we first tried them, that we have no better understanding of what those forms can do and when they should be used.

For a majority of the articles printed in newspapers, the various techniques of New Journalism are unnecessary and often detracting. Most stories are still printed for the information they contain; New Journalistic techniques often block presentation of that information.

We now see stories with Wolfian leads, rich and full of description, which quickly trail off into standard feature interviews with stock questions and stock answers. We see description for description's sake. Endless Salems and Winstons being smoked, legs continually crossed or uncrossed, glasses pushed up on the forehead. We are reading a lot more about the sky and the trees and the grass without really knowing why they are important to many of the stories in which they are used. We see endings tacked on with no sense of fulfillment or irony, or even—sadly—conclusion; pale descriptions of actions or movements of interviewees getting up and walking away, which do more to stop a story than to end it.

What this indicates is that articles aren't being "written" any more now than they were under the shackles of "old journalism," but now they are filled with all kinds of literary sidelights which often add only words and wasted space. Stories are written fractionally—a good lead here, some flourish in the body there, occasionally a thoughtful, conclusive ending; but rarely are there threads of continuity that show thought from beginning to end. It is, I'm afraid, the old journalism with a few frills being passed off as the new.

Why has this happened? Part of the reason is that, as young reporters, we came to believe we would be better journalists if we were allowed to write instead of just report, and so we began to try to write without studying the craft of writing in the ways we had studied reporting. We felt that the difference between writing and what we were accustomed to was simply a loosening of the old formulas, when in fact it was not that at all. It was a tightening of thought patterns and word associations and ideas, an extension beyond the old formulas, that demanded all the earlier skills, which added the discipline to subdue the easy phrases and combinations and to search for something better.

One way to do this, I was told a few years ago, is to read good writers. Unfortunately, this does not mean to read newspapers, because of the great bulk produced daily only a scant portion has good writing as well as good reporting. But if we are striving for a newspaper form which blends both, then we must read all we can.

We must read and study those reporters whose abilities to ferret out illusive facts stand above normal standards. And we must also read those who are experimenting successfully with the more elegant forms of nonfiction writing; writers like Ward Just, whose blend of reporting and writing gave his book *Military Men* dimensions far beyond the normal presentation of facts; like David Halberstam, whose proven abilities as a reporter have been enhanced by his more recent talents as a writer; like Richard Rhodes, who seems to end an article as well as anyone writing these days; like Gay Talese, who is perfecting the technique of the internal monologue; like Garry Wills, and Anthony Lukas, and others.

No, we do not need novelists on our newspapers, but if we could get some of our best young reporters to study the writing process, our writing standards would likely improve. But unless there is some impetus for this, some force apart from those of my generation who are using or abusing the newer forms, it will be a slow process. This is where the role of the editor becomes critical, for if he does his job properly, with intelligence and toughness, young writers won't fall into some of the habits of bad writing.

Journalists of my generation have not been edited severely, and this is unfortunate because we have not done it to each other. Many of us gained early experience on college newspapers, and—good training grounds as they are—they are not a place where critical editing takes place, either because we were too concerned with our own writing or because we did not know the functions of a good editor. But in any creative process there must be constant critical evaluation, and it is important for young journalists because we are not dealing with formulas as much as before.

There is the belief that once a young writer leaves the sanctuary of college and is subjected to the pencil of a pro, he will shake the bad habits. This is simply not true. On smaller papers, where most of us start, a young, aggressive reporter can write and write and write and see his experimentations appear in print nearly untouched. This gives him a false sense of his own talents, for on these papers it is difficult to find editors who will give the kind of thoughtful evaluation needed. This is where the excesses begin.

On larger papers it is difficult, I am told, to get editors to sit down long enough to give a young writer the kind of personal attention he needs. This is not a condemnation of editors, but as Paul Swensson told the American Society of Newspaper Editors a few years ago, there must be a change in philosophy in editing, one that moves away from editing sentences and paragraphs to one which considers the scope of the whole story, from changing faulty mechanics to eliminating faulty thinking.

Young writers could help accelerate this by demanding that editors really edit, by literally forcing editors to tell them where the soft spots are. They are hesitant partially because they don't often have confidence that editors will treat their stories as reporting and writing. It is difficult to watch a paragraph formed with thought and care excised thoughtlessly because it did not meet standards of formula journalism.

Editors could help also by recognizing some of the patch jobs that are crossing their desks as just that, and by explaining to young reporters the times to hammer and the times to write. We are not so unreceptive that we will not listen to reasoned judgments by editors who know their craft. Too often we have not gotten this, and now we are defensive when it happens because we believed we were good. I remember times when journalism professors gave me such talks, and although I argued with them, in the end I sat down and rewrote, and through those somewhat painful sessions began to realize the influence of good editing on a piece of writing.

If they do their jobs well, editors will not only find fault with the reporting, they will find fault with the writing. And most importantly, they will demand that a reporter rewrite, from top to bottom if necessary. Understandably, there is a problem of deadlines, but as newspapers move away from this fixation—especially on the kinds of stories which will demand good writing *and* reporting—editors should not feel the pressure of the clock and a large hole forcing them to print something they feel should be improved.

Those who say, "This is what you should do next time," will not make their points in the same way as editors who say, "This is what you must do before we print this." Such forcefulness may cause some bloodletting in our newsrooms, for who among us does not suffer from pride of authorship? But it will probably result in stories which come closer to achieving standards of New Journalism we now only pretend to meet.

A Fun-House Mirror

WILFRID SHEED

The worst news to come this way in some time (if you exclude the recent unpleasantness at the polls) is that Tom Wolfe is serious. I don't mean artistically serious—I always assumed that—but, *you* know . . . *serious.* He has been carrying on at some length lately about his baby, the New Journalism, but with none of his old nerve-racking audacity. More like a . . . *grandfather,* for God's sake.

This could have several dire consequences, even beyond the endless panel discussions it has already launched on "Is There a New Journalism," all of which are on Wolfe's head. It has also robbed us of one of our most resourceful literary performers in the middle of his act: rather as if Groucho were to come back at Mrs. Rittenhouse with a lecture on comedy. That sort of thing should be postponed till dotage, at the very earliest.

Wolfe at his best seemed to be impenetrable. No criticism could pierce the white suit or provoke a straight answer. One assumed that the effect was calculated, but one couldn't quite be sure. That is the essence of eccentricity-as-art (see Tiny Tim). He *is* kidding, isn't he? The clown bats his lids, seems not to hear the question. Gooses you, one way or another.

Wilfrid Sheed's latest novel is *People Will Always Be Kind.* He is also a film critic and writes frequently on literary matters for the *New York Times Book Review,* in which "A Fun-House Mirror" appeared December 3, 1972.

You have to conclude that Wolfe is either tired of acting—we don't have the stamina of the great Englishmen, your Waughs and Sitwells—or wants to try something else (not more essays on the New Journalism, I hope) or, more seriously, that he undervalues what he was doing. N.J. or no N.J. (the initials are ominous), Wolfe was never in the same racket as Gay Talese or Dick Schaap—or they with each other. Call A. J. Liebling, Paul Gallico and Jim Bishop the Old Journalism, and what have you added to any of them? It is surely for desperate graduate students to discover these schools and for writers to keep out of them.

To avoid any further aroma of the panel discussion (which Wolfe is now conducting with himself anyway in the December *Esquire*) let's allow that the boys he cites are doing something new in close-to-the-skin reporting. But did anyone ever read Wolfe for that? It is actually a quaint feature of his gift that readers assume his reporting to be inaccurate, even when he swears it isn't.

He claims that he and his friends evoke a subject for you as it really is, and maybe that's what his friends do. But in his own case, this is like El Greco boasting about his photographic accuracy. We enjoy Wolfe (or not) precisely for the distortion. We never supposed the Bernsteins were really like that. All the details may have been right in "Radical Chic," as Wolfe ponderously argues—and as his critics ponderously argue back—but the result was gorgeously unreal. Why? Because the Bernsteins probably don't give a damn about their canapés or what shoes they've got on. Wolfe does and, like the artist he is, makes you share his values. In this sense, Wolfe's Bernsteins are like the cartoon George Grosz's Germans, part them and mostly him. The real subject is his imagination, as affected by the Bernsteins.

Wolfe's prose is also a distorting mechanism. He maintains that he finds a language proper to each subject, a special sound to convey its uniqueness; but loyal readers may find that this language is surprisingly similar, whether dealing with stockcar racing or debutantes, and that it obliterates uniqueness and drags everything back to Wolfe's cave. This is what artists do, and it's strange that he refuses to recognize it. In his frenzied assault on the Novel, he allies himself with some quite talented but prosy journalists who don't do any of this, in order to beat up on a form much closer to his own.

Call it subconscious strategy, if you dabble in such superstitions; but his blindness on the point may serve an artistic purpose for himself. By muttering "Reporter, I'm a reporter" over and over, he reminds his nose to stay down near the details where it works best. But upon these truths he imposes his own consciousness, his own selection and rhetoric, and they become Wolfe-truths, and he is halfway over the border into the hated Novel. He ingenuously wonders why no novelist has ever used the reporting he did on the West Coast Beats in *Electric Kool-Aid Acid Test,* but doesn't realize he has already used it himself. That book may well be the best literary work to come out of the Beat Movement, yet the material is quite inaccessible to anyone else. I pity the poor writer following Wolfe to the Coast hoping to find what he found. It is all in Wolfe's skull. The Beats probably weren't like that at all, as far as anyone else could see. In fact, rumor has it that all they wanted to do was splash his white suit. Like everybody.

So let's hear no more social realism out of Wolfe, that supreme fantastist. The Truman Capotes may hold up a tolerably clear glass to nature, but Wolfe holds up a fun-house mirror, and I for one don't give a hoot whether he calls the reflection fact or fiction. But Wolfe seems to feel burdened by his uniqueness and is eager to be one of the boys in the pressroom again, so he has enrolled the Dublin-type story-teller Jimmy Breslin in his raggle-tag school and roaring Pete Hamill, who is not primarily a reporter at all but inspired street lawyer, and just about any writer he can find under 40. All he has done is give literary glamour to some good journeyman reporters, and some journalistic glamour to the essayists, and provide some company for himself.

So, now that we've drummed Wolfe out of his own movement, is there anything left to discuss? At least one good question came out of those lugubrious panel shows—from Pauline Kael, I believe. To wit: Is the New Journalism to be trusted with real history? Or does its natural tendency to personalize issues and to overvalue the reporter's own experience confine its usefulness to smaller units of material?

The best answer we've had to that so far is probably David Halberstam's Vietnam encyclopedia, *The Best and the Brightest,* although Halberstam cheats by adding much erudition to his own experience and by effacing himself almost squeamishly from the text. (When he does have to mention himself, you can practically sense him reddening.) But the personality is there all right and the imperious angle of vision, and Halberstam has dramatized his material into possibly the best novel yet written about the war.

As told to and by David Halberstam, this godforsaken war would seem to be the ideal subject for non-fiction fiction. Unlike most wars, which make rotten fiction in themselves—all plot and no characters, or made-up characters—Vietnam seems to be the perfect mix; the characters make the war, and the war unmakes the characters. The gods, fates, furies had a relatively small hand in it. The mess was man-made, a synthetic, by think-tank out of briefing session. At the top sits the boy President in his tree-house, smarting from the Bay of Pigs and even more from Khrushchev's personal put-down in Vienna, badly needing someone to push around for home consumption—and Vietnam was available. Underneath, there's his military guru Max Taylor, the kind of smoothy the boy President hits it off with, but by ill chance a devotee of brush-fire wars, needing a specimen to prove his point; and Bob McNamara, the chilly systems analyst itching to do for Saigon what he'd done for Ford Motors; and down through murkier quirks—Walt Rostow's mystical faith in bombing; and McGeorge Bundy, "the minister's son in the whorehouse" (L.B.J.), mesmerized by his first sight of blood at Pleiku.

It sounds dangerously like the Cleopatra's-nose school of history—could we have avoided war if Bundy weren't quite such a prig and Rostow such an excitable little fellow? But Halberstam is smart enough to sidestep this New Journalism trap: he suggests that behind the Bundys there were more Bundys, a whole class was involved. Vietnam was, above all, the effete snobs' war—the Eastern eggheads, who had been painted pink for girls by Joe McCarthy and were out to prove their manhood or bust. It wasn't just Lyndon Johnson who wanted to be John Wayne (though that was the topper); it was McGeorge Bundy, dean of Harvard, and Walt Rostow of M.I.T., tall in the saddle and heading for the quagmire.

Well, a whole class of manly Bundys may be even harder to accept than one—the sins of the New Journalism are not lessened by these multiplications. But I think reviewers have missed the subtlety of Halberstam's analysis here. He quotes Emerson's saying that "events are in the saddle" several times, which implies that the Bundy-Rostows were only allowed up there to pose with them. They were just the kind of people who like to pose with events. But it didn't matter. There was no stopping the runaway war. Max Taylor saw his brush-fire skirmish combust into a forest fire but was helpless to stop it; Mc-Namara's charts indicated an unmistakable Edsel, but he couldn't pull it off the market. The book ends with Nixon about to set off on his four-year plan to end it. And he may have had one at that. By then the war was devouring plans like a dragon chewing on paper.

The difficulty remains: If a whole class did it, why pick on Rostow? And, if events did it, why pick on a class? Well, because it's interesting, that's why. In respect to Kael's question, I would say that Halberstam's personalizing of issues makes for better reading and, occasionally, more dubious history. Some of the vignettes are wonderfully shrewd (Bundy again), some are blown-up cartoons (L.B.J.). All the Army officers tend to be stiff and reserved—Halberstam doesn't allow for how much of this is a standard professional mannerism. In each case, we are at the author's mercy, depending on his omniscience, psychological accuracy and personal honor (did Dean Rusk call him Fred by mistake one day? does this boy carry grudges?), a heavy burden even for a priest.

Because this isn't gossip and opinion anymore or Tom Wolfe zipping along the strip in his outasight Gucci-puccis. Vietnam has reached the war-criminal phase, at least in the public mind; and the reader starts out with blood in his eye. The historian doubles as prosecutor; and a sloppy, spiteful hatchet job goes into the record with the rest. We can thank God the task has fallen this time to someone as scrupulous and informed as Halberstam. Still, the fine malice of his portraits shows what one of the hairier new journalists might do with it.

Not that we need be too concerned with the reputations of Jack Kennedy's whizz kids, who seem to be doing very nicely for alleged war criminals. But, for the delicate task of analyzing how and why we get into wars, one has to doubt the capacity of the new personal journalism as practiced domestically, unless backed, as here, by massive scholarship and impersonal historical sense. Halberstam's dramatization of events is beyond praise, and for that he does need faces. But, if the space and skill lavished on these leaves us supposing that the war was caused by faces, we might have been better off without them at that.

Is There a
'New Journalism'?

JACK NEWFIELD

After participating in several panel discussions, attending (*More*)'s counter-convention, reading books and articles by Tom Wolfe and Michael Arlen, and being interviewed by several high school students about it, I have finally come to the conclusion that the New Journalism does not exist. It is a false category. There is only good writing and bad writing, smart ideas and dumb ideas, hard work and laziness.

Anyone who is less than thirty-five and owns a typewriter becomes known as a "new journalist." Writers as different as Richard Goldstein, Eldridge Cleaver, and Rex Reed get lumped together under a contrived umbrella.

Everyone has a different definition of what the New Journalism is. It's the use of fictional techniques, it's composite characterization, it's the art form that's replacing the novel, which is dying. Or it's anyone who use to write for the old *Herald Tribune* magazine, it's participation in the event by the writer, it's the transcendence of objectivity, it's anyone who makes up quotes, it's anyone who hangs out at the Lion's Head bar.

Seymour Krim, in a piece in *New American Review,* once made a reference to the "Cleaver-Rubin-Newfield style." And Mike Arlen, in

Jack Newfield's piece appeared in the *Columbia Journalism Review,* July-August, 1972. It's an adaptation of an article, "Of Honest Men and Good Writers," that originally appeared in the *Village Voice.*

the *Atlantic,* linked me and Tom Wolfe together: "The New Journalist is in the end, I think, less a journalist than an impresario. Tom Wolfe presents Phil Spector! Jack Newfield presents Nelson Rockefeller! Norman Mailer presents the Moon Shot!" *

This piece is to explain why I don't think there is such a thing as New Journalism, and why I don't think I am a new journalist.

To begin with, there is not that much new about the new journalism. Advocacy preceded the who-what-when-where-why of the AP by a couple of centuries. Tom Paine and Voltaire were New Journalists. So was John Milton when he wrote his *Areopagitica* against government censorship in the seventeenth century. "Objective" journalism developed with the teletype and radio news.

Defoe, Addison and Steele, Stephen Crane, and Mark Twain were all New Journalists according to most definitions. So was Karl Marx when he wrote for the *Herald Tribune.*

Yet something different and better does seem to have happened to mass publication journalism in the last fifteen years. I suspect it is nothing more profound than a lot of good writers coming along at the same time, and a few wise editors like Dan Wolf, Clay Felker, and William Shawn giving these writers a lot of space and freedom to express a point of view. I wouldn't refine the generality much more than that.

But this new rush of talent did not, as Tom Wolfe seems to suggest, spring Zeus-like from John Hay Whitney's banker's brow in the *Trib's* protean cityroom in late 1963. It appears, rather, to have crystallized at *Esquire* in the late 1950's, and to have been motivated by an economic desperation to compete with *Playboy*'s sexist centerfolds, then attracting considerable advertising revenue away from *Esquire.*

It was during this period that *Esquire* published brilliant profiles of Joe DiMaggio, Frank Sinatra, and Joe Louis by Gay Talese. Talese managed to get inside his subjects' private and interior lives, and give readers a deeper, truer sense of how things really are. At the same time Tom Morgan, now Mayor Lindsay's press secretary, wrote equally rich portraits of Roy Cohn, David Susskind, and Sammy Davis, Jr. These are preserved in a forgotten book, *Self Creations: 13 Impersonalities,* which some paperback publisher should wake up and reissue.

Then in 1960 an *Esquire* editor named Clay Felker had an idea, and assigned Norman Mailer to cover a real event, the Democratic national convention in Los Angeles. Mailer's piece was a masterwork of good writing and clear thinking. It was not a new form. John Hersey, also a novelist, had written about a real event—Hiroshima. George

---

Orwell had written about the Spanish Civil War. James Agee had written about the life of white tenant farmers in *Let Us Now Praise Famous Men*.

So Mailer, who happened to be a novelist of distinction, wrote a great work of journalism. And *Esquire*, in an economic war with *Playboy*, published all 30,000 words. I was attending Hunter College then, and Mailer's piece blew my mind. It also blew Pete Hamill's and Jimmy Breslin's. Mailer opened a door with that piece, and the one he did on the Liston-Patterson fight. But it was not a new art form. He did not invent anything. He just wrote great liberating prose. Just like Lillian Ross, or Joe Mitchell, or A. J. Liebling, or Westbrook Pegler and H. L. Mencken.

I grew up on three journalists: Murray Kempton, sportswriter Jimmy Cannon, and I. F. Stone. From Kempton I tried to learn irony and a sense of history; from Cannon a love for the city and a sense of drama; from Stone a reverence for facts, truth, and justice. Later, from Hamill and Breslin, I would learn the legitimacy of rage, the folly of politeness, and a sense of concreteness about the lives of ordinary people.

Then along comes Tom Wolfe, the Boswell of the boutiques, with a history of the New Journalism that never mentions Kempton, Cannon, or Stone. Or Lillian Ross and Joe Mitchell, who wrote for the rival *New Yorker*. Or any *Village Voice* writer, for that matter. Like any faithful Boswell, Wolfe only mentions his friends.

I've had a lot of shop talk conversations with Hamill and Breslin, and both feel a special debt to Cannon for the shaping of their craft. Hamill, in fact, dedicated his book *Irrational Ravings* to Cannon.

This is how Pete described Cannon's influence on him: "But it was Cannon who made me want to be a newspaperman. He wrote a sports column, but it was always more than that. In some ways the hero of the column was its style, an undisciplined personal mixture of New York street talk, soaring elegance, Hemingway and Algren, deep Celtic feeling, city loneliness, Prohibition violence, and a personal belief in honor."

But is the sixty-three-year-old Jimmy Cannon a "New Journalist"? Or just a good one?

Another exceptional sportswriter of the Fifties left his mark on many of us: W. C. Heinz. Heinz' classic 1952 piece on Rocky Graziano can be found in the anthology *The Best of Sport*, published by Viking. Heinz also authored a lean, beautiful novel about boxing, *The Professional*. Breslin calls Heinz "the best I ever saw." Yet Wolfe and most students of the New Journalism have never even heard of him.

What's called the New Journalism is really a dozen different styles of writing. Talese and Capote do one thing very well. Rex Reed has his own act. Breslin, Hamill, and I have certain things in common—a populist politics, working-class backgrounds, respect for Mailer, Kempton, Cannon, and Heinz, and a love for this wounded city. Sometimes I think the three of us, one pusher, and one junkie will be the last five people left in town.

And Tom Wolfe represents another strand in all this. He is a gifted, original writer, but he has the social conscience of an ant. Wolfe is a dandy. His basic interest is the flow of fashion, in the tics and trinkets of the rich. But if Wolfe represents a conservative, or perhaps apolitical approach, there is also the committed school of Stone, Kempton, Royko, Halberstam, Wicker, Cowan, Hentoff, and many others.

Some alleged New Journalists, like Robin Reisig and James Ridgeway, are really part of an older muckraking tradition that stretches back to Lincoln Steffens and Ida Tarbell. So is Jack Anderson, who is considered an "old journalist" because he has a syndicated column.

Actually, I think the only really new journalism in America today is being done by people like Studs Terkel and Robert Coles, who are trying to record history from the bottom, through the eyes of average, unfamous people, rather than through presidents and celebrities.

Paul Cowan's *Village Voice* stories on coal miners and the residents of Forest Hills are also in this democratic vein. So are my own prison articles, where I try to present the prison reality from the point of view of powerless unknown inmates, rather than wardens, or expert penologists, or corrections bureaucrats, or liberal politicians.

The New Journalism is not going to become an evolutionary substitute for the novel, as Norman Podhoretz first suggested in a 1958 essay, "The Article as Art." * Tom Wolfe also made this excessive claim in his recent essay in *New York* magazine. The New Journalism, Wolfe wrote, "is causing panic, dethroning the novel as the Number One literary genre, starting the first new direction in American literature in half a century."

Nonsense.

First of all, there are still plenty of fine novelists around: Barth, Roth, Updike, Bellow, Ellison, Pynchon, and Malamud are all working. Plus fresh talents on the way up like Fred Exley, Robert Stone, Marge Piercy, Sol Yurick, and Robert Coover, who assure the vitality of the genre.

Second, some of the best "New Journalists' have found their own expanded form still so inhibiting they have turned to writing novels themselves—Hamill, Breslin, Joan Didion, Jeremy Larner, David Halberstam, Joe McGinniss, and earlier, Mailer, Baldwin, and Heinz. Breslin and Joe Flaherty have spent the last year working on novels.

---

* [Editor's note: See Norman Podhoretz, "The Article as Art," page 125.]

Third, most of us alleged New Journalists have read a lot of naturalistic novels, and have been influenced by Dreiser, Dos Passos, Farrell, Steinbeck, and Algren. This tradition seems out of fashion now, but what's called the New Journalism owes a lot of dues to it.

There is room for both good novels and good journalism. The need for newness, the competition of categories, is just a game of egos. Why deny our roots? What is the need to claim historical novelty? What's wrong with giving credit to Jimmy Cannon and John Steinbeck?

The distinction has also been blurred between what is called New Journalism and underground journalism. If New Journalism can at least be recognized as good writing and lucid thinking, there is little of that in most of the underground press. (I exempt sea-level papers like Boston's *Phoenix* and Chicago's *Daily Planet*.) New York's *East Village Other* proved that postlinear heads couldn't write linear prose. The dumbest political column of the year—even worse than Evans and Novak—was Al Goldstein's romanticization of George Wallace recently in the New York *Ace*.

Most political writers for most underground papers don't know how things really work, and lack the Breslin-Hamill instinct for the concrete. At this point, conventional "old journalists"—like David Broder, Jim Perry, Alan Otten, Martin Nolan, and Mary McGrory write better and see clearer than the underground pundits.

The underground press has been very good at writing about certain things—the war, women's liberation, prisons, rock music. But it has been very bad reporting on other things—electoral politics, original muckraking, neighborhoods and ordinary people, crime and the fear of crime and violence and arrogance when they appear on the Left.

It was *Life* magazine that broke the Abe Fortas and San Diego scandals. It was Hamill's piece in *New York* magazine that first noticed the swelling rage in white workingmen's neighborhoods. It was the Staten Island *Advance* that first exposed the horror of Willowbrook. It was Jack Anderson who exposed ITT. These are the sort of stories a better underground press might have dug out first.

Some press critics have tried to make "advocacy" the line that divides "biased, irresponsible" new journalism from professional, objective mainstream journalism. But it seems to me that the most blatant advocacy journalists have almost always been on the Right.

Joe Alsop has been advocating (and predicting) an American military victory in Vietnam for a decade. William F. Buckley might be the purest advocacy journalist in the country. He helped elect his brother to the Senate in 1970. He campaigned for John Ashbrook in New Hampshire this year. He is editor of a magazine with an ideological line much more narrow and rigid than the *Village Voice*. He even ran for mayor in 1965.

Somehow the concept of advocacy in journalism has become identified with the Left. But what about the *Reader's Digest?* They've published seventy-seven pieces on Vietnam since 1951, seventy-six of them in favor of the war. Does *U.S. News & World Report* present a balanced view of capitalism? Is New Hampshire's *Manchester Union Leader* fair and objective?

Objectivity can be defined as the way the mass media reported the history of the Vietnam War before the Pentagon Papers; the way the racism in the North was covered before Watts; the way auto safety was reported before Ralph Nader. Objectivity is the media printing Nelson Rockefeller's lies about Attica until the facts came out that the state troopers and not the inmates had killed all the hostages; that the troopers used outlawed dum dum bullets; that 350 inmates, including some badly wounded, were beaten after they gave up. Objectivity is printing a dozen stories about minor welfare frauds, but not a word about the Mylai massacre until Seymour Hersh. Objectivity is not shouting "liar" in a crowded country.

The goal for all journalists should be to come as close to the truth as possible. But the truth does not always reside exactly in the middle. Truth is not the square root of two balanced quotes. I don't believe I should be "objective" about racism, or the conditions inside Clinton Prison, or lead poisoning, or the fact that parts of New York's Brownsville look like Quangtri. Certain facts are not morally neutral.

So, I think there is no such thing as New Journalism. It still comes down to good writing, and hard work, and clear thinking. The rest is bullshit. The best motto for all of us is still the last line of James Baldwin's introduction to *Notes of a Native Son:* "I want to be an honest man and a good writer."

Amen.

Further Readings

Tom Wolfe's commentaries on the New Journalism are collected in his book *The New Journalism* (Harper & Row, 1973).* There's also a piece by Wolfe, "The New Journalism," in *The Bulletin* of the American Society of Newspaper Editors, September, 1970. Book-length studies include Michael L. Johnson's *The New Journalism* (The University Press of Kansas, 1971) and Everette E. Dennis' and William L. Rivers' *Other Voices: The New Journalism in America* (Canfield Press, 1974). *The Magic Writing Machine: Student Probes of the New Journalism* (School of Journalism, University of Oregon, 1971), edited by Everette E. Dennis, is a collection of student essays on the New Journalism. Individual articles treating the New Journalism include the following: W. Stewart Pinkerton, Jr., " 'New Journalism': Believe It or Not," in *The Press*, edited by A. Kent MacDougall (Dow Jones Books, 1972); John Tebbel, "The Old New Journalism," *Saturday Review*, March 13, 1971; John Madigan and Curtis MacDougall, "The 'New Journalism' Debate," *The Quill*, September, 1971; David McHam, "Old Ain't Necessarily Good, Either!", *The Bulletin* of the American Society of Newspaper Editors, January, 1972; Seymour Krim, "Letter to Nat Hentoff" and "Letter to Jack Newfield," in *Shake It For the World, Smartass* (Dial, 1970); Alfred Kazin, "The World as a Novel: From Capote to Mailer," *The New York Review of Books*, April 8, 1971; William Wiegand, "The 'Non-Fiction' Novel," *New Mexico Quarterly*, Autumn, 1967; Robert Kiener, "An Exclusive Interview with Herbert Gold," *Writer's Digest*, September, 1972; "The Editor Interviews William Styron," *Modern Occasions*, Fall, 1971; Remarks by Seymour Krim and Wilfrid

---

* For a perceptive analysis of the book see Michael Wood's review in the *New York Times Book Review*, July 22, 1973.

Sheed in "The Writer's Situation: II," *New American Review 10* (Signet, 1970); Everette E. Dennis and William L. Rivers, "What Is The New Journalism," in *Communication*, Fall, 1973.

INDEX

LIBRARY
OKALOOSA-WALTON JUNIOR COLLEGE